The Movie Greats

Barry Norman
The Movie Greats

HODDER AND STOUGHTON
BRITISH BROADCASTING CORPORATION

British Library Cataloguing in Publication Data

Norman, Barry
   The movie greats.
   1. Moving-picture actors and actresses
   I. Title
   791.43′028092′2   PN1998.A2

   ISBN 0 340 25972 8

*Printed in Great Britain for Hodder and Stoughton Limited, Mill Road, Dunton
Green, Sevenoaks, Kent and the British Broadcasting Corporation, 35 Marylebone
High Street, London W1M 4AA, by Morrison & Gibb, Limited.
Hodder and Stoughton Editorial Office: 47 Bedford Square, London WC1 B3DP*

Preface

"The only trouble with Hollywood," said Joan Fontaine, "is that you know you're running out of it. You go right through it and out the other end. It's not a cul-de-sac."

This book, like its predecessor, *The Hollywood Greats*, consists for the most part of brief biographies of some of the people who ran into Hollywood and came out, sometimes willingly, sometimes not, at the other end. It is also, like its predecessor, based on and developed from a number of documentary programmes which I wrote and presented for BBC television. Some of the stars I deal with are American, some are British, but all of them, at one period or another and for greater or shorter lengths of time, worked in Hollywood and indeed had they not done so they could probably not have been called stars. Hollywood was, and to a considerable extent still is, a kind of Mecca for actors, especially English-speaking actors. Hollywood makes bigger films, Hollywood pays fatter salaries, Hollywood productions reach larger audiences. Hollywood stardom, in short, means world stardom and in the cinema today there is little point in aiming for anything less. If Hollywood hasn't called at least once or twice, no English-speaking actor, no matter how talented, can be considered more than a very minor star.

Among the nine actors and actresses who feature in this book there are some whose experience of Hollywood was comparatively limited. Jack Hawkins is one example but then his career and opportunities were drastically curtailed by cancer; Gracie Fields is another but she disliked the place and opted out. Much the same may be said of Robert Donat who was constantly wooed by Hollywood studios, made several films for them but only worked there once.

Nevertheless, they were all stars (though Gracie Fields' greatest fame and popularity were not achieved in the cinema) and some of them were even very good actors — not that this is terribly important in any consideration of stardom. The two things are by no means synonymous: a very great actor may not be a star, a very great star may be a truly lousy actor. For this reason, among others, I have not attempted to analyse the individual qualities possessed by the people I deal with here. If you want to know what makes a man a good actor the *best* way is to go and watch his performances; if you want to know what makes a man a star the *only* way is to go and watch his performances. Acting ability can be examined and identified; the quality of stardom cannot. Acting ability can be acquired; the quality of stardom is innate. Ellen Terry once described it as "that little something extra" and nobody, I think, has ever come closer to defining it.

So I merely ask you to accept, as I did before I started on the TV programmes, that all these people were stars and a few of them were also good actors. And having accepted that, the question that interested me most was: what kind of people were they? The documentaries and the following chapters are an attempt to answer that — and only an attempt, for I do not claim to have discovered the ultimate truth about any of these people. Who knows, after all, what the truth is? Quite apart from the fact that in too many people too many memories have been altered subtly but significantly by the passing of time, the truth can often depend on the mood of the person you are talking to.

If you catch an old man on a good day when he is feeling well and ask him what, say, Edward G. Robinson was really like he may tell you, being in benevolent mood, that Edward G. Robinson was a saint. But if you catch him on a bad day when his bowels and bladder are performing at less than par and his arthritis is giving him hell, he may declare that Edward G. Robinson was the devil incarnate.

Who knows which of these versions is the truth? Maybe they're both true or maybe — more likely, of course — the truth lies somewhere in between. But whereabouts in between?

So, in many ways, the piecing together of these mini-biographies has been rather like detective work: comparing one statement with another, weighing this evidence against that in a bid to find the most logical, the most reasonable, explanation for the apparently illogical and unreasonable behaviour of, let us say, Charlie Chaplin or Marilyn Monroe.

What, after all, is most likely: that Marilyn Monroe died of an accidental overdose of drugs; that she committed suicide; or that, as somebody claimed in one book, she was actually murdered by or on behalf of Robert Kennedy, the Attorney General of the United States? All one can do is listen to the various arguments and from them try to form a pattern of probabilities. No biography, long or short, can, I maintain, ever amount to much more than that.

Nor, I think, could I have come appreciably closer to the ultimate truth if the subjects had been alive and thus available for questioning. Very few people tell the whole truth, least of all about themselves. In any event, for me the matter didn't arise since all the subjects were dead and had indeed been selected — not only but partly — because they were dead. Now this sounds rather sinister, like a form of literary body-snatching. You can't libel the dead, right? The dead can't answer back. True in both cases but that is not why I chose to look at the late, rather than the living, greats. Portraits of living people tend to be bland, sometimes even eulogistic and, at best, careful. The subject's strengths are emphasised, his weaknesses played down or ignored altogether. Yet a person's weaknesses are often far more interesting and more indicative of his character than are his strengths.

If I had been preparing my TV series or this book when Marilyn Monroe was alive and I had gone to any of my interviewees and said, "Tell me about her drug problem," it's virtually certain that each of them would have said, "You'd better ask Marilyn herself about that." But it's equally certain that Marilyn herself wouldn't have told me. Quite right, too, you may say. Why should she? None of your business. Yet it is, in a way, one's business — it's the business of any biographer (even a mini-biographer) to find out everything he can about the subject under review and then try to put each of the discoveries into perspective. But this only becomes possible when the subject is dead and his or her friends, acquaintances and associates no longer feel themselves constrained by social niceties, a fear that their motives may be misunderstood or by a kind of unwritten, unspoken embargo. In short, people are franker (which is not, by any means, to say more malicious) about their friends when they are dead than when they are alive.

But what, you may say again, does it matter anyway? These people were only mummers and strolling players, mere butterflies who appeared and fluttered prettily and went and changed nothing. And that, too, is true. But they were, if such a thing is possible, immortal butterflies. It is said that there are five stages in a star's life as seen by a casting director. In stage one he says: "Who is Hugh O'Brian?" In stage two he says: "Get me Hugh O'Brian." In stage three he says: "Get me a Hugh O'Brian type." In stage four he says: "Get me a young Hugh O'Brian." And in stage five he says: "Who is Hugh O'Brian?"

With profuse apologies to Hugh O'Brian (who must certainly have heard it all before) I submit that the progression is cruel but accurate. What I also submit is that none of the people in this book ever reached stage five, before or after death. And it is not only the fact that their work is recorded on film which, if treated properly, is more or less imperishable, that makes their memory imperishable too.

Many of their contemporaries are also on film but their names are almost forgotten. What each of my nine had in common was star quality and they had it in such abundance that they can reach out beyond their time and bring to succeeding generations as much pleasure as they brought to their own. And people who can do that are rare enough for their lives to be worth recording.

But I speak of nine while there are in fact ten chapters in this book. Well, the tenth chapter is a brief sketch of Hollywood itself — not the Hollywood of today but the Hollywood that existed in the 1930s and 1940s when it was rich and grand and powerful. Hollywood today, so everyone tells me, is not what it was and I am sure they are right. But even when it was what it was it must still have been an odd place in which to find the headquarters of the most influential medium of mass entertainment there has ever been. It is, in fact, merely a stretch of urban sprawl set in the hills overlooking the smog of downtown Los Angeles — a city, as Raymond Chandler said, "with all the personality of a paper cup" — and joined to it by a multi-lane freeway.

It's a combination of opulence and tat, a factory town with palm trees and swimming pools. Its wealthy residents live in the dormitory suburbs of Bel Air and Beverly Hills, where the only people you ever see are Mexican gardeners and nobody walks the streets, not even the Mexican gardeners, because a man walking the streets is naturally assumed to be a man who has no car and a man who has no car is a bum who has no right to be in Bel Air or Beverly Hills in the first place. The unseen residents all have cars. The men have Rolls-Royces or Cadillacs and their wives go shopping in brand-new Mercedes and a Porsche is just a toy that you give to your younger daughter on her seventeenth birthday.

This strange place became the headquarters of the film industry quite by accident. The odd movie had been made in or around Los Angeles since about 1912 but it was Cecil B. de Mille who inadvertently established Hollywood as the world's film capital when he made *The Squaw Man* there in 1913. *The Squaw Man* was actually a western set in Wyoming so naturally, following the inscrutable logic of the movie business, de Mille originally planned to make it in Arizona. But Arizona didn't look at all like Wyoming so he went to California instead. You may wonder why he didn't just go to Wyoming but I expect that was too simple. Still, thanks to de Mille and his peregrinations, his company, Paramount, was the first to put down roots in Hollywood. By the mid-1920s six other companies — Universal, Fox, MGM, Warner Brothers, United Artists and Columbia — were also established there.

From such unlikely beginnings Hollywood — the place you ran into at one end and out the other, clutching, if you were lucky, a large wad of loot — prospered and grew and then declined and fell. Dreams and reputations and fortunes were made and broken, found and lost there. For three decades, at least, it attracted the brightest talent — actors, writers, producers, directors — to be found anywhere in the world. What they produced there was instant entertainment on a scale more massive than anybody could ever have imagined possible. Sometimes, too, they even produced art but that was an accident. Nobody in Hollywood ever set out to produce art.

What they set out for was success. "Our town," said Hedda Hopper, the gossip columnist, "worships success, the bitch goddess whose smile hides a taste for blood." Success was a hit picture, long queues around the block, a fortune at the box office and a renewed contract at double the previous salary. But the competition was fierce and there is never enough success around for everyone. Nobody's bread is dipped in the gravy all the time. And so, between the bouts of success, for most of the people most of the time the true name of the game was survival. But sometimes, as you will discover if you read on, not even the biggest stars were tough enough to manage that for very long.

Contents

1 Marilyn Monroe   15

2 Peter Finch   57

3 Groucho Marx   87

4 Jack Hawkins   115

5 Edward G. Robinson   139

6 Robert Donat   171

7 Gracie Fields   199

8 Leslie Howard   225

9 Charlie Chaplin   253

10 Hollywood   281

   Index   309

Illustration Acknowledgments

Associated Press: pp 142 (bottom), and 226

BBC: pp 89, 119 and 228 (top)

The Bodley Head: p 257 (bottom)

John Donat Photography: pp 173, 174, 175 and Robert Donat portrait on jacket

Fox Photos: p 201

Mrs. Doreen Hawkins: pp 116, 117, 118 (bottom) and 119

Ronald Howard: p 229

Keystone Press Agency: pp 58 (top), 59, 90 (top), 118 (top), 202, 255 (bottom), 256, 257 (top) and 283 (top right)

The Kobal Collection: pp 15, 16, 17 (left), 18 (right), 19, 60 61, 87, 88, 90 (bottom), 91, 115, 139, 140, 141, 171, 172, 199, 225, 227, 228 (bottom), 254 (top), 255 (top), 257 (bottom), 282, 283 (bottom), 284 (bottom), 285 and cinema posters and portraits on jacket of Marilyn Monroe, Gracie Fields, Groucho Marx, Peter Finch, Edward G. Robinson, Leslie Howard and Jack Hawkins

Metro-Goldwyn-Mayer: pp 171, 225, 285 and *Gone With the Wind* poster on jacket

National Film Archive: p 89

National Telefilm Associates: p 228

Paramount Pictures: p 60

Picturegoer: p 199

Popperfoto: pp 17 (right, top and bottom), 18 (left), 57, 58 (bottom), 142 (top), 143, 200, 203, 253, 254 (bottom), 281, 283 (top left) and 284 (top and inset)

Twentieth Century Fox: pp 16, 19 (bottom), 175 and Gracie Fields portrait on jacket

United Artists Corporation: pp 15, 19 (top), 61, 140 and *Modern Times* poster and Edward G. Robinson portrait on jacket

Warner Brothers Inc: p 18 (top right)

The Movie Greats

Marilyn Monroe

Monroe the starlet, aged twenty-two, and just another plump, near-blonde around Hollywood.

above: In her first film, Scudda Hoo! Scudda Hay! *Monroe's role, minuscule to begin with, was deleted entirely in the cutting room.*

below left: 1950. The year of The Asphalt Jungle *and* All About Eve. *The familiar sex goddess of the next decade is just beginning to emerge.*

below right: By 1953 everyone, not just Monroe, had discovered that Gentlemen Prefer Blondes. *For her stardom started here.*

above : With Yves Montand during the filming of Let's Make Love *which, misguidedly perhaps, is what they did.*

inset top : Her second husband Joe di Maggio, the baseball star. It was the marriage of the all-American hero and the all-American heroine and, perhaps not surprisingly, it didn't last.

inset bottom : Husband No. 3, the playwright Arthur Miller. The Body and the Egghead. This didn't last either.

*above left : The notorious — but by today's standards curiously
innocent — nude calendar. "What did you have on, Marilyn?" she
was asked. "Just the radio," she said.*

above right : Posing in England during the making of The Prince
and the Showgirl. *The cheesecake shots were better than the film.*

opposite page :

above : In The Misfits, *Monroe's — and Clark Gable's — last film
and for each of them one of their best.*

*below : One of Monroe's last publicity shots, taken just before she was
fired from* Something's Got To Give. *Within a week or two she was
dead.*

I only ever saw Marilyn Monroe once. She and I were in the audience at a Sunday-night performance at the Royal Court Theatre in London in 1956 when she was in England to film *The Prince and the Showgirl*. God knows what play they were doing that night: I only remember Monroe — white-blonde hair like vanilla-flavoured candyfloss and an oddly timid expression, as if she were afraid of something. The audience perhaps, people like me who just stared at her. It's a very un-English activity to stare at complete strangers but you couldn't help staring at Monroe. She simply sat there in the stalls, doing absolutely nothing to attract attention and yet arousing so much interest that the play itself was a mere diversion in the background, performed valiantly and no doubt excellently but more or less unnoticed.

She was married then to Arthur Miller and him I met twice. The first time was at the gates of the house in Surrey where they were living and where she had been taken ill. He came out courteously enough to tell me and other members of the Press that he had nothing very much to say.

Our second meeting was in Ireland some years later when Miller was visiting John Huston to discuss the forthcoming production of his screenplay *The Misfits*, Monroe's last completed film. I arrived at the house a few minutes behind Miller, just in time to see the butler, a young Irishman in a white coat, accost him on the doorstep.

"Yes? What do you want?" asked this butler.

Miller said: "My name is Arthur Miller. I have an appointment with Mr. Huston."

"Just wait a minute," the butler said and then, glancing back over his shoulder into the house he called, in the formal manner of Irish butlers, "Mr. Huston, there's a feller here to see yez."

On such flimsy evidence it is, I know, quite unfair to say that I was not much impressed by Arthur Miller, but I was overwhelmed by Monroe. I admired Miller, of course, as a writer but sitting there in the house with him and Huston I wondered what Monroe had ever seen in him. No doubt Miller's friends, especially later when she was dead and ever more scurrilous memoirs of her were coming out virtually every hour on the hour, must have asked themselves the same question in reverse. But that's how it always was with Monroe: either you were for her or against her; there was no intermediate course, no room for indifference.

Norman Mailer once described her as "every man's love affair with America" and at her peak she was certainly that: an object both of lust and adoration, the most marvellous symbol of sheer femininity in the history of the cinema, the ultimate Sex Goddess proudly presented to the world by the United States of America in general and 20th Century Fox in particular. There were other sex goddesses around at the time, not least Sophia Loren and Brigitte Bardot, but they stood on pedestals slightly lower than Monroe's. Loren was totally a woman, sophisticated and un-girlish; Bardot was a petulant, dangerous child and Monroe was a devastating combination of the two.

It was America who created her, set her up way on high (the better no doubt to stare up her skirt) and it was America who tore her down again. I wonder why. When you look at the books and the magazine articles that have been written about her and are still being written about her, nearly two decades after her death, it almost seems as if there was a national need to believe that this woman, who once had been idolised, was not only no better than but in fact a great deal worse than anybody else. Perhaps it's something in the egalitarian American soul that denies anybody the right to be different, to be "special". All right, the argument seems to run, so Monroe was sexy. So what? She was also a slut and a whore; she was a no-talent; she was neurotic and megalomaniac; she was undependable; she was a drug addict. Columns of personal reminiscences, ghost-written on behalf of people who barely knew her, make these points again and again and are eagerly devoured by a public that says, "See? I told you so."

What on earth had she done to deserve such treatment? Whom, apart from herself, had she ever really hurt? Well, it's true that she often made life extremely difficult for film directors and producers but these are big, strong men (or, if you prefer, since men of power in the film industry are often of diminutive stature, small, strong men) well equipped and handsomely paid to deal with temperamental actresses. It's also true that she had three marriages and none of them worked out but at least one of her three discarded husbands continued to love her until the day she died and indeed he probably loves her still.

I find it hard to believe, in fact I refuse to believe, that she was the monster posterity has decreed her to be. I believe rather that she was a victim, a sexual Wizard of Oz, a confused and bewildered creature who used the remarkable physical gifts with which nature had endowed her to keep at bay a world that, on the whole, simply frightened her.

Heaven knows she started off with the kind of background, the kind of handicaps, that were most likely to set her off in any direction other than upwards — into delinquency, perhaps, into crime, into prostitution. She was born on June 1st, 1926 in Los Angeles and was registered as Norma Jean Mortensen. She was registered thus because Mortensen happened to be her mother's married name but whether her father was Mortensen himself or another fellow entirely, named C. Stanley Gifford, is very much open to question. Not that it really matters a great deal because Mortensen, a baker, and Gifford, an employee of a firm called Consolidated Film Industries and her mother's more or less casual lover, had disappeared from the scene before Norma Jean put in her appearance. Thus she was either the legitimate daughter of a vanished husband or the illegitimate daughter of a vanished boyfriend, neither of which is a particularly desirable start in life. In any event she was certainly the child of a one-parent family.

This, of course, is not necessarily an insuperable obstacle to a happy life but Norma Jean's mother was a considerable handicap in herself. She had been born Gladys Pearl Monroe, later — on her first marriage — became Gladys Baker, then Gladys Mortensen and, at the time her daughter was born, she was working as a negative cutter in the film industry. But she was also mentally ill and came from a family with a long history of mental illness. She suffered from paranoid schizophrenia and spent lengthy periods in various asylums, clinics and mental hospitals.

So, in effect, Norma Jean grew up without a father and, for much of the time, without a mother, too. Because of Gladys' mental condition she was shunted about from one foster home to another and in 1935, when she was only nine, she was placed in the care of the Los Angeles Orphans' Home in Hollywood. There she stayed for nearly two years, a traumatic experience because she knew all along that she was not an orphan. She kept telling people so but nobody took any notice. Once she tried to run away but was found again and taken back. In later years she told positively Dickensian stories of the way she was treated in the orphanage, alleging that she was made to wash up and scrub floors all day long. These tales were, at best, exaggerated. Life in the orphanage cannot have been easy but it certainly wasn't brutal. Norma Jean's memories of it probably reflect her mental, rather than her physical, wretchedness at the time.

In June 1937, however, she was rescued from this place by Grace Goddard, a friend of her mother, who first placed her briefly with foster parents and then took her into her own home. That time with Grace and Erwin Goddard was the happiest period of Norma Jean's childhood. Grace was perhaps the closest approximation to a mother of her own that she ever had and Grace's aunt, Ana Lower, was also a considerable influence on her, introducing her into the local Christian Science Church (Gladys, incidentally, was also a Christian Scientist) and giving her a religious belief to which she clung devoutly at least until she was in her twenties.

The Goddards lived in the town of Van Nuys, California, and Norma Jean attended the high school there from September 1941, until March 1942. She was then nearly sixteen, 5 feet 6 inches tall and already capable of doing wondrous things to the shape of a sweater. It was at this point that she met James Dougherty, who was around twenty-one, had a good job at the Lockheed aircraft plant and had been something of a celebrity in his day at the Van Nuys High School; an easy-going, athletic young fellow who, at the time Norma Jean entered his life, was much involved with another girl who had attained the lofty title of "Queen of the Santa Barbara Festival".

Dougherty had long been aware of Norma Jean as just another kid around the neighbourhood, nice looking certainly, but not to be compared with a Queen of the Santa Barbara Festival. It was only when Grace Goddard asked him to take the kid to a local dance that he realised that what he held in his arms was not a kid at all but a very nubile young woman and matters, he said, progressed from there in a way that was not necessarily in the best interests of the Queen of the Santa Barbara Festival.

Indeed, they progressed so rapidly that on June 18th, 1942, Norma Jean became Mrs. James Dougherty. To some extent the match was arranged by Grace Goddard, who believed that marriage was the best and most convenient way to get Norma Jean settled down. But Dougherty was at least willing and Norma Jean was enthusiastic since her groom was a good-looking young man, much sought-after by the neighbourhood girls and thus an excellent catch for her.

The bride herself was hardly more than two weeks past her sixteenth birthday, straight out of school and a virgin. This latter piece of information is not as impertinent or as irrelevant as it might sound because later on as Marilyn Monroe's tales of her childhood became ever more lurid and unreliable one of the claims she would most frequently make was that she had been raped by a lodger at one of her foster homes when she was only nine. Another claim was that she had had an illegitimate child when she was fifteen. Dougherty, however, would lend no credence whatsoever to either of those stories. "I was the first," he said. "Believe me; I know. There's no way she could have had a child and there's no way she could have been raped."

To begin with the marriage was happy and carefree enough. Dougherty taught his bride to shoot, fish and skin rabbits and she in return taught herself to be a neat and efficient housewife and an original cook who planned her dishes according to the colours of the ingredients. Peas and carrots featured prominently on the Dougherty dining table because she thought they looked pretty nestling side by side on a plate.

Dougherty's memory of his first wife, nearly forty years later, was of a bright, warm, attractive girl with few friends of her own (mainly, he thought, because other women regarded her as a potential threat), who then — as later — was in urgent need of love, recognition and attention. "I imagine," he said, "that I was kind of like a father and a brother as well as a husband to her." But she needed to love as well as to be loved and so, early in the marriage, she wanted to start a family. Dougherty, however, dissuaded her. "I felt she was too young emotionally to begin raising children. I wanted her to wait at least until the war was over. She begged me to let her have a baby but I said, 'No, not yet, not yet. Wait until you're a little older .'"

Generally speaking this was the only point of disagreement between them although there was, he recalled, another occasion when he upset her rather badly. "She wanted to bring a cow into the house one time because it was raining and the cow was getting wet and was mooing and I told her, I said, 'You can't do that. That's crazy.' She felt very bad, you know, because I mentioned the word 'crazy'." From then on he was careful not to repeat the error because even the most jocular accusation of craziness would "make her become pensive and worried", and this was due to the family background of mental illness. Of that she was reminded during the early days of her marriage when she was reunited with her mother. "When they first met," said Dougherty, "it was almost like strangers because Norma Jean hadn't seen her since she was a small child."

Gladys was then spending one of her increasingly brief periods out of hospital but, as Dougherty said, she was never really cured and even at that time was showing signs of the religious mania that later was to dominate her personality and that was to confine her to an institution where she was supported by her daughter.

The idyllic part of the Dougherty marriage ended when Jim was inducted into the Merchant Marine and was sent overseas. There was little he could do about that, America being at war at the time, but nevertheless Norma Jean regarded his leaving her as a form of rejection. Dougherty argued, reasonably, that it wasn't anything of the kind and that he was hardly a free agent in the matter but she was not to be convinced. "I think one of the worst things her childhood left her with was a sense of rejection," he said. "So many times she was transferred from one foster home to another and each time to her it was a rejection. When I went overseas she saw it as another rejection and I think that was one of the things that started the beginning of the end for us."

When her husband went away, Norma Jean's security went, too. She was obliged to give up her own home and move in with Ana Lower, Aunt Ana as she called her, and fond as she was of Aunt Ana she was lonely without Dougherty. To counteract this her mother-in-law found her a job at the Radio Plane factory. It was a fairly humble, manual job but one day an Army photographer called in to take propaganda pictures on behalf of the war effort and decided to use Norma Jean as a model. She revealed a natural talent for the work and the photographer recommended her to a modelling agency in Los Angeles.

From that moment she was embarked upon a new career: the agency signed her up and soon her photographs began to appear in a large number of magazines. Dougherty had no objection to the modelling work but gradually, as she developed the ambition to become an actress, he began to grow worried. "I knew that if she got into the movies she was going to run into problems. It's a dog-eat-dog world with a lot of phonies in it and I knew she wouldn't be able to handle that."

Norma Jean, on the other hand, believed she could handle it. The modelling work became more and more important to her and by the time her husband came home on his second leave from the Merchant Navy she was on the covers of twelve different magazines. On that occasion she was an hour late meeting him off the train. He didn't think it too significant at the time because punctuality was never one of her virtues but, as he learned later, her failure to be at the station waiting for him was due to the fact that she had been taking a film test. "She never told me," he said, "because she knew I wouldn't approve." More accurately she didn't tell him then; she waited until he had returned to his ship in Shanghai and then revealed all in the "Dear John" letter that is dreaded by every serviceman abroad.

"She wanted a divorce," he said. "Of course, she couldn't divorce me while I was overseas because I wouldn't sign the papers until I could get home and talk to her. Then she told me she was going to be an actress and said they wouldn't even consider her until she was divorced, because they didn't want her having babies once they'd spent the money to bring her from a starlet to a star. She said, 'Even though we're divorced it doesn't keep us from being together. You can come and see me, take me out.' I said, 'No, thanks,' and that was it."

At first Dougherty rejected the idea of a divorce altogether, but by now Norma Jean was sharing a tiny apartment and indeed a bed with her mother and when, on his next leave, her husband arrived at three o'clock in the morning there was nowhere for him to sleep. The following day they met to discuss their future and: "It was very emotional. We both cried and she said, 'I've got to go this way. This is my chance,' and I said, 'Well, that's it,' so I signed the papers."

If all this appears to be ruthlessly self-centred behaviour on Norma Jean's part, it's perhaps worth remembering that she had, rightly or wrongly, felt rejected by her husband's absence abroad and that in the modelling and cinema worlds she was for the first time in her life being treated as an individual in her own right, as somebody of importance. She was at last being given recognition and attention and these can be highly seductive to someone who has been totally deprived of them.

The divorce from Dougherty became final in September 1946, and by then Norma Jean was twenty, although she wasn't to remain Norma Jean for very long. Three months earlier she had been to see Ben Lyon, the head of casting at 20th Century Fox, who was sufficiently impressed to offer her a contract at 75 dollars a week. He also decided that she should change her name. Henceforth she was to be Marilyn, after the musical star Marilyn Miller whom Lyon very much admired, and Monroe because that was the maiden name of Norma Jean's mother.

The name was not the only thing that was changed. Some time after she had signed the contract she talked on the telephone to Dougherty who asked her, with some concern: "What's the matter, you got a cold or something? Your voice sounds so low, so different."

"Oh," she said, "I had to lower my voice because they told me it was more sexy."

But what kind of person was this newly-created Marilyn Monroe with the low, sexy voice and the tight clothes that caused her to wiggle so devastatingly when she moved? It has been suggested that at this time she was busy working her way to the top on the casting couches of Hollywood. But if so this would seem to indicate that she had changed her personality as drastically as she had changed her name because Dougherty was convinced that she had been faithful to him, despite his absence abroad, until the marriage ended.

And Ben Lyon, too, refused to believe the stories of her early promiscuity. When I talked to him a few months before he died he remembered her as a very nice girl, a rather lonely girl who lived modestly and — on her small salary — quite often in debt at the Studio Club, a sort of YWCA for young actresses. Once she was so broke that she asked him to lend her a few dollars, an occasion he recalled vividly because, he said, she was the only person in Hollywood who ever borrowed money from him and insisted on paying it back.

At the same time he didn't exactly deny that the opportunity to advance her career prostrate on a casting couch was absolutely denied to her. Quite often, he said, producers at the studio would call him up and remark casually, "That new blonde you've got, what's her name, Monroe, is it? Well, I may be able to offer her something. Send her up to my office at six o'clock." Both Lyon and Monroe were perfectly aware that anything that was likely to be offered to her in a producer's office at six o'clock in the evening would have very little to do with films and he didn't believe she ever accepted any of these invitations. The circumstantial evidence at least suggests that he was probably right, for had she been more sexually compliant her career at Fox would surely have prospered far more than it in fact did. During her brief initial spell at the studio she appeared only in two minuscule parts in very negligible films and after a year her contract was dropped. In the first, *Scudda Hoo, Scudda Hay*, a romantic comedy starring June Haver, she was virtually an unidentifiable figure in the background in a boating sequence and in the second, *Dangerous Years*, a story of juvenile delinquency, she was seen for about two minutes.

Had she been promiscuous the most significant thing that happened to her at Fox might have been the fact that she attracted the attention of Joseph M. Schenk, an executive producer at the studio, who was already about seventy years old. He was a prominent figure in Hollywood who had been married to Norma Talmadge and at one time or another had been chairman of Universal Artists, founder of 20th Century Productions and head of 20th Century Fox. On a less fragrant note he had also been involved with union racketeers and, during the early 1940s, served a prison sentence for tax evasion.

If she had offered such a man more than friendship, the studio would hardly have treated her in so cavalier a manner as it did. But Schenk, who had set himself up as the young starlet's protector, failed to intercede on her behalf — or certainly failed to intercede effectively — when Fox decided not to take up its option on her services, though he did persuade Harry Cohn of Columbia to put her under contract and it was at that studio that she played her first significant role in *Ladies of the Chorus*.

It was there, too, that she acquired her first drama coach, Natasha Lytess, who, from then on, was always on the set when Monroe was working. (Always, that is, until her pupil discarded her some years later in favour of Paula Strasberg.)

In Monroe's early days at Columbia there was talk of giving her a screen test for a certain role and John Huston, the director, overhearing this talk came to the conclusion, no doubt accurately, that what the test in fact amounted to was an elaborate trap to get her into somebody's bed. Rather nobly and without even knowing her Huston sprang to the damsel's rescue by volunteering to direct the test himself in colour and with John Garfield playing opposite her, thus making the proposition so expensive that it was reluctantly dropped by its proponent. Huston claimed that by his action he had "warded off a fate worse than death for Marilyn Monroe". Whether he did or not, the episode casts an interesting light both on her character and her relationship with Joe Schenk. In the first place it seems unlikely that anyone would go to such lengths to bed her if she were, as has been alleged, already a willing occupant of casting couches. And in the second place if Schenk, still a powerful man around Hollywood, was, as has also been alleged, more than just a protective grandfather figure it seems equally unlikely that some studio producer or director would risk incurring his wrath by trying to seduce his girlfriend. There was, after all, no noticeable shortage of pretty blondes around, most of whom could safely be lured to a casting couch without upsetting anybody. The blondes themselves might be upset, of course, when having given their all they found themselves discarded but they were hardly important and certainly not in the way that the likes of Joe Schenk were important.

Around this time, too, there was another small but significant event: one day, while she was filming *Ladies of the Chorus*, Monroe failed to report for work. An emissary was sent to enquire the reason for this absence and found her in her room at the Studio Club quite ill with hunger. Her salary was small, her debts — for clothes and rent — were large and she had simply been unable to afford the money to eat. Once again the strong implication seems to be that, no matter what might be claimed to the contrary, she was not Schenk's mistress; or if she was his mistress it was clearly a role she played for love and not for money.

With the completion of *Ladies of the Chorus* Columbia, like Fox, decided she had no future to speak of and dropped her contract. Once more Joe Schenk appears to have been of very little help. So in the autumn of 1948, aged twenty-two, she was again a free agent. She appeared briefly, though quite memorably, in *Love Happy* when she wiggled outrageously into the office of private detective Groucho Marx and said: "Some men are following me", and just as briefly and far less memorably in *A Ticket to Tomahawk*, but by the summer of 1949 she was so hard up that when the photographer Tom Kelley asked her to pose in the nude for a calendar picture and offered her fifty dollars to do so, she agreed.

These days when it's comparatively rare for even the most serious young actress to be allowed to keep her knickers on in a film for more than about ten minutes, posing nude for a calendar is hardly sensational. But in 1949 it was considered that only tarts went in for that kind of thing and it's a measure of Monroe's desperation that she agreed to Kelley's suggestion. From that low point, however, her fortunes began to improve. After a promotion tour for *Love Happy* she returned to Hollywood and met the second, and by far the more important, of her elderly protectors, Johnny Hyde, executive vice-president of the William Morris Agency. Hyde had been born in Russia and had come to America as a child acrobat with his parents' vaudeville act. When he grew too big to be hurled about with any degree of safety either to himself or the fellow acrobat responsible for catching him he became an agent and swiftly rose to the upper echelons of agency by discovering Betty Hutton and bringing Rita Hayworth to prominence. By the time he met Monroe he was fifty-three, suffering from a heart complaint and separated from his wife.

According to Rupert Allan, who was to become Monroe's Press

agent, Hyde was "brilliant and very successful, a very wealthy man. He was small and unattractive-looking, no physical presence to speak of, but he was devoted to Marilyn and she was very fond of him." He was in fact so devoted to her that he bought her contract from her original agent and set about making her a star, an aim in which he was somewhat hampered by the fact that Monroe was only the latest in a swiftly changing line of blondes in whom Hyde had interested himself.

It took some while before the rest of Hollywood began to realise that this time it was different, that this time he was really serious both in his love for and his belief in the girl. Hollywood woke up to this fact about the same time as Hyde's wife did. Producers reacted by looking at Monroe with new interest and Mrs. Hyde reacted by suing for divorce.

Hyde's promotion of Monroe was simple: he took her to every important function, restaurant and party in Hollywood and he talked about her to everyone he met. The first man of influence to succumb to this bombardment was John Huston who, on Hyde's insistence, let her read for the part of the dumb blonde in *The Asphalt Jungle*, which she did effectively enough for him to give her the role. When filming began Monroe reported for duty with her drama coach, Natasha Lytess, who had given up her job at Columbia to devote herself to her young protégée.

Huston said he didn't object to this attendance though he was surprised by it since it was "unique in my experience" for a supporting actress to turn up with her own individual drama coach. Whether the presence on set of Miss Lytess actually did any good he wasn't sure but on the other hand it didn't do any harm.

Johnny Hyde's next move on Monroe's behalf was to persuade Joseph L. Mankiewicz to give her the small but eye-catching role of Miss Caswell, another dumb blonde, in *All About Eve*.

Mankiewicz, who had been quite impressed by her work in *The Asphalt Jungle*, agreed to take her on and found that all went well as long as "I pointed her in the right direction and said, 'Repeat after me' every now and then, because she didn't know much about acting, she didn't know what to do with a line."

She seemed to him a lonely girl. When, at the end of a day's shooting, Mankiewicz and others would go out for a drink before dinner "we'd find Marilyn having a drink by herself and we'd ask her to join us, which she would. But the next evening we'd again find her alone. She would never assume that we wanted her to join us or that she was indeed a part of our group."

Mankiewicz said this struck him as rather sad and added: "I also found it sad when one day she came on the set carrying a book under her arm. I thought it was a little odd for her and I said, 'Marilyn, let me see what you've got there.' It was *Letters to a Young Poet* by Rainer Maria Rilke, which was even more astonishing, because she had no idea who Rilke was. She said, 'I just go into the bookshop on Hollywood Boulevard and I pick up a book and open it at random and if what I'm reading interests me, I buy it. Is that wrong?' " Mankiewicz told her it wasn't wrong, that it was in fact an excellent way to go about reading; but what saddened him about the incident was the reflection it cast on her desperate need to improve herself. Together with her dependence on her drama coach, the carrying about of books which she might, or might not, actually have read all the way through indicates that even at that early stage in her career she was not content merely to be the dumb blonde that all of Hollywood assumed her to be.

All of Hollywood, that is to say, except Johnny Hyde, who doggedly continued pleading her cause in the offices of the mighty. In 1950 she was seen in six films and four of them, including of course both *The Asphalt Jungle* and *All About Eve* — the most significant of the six — had been set up for her by Hyde. That same year he also negotiated a seven-year contract for her with 20th Century Fox. But apart from providing plastic surgery to remove a minuscule bump on her nose, this was virtually the last thing he was to do for her. At the end of 1950 Johnny Hyde died of a heart attack. By then Monroe was living with him at his home in Beverly Hills, having moved in to recuperate after her nose operation.

Almost from the first time they met Hyde had been eager to marry her but she always refused on the grounds that, fond though she was of him, she didn't love him enough for marriage. And she turned him down again when he proposed to her for the last time when literally on his death bed. His reason for doing so then was to safeguard her future, for as his widow she would inherit his very considerable estate and be financially secure for life. But the idea of marrying a dying man just for his money appalled her.

With Hyde gone, however, life became more difficult. 20th Century Fox did little to promote her career because the head of the studio, Darryl F. Zanuck, had scant regard for her acting ability and thought of her merely as a marketable commodity, which indeed she was because the public swiftly took to her.

And that was just as well, for in 1952 there came the potentially destructive revelation that she had posed in the nude for Tom

Kelley's calendar. "What did you have on, Marilyn?" the reporters asked her. "Just the radio," she said. In the circumstances this was the perfect answer since it apparently showed her to be precisely the delicious but empty-headed blonde that she played in most of her films and the public can forgive a delicious but empty-headed blonde almost anything. Far from destroying her career, the calendar revelation gave an enormous boost to the box-office receipts of her current film, *Clash by Night*.

At this point Monroe was constantly working. In three years, from 1950 to 1952, she appeared in seventeen films but despite that, despite her increasing popularity, she was unhappy about the way her career was progressing. Neither her work with Natasha Lytess nor her enrolment in the acting classes run by Michael Chekov, a disciple of Stanislavski, could convince Zanuck that she was a serious and gifted actress. Furthermore, since the death of Johnny Hyde she had been living a more or less solitary life. True, in 1951 she had met, been greatly attracted by and begun an affectionate correspondence with the playwright, Arthur Miller. But he was married and living in New York and it was not until April 1952, when some friends invited her to make up a foursome at an Italian restaurant on Sunset Strip, that she formed any lasting romantic attachment. On that occasion her dinner partner was Joe diMaggio, a recently retired baseball player so revered as to be a national institution. Monroe had no interest whatsoever in baseball but even she had heard of diMaggio and the attraction between them was instant.

Inez Melson, who was Monroe's business manager from 1951 onwards, said: "I'm quite sure she loved Joe but one of the attractions was that he belonged to a big family. Every weekend, before they were married, Marilyn flew up to San Francisco to be with his family and I think she liked the idea of being part of it. I know she would have liked a family of her own. The thing she wanted most in the world was to be a mother."

In many ways 1953 was Monroe's best year. DiMaggio was a constant, devoted presence in her life, eager to marry her, and suddenly her career began to blossom. *Photoplay* magazine selected her as "the best newcomer of the year", thus proving that it takes many years to become a newcomer in Hollywood. Her eighteenth film, *Niagara*, in which she played an unfaithful wife plotting to kill her husband, established her at last as a star and she followed this with two delightful comedies, *Gentlemen Prefer Blondes* and *How to Marry a Millionaire*. On the debit side there were, as ever, differences of opinion with her directors, partly because she would only put her trust in Natasha Lytess. Never mind whether the director was satisfied with a particular take, if Lytess gave it the thumbs down Monroe would insist on doing it again. And again. And again. Still, by and large, the only event that seriously marred her onward progress that year was the furore that attended the gala evening at which she picked up her *Photoplay* award.

Monroe chose for this occasion a dress so revealing that diMaggio refused to escort her and even Joan Crawford, hardly the most demure of women, was moved to attack her in print for "flaunting her sex". Monroe was deeply distressed and yet later in the year, when she and Jane Russell were jointly granted the accolade of being asked to leave their hand and footprints in the cement outside Graumann's Chinese Theatre on Hollywood Boulevard, she suggested that being who they were they should perhaps leave the imprints of their breasts and buttocks as well.

It was the kind of impish remark which, taken together with her lapse of sartorial taste at the *Photoplay* award, underlined the contradiction in her character which she was never really to resolve. On the one hand there were the acting lessons, the drama coaches, the desire to be taken seriously; and on the other her almost narcissistic pleasure in and display of her magnificent body. (A few years later when she was making a film for George Cukor it became so apparent that she wasn't wearing any underwear at all that the continuity girl approached Cukor and said: "We've just got to do something about that five o'clock shadow.")

Such incidents merely lent ammunition to those who mocked her longing to be taken seriously. How could she hope for respect, they argued, how could she expect her ambition to make a film of *The Brothers Karamazov* to be greeted with anything much better than ribald mirth, when she flaunted herself like that?

The answer quite possibly is that Monroe was an innocent who saw no connection between the way she looked and her acting ability and if that were so she at least had an arguable point. There's nothing in the rules that says actresses who wish to play in films based on classic novels must be built on the general lines of broom handles; equally there's nothing in the rules that says a woman as superbly constructed as Monroe should not take pride and pleasure in her body and, by transmitting her own pleasure, enable countless millions of cinema goers to enjoy it too.

In January 1954, Monroe and Joe diMaggio were married. It was a curious match because, apart from the fact that by then they were both national institutions, they would appear to have had very little in common. He was a shy and reticent fellow who disliked and distrusted Hollywood and was perfectly happy to sit around watching television of an evening; and she was, well, she was simply Monroe. What diMaggio offered her, though, was love and the part of her that was still Norma Jean was always in search of that.

As it turned out, however, love alone was not enough. As part of their honeymoon Mr. and Mrs. diMaggio went to Japan, where he was to promote baseball, and to Korea, where she did no end of good for the morale of the American troops by waving her hips at them.

In both countries there is no doubt that Monroe was the greater attraction and diMaggio began rapidly to understand that he had acquired more than a wife: he had acquired the world's Number One sexpot, an object of adoration and lust. Another movie star might have been able to accept that; a retired baseball player could not so easily do so.

Thus the problems that were to end the marriage were already starting to reveal themselves. Eight months after the wedding Monroe was beginning to drink too much and was going to a psychiatrist. This was not diMaggio's fault; true he was possessive and, understandably, a little jealous since no husband could take much pleasure in watching other men openly leering at his wife. But the main problem was that Mr. and Mrs. diMaggio were simply incompatible, no matter how much fondness existed between them.

And so when Monroe set off for New York to film *The Seven Year Itch* diMaggio did not accompany her. He did join her later but, in retrospect, it might have been better had he stayed at home because he arrived just in time to watch the filming of that famous scene when Monroe stands over a grating and the breeze from below blows her skirt up around her neck.

Billy Wilder, the director, described the occasion thus: "Two things happened which amused me greatly: (a) there were 20,000 people watching, held back by police and barricades and (b) there were fourteen electricians killing each other over who was going down under that subway grid and working the fan that was to blow her skirt up. Well, it all got so out of hand that we couldn't shoot the scene there on Madison Avenue. The crowd and the electricians got unruly. So we went back to Fox and dug a hole there and twelve more electricians fought for the job."

Meanwhile, on that night in Madison Avenue, diMaggio was standing on the sidelines, shocked and embarrassed.

Wilder said: "I'd have been upset, you know, if there were 20,000 people watching my wife's skirt blow over her head. (She did wear panties, mind you. Please.) But there was take after take and, well, you know the New Yorkers. There were various little comments being shouted from the sidelines and diMaggio didn't like it very much."

Not surprising, really. In the mid-1950s a glimpse of a lady's knickers, be they ever so chaste, was a rare sight and not one which any husband would wish to share with 20,000 cheering strangers. Questioned by a reporter, diMaggio refused to comment on what he had just witnessed and the following day he returned to California. A few weeks later, in mid-September 1954, Monroe consulted a lawyer and soon afterwards the Press was formally told that the diMaggios were separated. Billy Wilder said: "It was always a kind of strange marriage to me, the kind you invent for an MGM picture — you know, the Lady and the Boxer, with Max Baer and Myrna Loy. Only in the picture they would never be married."

The break with diMaggio also coincided with Monroe's first temporary break from Hollywood. Soon after she completed *The Seven Year Itch* in November 1954, her previous film *No Business Like Show Business* was released and her notices were dreadful. If that were not bad enough Fox, unimaginatively, offered her yet another sex comedy entitled *How to Be Very, Very Popular*. In *No Business Like Show Business* she had performed a highly erotic dance number called "Heat Wave" in which she had worn very brief black panties and the effect, to the casual and prurient observer, was that she wasn't wearing pants at all but was, in fact, flashing her pubic hair. The prurient Ed Sullivan, a powerful columnist, described the scene as "frankly dirty". Embittered by this attack and the latest rubbish offered to her by her studio, Monroe declared that she no longer felt contractually bound to Fox and flew to New York to launch her own company, Marilyn Monroe Productions, which she had formed with the photographer, Milton Greene.

In New York Arthur Miller came back into her life, she began to study under Lee Strasberg at the famous Actors' Studio, *The Seven Year Itch* opened and was an immediate box-office success and she and Joe diMaggio were divorced. At the Actors' Studio (where a fellow student Eli Wallach found himself "amazed at her desire, her eagerness to learn") Natasha Lytess was replaced as her resident coach and guru by Strasberg's wife, Paula.

And on the advice of Milton Greene, and no doubt of Paula Strasberg too, Monroe renegotiated her contract with Fox on terms more advantageous to herself. She signed a new seven-year contract under which she would make only four films for Fox and would be free to do outside productions.

The first picture she made under this revised deal was *Bus Stop* in which, playing opposite Don Murray and directed by Joshua Logan, she gave what is still generally considered to be the best performance of her career. It's a minor tragedy that she was rarely allowed to play roles of such weight again, in this case the role of a pretty but shop-soiled singer in a tawdry night club who appears, to the young and innocent cowboy portrayed by Don Murray, as a sort of angel. With a few more films of that calibre in her record her reputation would have stood even higher than it now does. As it is — and in the words of Billy Wilder, one of the shrewdest and most percipient of Hollywood directors — "she made her name playing trivia, absolute, total trivia and to make it playing trivia is much tougher than playing Ibsen".

The film with which she followed *Bus Stop* was not exactly trivia but even so it was something of a disappointment. In 1956, Monroe now aged thirty went to England to co-star with Laurence Olivier in the screen version of Terence Rattigan's *The Prince and the Showgirl*.

On the face of it this should have been quite a sensational pairing: the greatest English-speaking actor in the world and the sexiest woman in the world. But in the event — and for reasons that were totally beyond the control of Olivier, the director as well as the co-star — it was no better than mediocre.

Before she left for England Monroe had finally married Arthur Miller. The old friendship between them, rekindled by her arrival in New York in late 1954, had swiftly developed into something deeper and more passionate than that. Miller had left his wife and obtained a divorce in Nevada. But at the same time he was under investigation by the House Un-American Activities Committee on suspicion of harbouring Communist sympathies. It was an extremely awkward time for him but the pressure was greatly relieved by his public announcement that he was going to marry Monroe. At once the HUAC lost interest in him on the grounds, no doubt, that anybody who was about to marry the national sex symbol could not possibly be a Commie.

It was an odd time and they were odd circumstances in which to reveal an impending marriage and there are those among Monroe's staunchest friends who feel that Miller's behaviour was not entirely selfless. Rupert Allan, her Press agent, said: "She thoroughly admired him. She thought he was a father figure and she thought he was a great talent and a great writer and a great intellect, all of which he was not. The way he announced their engagement was rather bizarre. He announced it to the Press in Washington when he was up there for the HUAC, then he telephoned her in New York and told her what he had done."

How did she react to that?

"She was surprised, she told me, but she was very happy."

Did she blame him for his action?

"No, no. She went out and campaigned for him. It was good for him, you see, to marry the All-American Girl image."

Leaving aside that parenthetical dismissal of Miller's professional ability, what he had done would certainly seem to be pragmatic, though not necessarily as cold-blooded as Mr. Allan makes it seem. There was no doubt that bride and groom were equally attracted to each other. Eli Wallach, a friend of them both, said: "I think they were very much in love. I found them a place to spend their honeymoon on Long Island and they were very happy together."

Yet Wallach, too, said he thought Miller was "very smart" to make his announcement at the time he did and it certainly helped him to get back the passport that had been confiscated from him in 1954. Even so: "I think he saw in her a vulnerable lady whom he could protect against all hostile forces and she saw in him a father, a man with knowledge, a creative person and that's what she wanted. I'm sure she entered the marriage with the idea that she was going to make a go of it this time, with the feeling that 'this is going to work'. I think both Marilyn and Arthur Miller were determined to make a go of their marriage, to prove to all the scoffers, to the Press and all the intellectuals who said, 'How could you do this — Beauty and the Beast, the Brain and the Body — how could you do that?' that it could come true."

The couple were married in June 1956, and almost immediately left for England and the filming of *The Prince and the Showgirl*. For newly-weds this should have been an idyllic interlude; instead it was an unhappy time for all concerned. Monroe was insecure at the thought of acting with a man of Olivier's stature and insecurity meant that she was perpetually late on set. Paula Strasberg constantly interfered, overriding Olivier's direction and making Monroe insist on countless retakes. In turn, Olivier became quite naturally irritated by the pair of them. By now Monroe was taking uppers and downers as a matter of habit and even her new husband was growing a little disillusioned.

Norman Rosten, the poet, who, along with his wife, had befriended Monroe during her spell in New York, said: "She was a difficult woman, you know. We liked her and we say the nicest things about her and she deserved them: she was a very gallant person. But she was trouble and she brought that whole baggage of emotional difficulties of her childhood with her. She was very insecure and she had psychiatrists in attendance, if not every day then a number of times a week."

One of the reasons for her emotional problems was the fact that she desperately wanted but was unable to have a child. Soon after she and Miller returned to America she did in fact become pregnant but it was tubular and had to be aborted. The inability to have children caused her deep depression — it was as though she were merely some kind of sexual toy and not a complete woman at all.

Whitey Snyder, her favourite make-up man in Hollywood, believed that "If she could right away have had a child — because she loved children so much — if she could have had one of her own to take care of I'm sure it would have helped her immensely."

But that, alas, was not then possible; nor was it ever possible. What she had, instead, was the bitter disappointment of an obligatory abortion. For a year afterwards she was away from the cameras, recovering from this personal tragedy and doggedly studying acting. Her partnership with Milton Greene was dissolved; she and Miller moved into a farm and then to an apartment on New York's East Side and it was August 1958, before she returned to the film studios to star with Jack Lemmon and Tony Curtis in Billy Wilder's *Some Like It Hot*.

By now her working pattern was fully established: as always she arrived on set with her drama coach (still Paula Strasberg) but now the entourage had grown to include her personal hairdresser, make-up man, Press representative and various others whose titles and duties were unspecified.

A great deal has been made of the fact that at about this time Monroe was notoriously unreliable, that she was either late reporting for work or that she didn't turn up at all. The implication is that she was carried away by delusions of grandeur, believing herself to be so important that it didn't matter if she kept others waiting.

But against that it must be remembered that she had *always* been late, even when she was a mere starlet and a moment's lateness could have led to her dismissal. To attribute her apparently selfish and careless behaviour to conceit is to miss the point. Monroe's inability to be anywhere on time stemmed from her basic insecurity: it was not a lack of belief in herself but a lack of confidence in herself and these are by no means the same thing. You can, as she did, believe you have the ability to do a thing well but at the same time you can lack the confidence to go out there and do it. So even at the peak of her success there was an anxiety about her, a desire to please that spilled over into her performances and could be quite heartbreaking, invoking in both men and women a powerful urge to protect her. That insecurity stayed with her throughout her life and in her later years she tried to deaden it with drink and barbiturates. One of its manifestations was the fact that despite her status in Hollywood her friends were not other stars or directors or producers or executives but men and women in rather humbler walks of life: make-up men like Whitey Snyder, publicity men like Rupert Allan and theatrical gurus like Natasha Lytess and Paula Strasberg.

And another of its manifestations was her amazing inability to be anywhere on time, a trait noticed by her first husband Jim Dougherty in the days before she even became a photographic model.

Now the psychological explanations for chronic lateness for appointments are too numerous to list but Monroe's own explanation is worth considering. Whenever she had an important date, she once said, she would lie for hours in a bath and quite forget the time. The bath was a treat not for Marilyn Monroe but for Norma Jean who, she claimed, as a child had invariably been obliged to bath in water already used by other people. And the subsequent lateness was a form of punishment, a rebuke — again not to the people who were waiting for Marilyn Monroe but to all those who had never waited for and never had time for and never paid attention to Norma Jean.

But touching and even true though this plea might have been it would have brought very little comfort to Billy Wilder, to Tony Curtis and to Jack Lemmon as they waited, hour after hour, for their tardy colleague to arrive.

Wilder said: "I wanted to strangle her because she was never on time and she never knew the lines. What I think it comes to is that she had no sense of time. She had a superb sense of timing, which is a totally different thing. She could be just extraordinary — she could be sweet, she could be warm, she could be trying very hard and then again she could be miserable, she could be offensive, she could be rude, she could be unapproachable and, worst of all, she just wouldn't show up, she wouldn't be around.

"I treated her every which way I could imagine to kind of help her along but it was very difficult. We were working at Fox — now she'd worked there for six or seven years and we'd have like 300 extras and she'd show up at two in the afternoon. I'd say, 'What happened?' and she'd say, 'I lost my way.' Now she was living at the same house, the studio wasn't moved overnight and yet she'd lost her way."

As a possible explanation for such conduct it might be worth pointing out that at this time Monroe was pregnant again. "One day," said Wilder, "Arthur Miller took me to one side. He said, 'Look, do me a favour, please. We've just found out that Marilyn is pregnant and we don't want anything to happen to the baby. So why don't you let her go home at four in the afternoon? Don't keep her here till six.' I said, 'Arthur, you know what time she turns up here?' He says, 'Well, she leaves the house at seven in the morning.' I says, 'She may leave the house at seven in the morning but she shows up here at eleven thirty and if I can get one shot by two thirty or two shots by four I'm very lucky. If she came on time she could go home for lunch and stay there.'"

If the lateness were not enough to complicate Wilder's life there was also the presence of Paula Strasberg and Monroe's occasional and in a way magnificent inability to remember her lines. Of the drama coaches and their importance to her, Wilder said: "I guess she was kind of like somebody who's not too steady walking and hangs on to a railing or a piece of furniture."

(There were others who said the drama coaches simply confused her and that she would have been a better and easier actress without them. But Rupert Allan believed they were psychologically important to her because "acting wasn't easy for her. It was a torment. She worried. She was filled with anxiety and apprehension.")

Of the inability to remember her words Wilder said: "For a good part of the picture she never fluffed a line but when she fluffed, boy, did she fluff. I remember a scene when the two boys [Lemmon and

Curtis] were in a room disguised as girls and she was to knock on the door and say, 'It's me. Sugar.' [That was her name.] And she was to come in and since she was having problems in the love story she was depressed and she wanted to have some whisky. So they brought some whisky along and put it in the dresser and she was to ask 'Where's the whisky?' and she was to go to the dresser and find it. Well, we ran like forty-seven takes — and that was just outside the door. She would knock, the boys would say, 'Who is it?' and she would say, like, 'Sugar, it's me,' and we'd do it again. So finally, since she was outside the room we printed it up and pinned it on the door — 'It's me. Period. Sugar. Period.' Well, when she got that and actually got into the room she couldn't remember 'Where's the whisky?' So we went into every drawer in that damn dresser; no matter which one she opened there it was in huge letters, 'Where's the whisky?' She couldn't miss it but by now we're on take sixty-three and the boys, you know, they've been standing there since six-thirty in the morning in high-heeled shoes and they're crying with pain.

"So I say, 'All right, let's take ten minutes,' and I took Marilyn aside and I said, 'Marilyn, don't worry,' and she looked at me and said, 'Worry about what?' It just meant nothing to her."

This, alas, was not an isolated incident. There were several other occasions when they ran into thirty or forty takes and before the film was over Tony Curtis had developed such a passionate hatred for her that when he was asked one day what it was like kissing her, he replied that he'd rather kiss Hitler, which is a fairly considerable admission from one who had started his life as Bernie Schwarz in the Jewish sector of New York. No doubt he would withdraw that statement today but there's little doubt that he meant it at the time. And clearly the fact that she caused so much aggravation helped to account for the popular image of her around Hollywood as a temperamental monster.

Jack Lemmon, however, did not believe that the fluffing of lines or the lateness had anything at all to do with temperament. In particular the lateness, he said, "must have gone all the way back to her childhood. There were a number of things, I'm sure, that caused her to be unable, literally unable, to face something until psychologically she could do it. Nobody could say, 'Look, this is a professional commitment. You must do it.' She couldn't face it until she herself was ready. It was the same thing during takes. Very seldom do I remember Billy Wilder saying, 'Cut.' Marilyn would stop, because if she thought the scene wasn't going well, even though I did or Billy did or Tony did, she would suddenly stop in the middle and wring her hands and say, 'I'm sorry' and walk off for a minute. She had a built-in alarm clock and it just went off when things weren't going well for her."

Now that would appear to be an exceedingly self-centred attitude but Lemmon was convinced that there was far more to it than that.

"She wasn't just the giddy blonde, you know. She had a certain intelligence about her work and she was a gifted comedienne. There's no question about that. She understood comedy and she developed herself. Nobody gave her those marvellous mannerisms — that thin, high voice, the funny look, whatever it was that was Marilyn and that people imitate and never come up to. That was all her. She developed that character and most of the time she bent the part to her. She didn't try to be totally different as a character actor; she was smart enough not to do that. Ultimately I think she used what talent she had more fully than maybe any other actor I've ever known. Olivier, for example, probably uses eighty to eighty-five per cent of his talent and the rest of us use about the same: you try but you can't get it all. But I think Marilyn came close to using a hundred per cent of her talents. They weren't that big but, damn, she used them all. That's why she would stop in the middle of a scene — it may seem selfish and it is but it wasn't meant that way. It was the only way she could work. She knew her limits and she went to those limits. It wasn't easy for her: she was fighting all the time, struggling to achieve what she could, trying as hard as she could. She didn't have the talents of some other actors, there's no question, but she was using more of what she had. It fascinated me to watch her work."

Whatever trouble she caused and whatever her reasons for causing it, *Some Like It Hot* was financially Monroe's most successful film. Professionally she had arrived at another peak but her life was once again in a mess. In November 1958, she had a miscarriage and the following year, still intent on having a child, she went into hospital for corrective surgery, although by then her relationship with Arthur Miller was under constant strain.

Her use of sleeping pills and wake-up pills had led on more than one occasion to an accidental overdose but the usage was in itself only a reflection of the fact — noted by Jack Lemmon during the filming of *Some Like It Hot* — that she was essentially unhappy. No doubt Arthur Miller was unhappy, too, and this shared state of wretchedness was only enhanced when early in 1960, while filming

Let's Make Love, she had a celebrated love affair with her co-star, Yves Montand.

Montand himself was married to Simone Signoret and it seems fairly clear that neither he nor his wife took the dalliance with Monroe too seriously. Monroe, however, did.

During the preparations for the picture both couples, the Millers and the Montands, lived in adjoining bungalows at the Beverly Hills Hotel. They became friends, though nothing more than that until Simone Signoret had to return to Paris and Miller to Connecticut to get on with his writing. "And that," said Rupert Allan, "left the two alone, working together very closely and both physically attractive. What happened was inevitable I would have thought."

Inevitable or not, it wouldn't necessarily have been too damaging if the affair had remained secret. In any event it would have passed soon enough because Montand had no intention of wrecking his marriage on Monroe's account. Unfortunately it didn't remain a secret. "It was Yves," said Rupert Allan, "who let the cat out of the bag. He let Hedda Hopper, the columnist, come to interview him. He didn't know English that well and he admitted they were having an affair. Marilyn was unhappy that it came out in the open, I'm sure, because first of all it had to hurt Arthur Miller — in fact it enraged him — and she also didn't want to hurt Simone Signoret, of whom she was very fond."

The liaison continued throughout the making of the film but not for a great deal longer and Monroe, according to Rupert Allan, was "very much upset" when it ended with Montand's departure for France and a return to the conjugal home. It was a far deeper affair for her than it ever had been for him.

What is more it virtually ended Monroe's marriage, although both husband and wife agreed not to announce their decision to divorce until after the filming of *The Misfits*, the picture which Miller had written especially for her.

The shooting, directed by John Huston who had earlier saved her from that fate worse than death and then given her her first real chance in *The Asphalt Jungle*, took place in Reno. Clark Gable was the co-star and others in the cast included Montgomery Clift and Eli Wallach. Miller and Monroe, maintaining the pretence that all was well in their private life, lived in the same hotel, though she spent little time with him off-set, preferring the company of her entourage of six.

Eli Wallach said: "What was happening away from the film was infinitely more dramatic. He was in one suite, she was in another. They'd get together for a Press conference but there was a coldness and a hardness in their relationship. And yet on the set in the film she had to be this lovely lady falling in love with this cowboy, Clark Gable. There was a turmoil in her that, I think, was making her ill.''

And indeed she was ill. John Huston said: "The girl that did *The Asphalt Jungle* was tremulous, young, aspiring, ambitious and obviously glowing. The one that was in *The Misfits* was not tremulous but trembling, an addict, hooked. She'd dived off the high board and the swimming pool was empty."

By this time, he said, she had become quite dependent on drugs to put herself to sleep. "I think she was afraid of not being herself the next day, of not being her most beautiful. That's the way it started and she became so hooked that she had to take drugs to wake up. Sometimes she would take overdoses and they'd have a hell of a time to get her to wake up at all."

Eli Wallach believed that Huston was "a genius" in dealing with Monroe on that film. "He handled her with great delicacy, never pressured her, never blamed her for anything, always made her welcome and comfortable off the set." Nevertheless the drug problem and her consequent lateness on or even absence from the set created numerous difficulties. In the middle of the production they had to abandon shooting for two weeks while Monroe was sent back to California to a hospital to be weaned off the pills.

Huston said: "She was a very sick girl, sick like an addict is sick. They took her to a hospital in Los Angeles and she was put under the care of psychiatrist to get her off the drugs." When she returned she seemed quite recovered but "it was only a few days before I discovered she was back into the drugs again".

And yet, despite the off-set drama, *The Misfits* is generally regarded as one of Monroe's very best films, one whose acclaim has increased over the years. Of Monroe's contribution to it Huston — not a man lightly to give praise — said: "I thought it was beautiful. I liked it very much. What I saw on the screen erased the anxieties and the pains that went into getting the performance."

It was her last completed film and I asked Huston, who had directed her at both ends of her career, how he thought she had developed since *The Asphalt Jungle*. He said: "Well, she wasn't an actress in the sense of the English, Shakespearian-trained actor who does a variety of roles and has virtuosity. She was herself and she could present herself very well. She wasn't an actress in the legitimate stage sense but in the motion picture sense she was a very fine actress indeed.''

Even so he could not imagine her carrying on, as an actress, into middle or old age. ''I think she would have gone on for a few years and then, as her beauty faded, she would have retired.''

Did he, I asked, mean that, unlike other actresses who were also beautiful in their time but managed to weather the inevitable fading of their looks and moved on into playing character roles, Monroe was entirely dependent on her beauty?

''No, not beauty alone,'' he said. ''But beauty was part of her fascination. It contributed largely to it because it was unique. There was an article in a magazine once in which her masseuse was quoted as saying that Marilyn's flesh was different from other flesh. Well, there was something honeyed about her, something fetching. But as time went on her beauty would have coarsened and that fragile, tremulous, lovely thing that we all witnessed would have been gone and then she would have lost her appeal because her appeal was largely physical.''

Perhaps Monroe, too, was aware of that and perhaps that's why her drug addiction was more noticeable and caused more concern on *The Misfits* than it had on any of her previous films. By the time it was finished she was already thirty-five and her body, though still superb, was no longer that of a young girl. Facially, too, she was not quite so pretty as she had been and, unlike actresses such as Garbo, Dietrich and Katharine Hepburn, whose beauty is based not so much on prettiness and youthful sexuality as on delicate bone structure, her looks — as Huston said — would probably have coarsened with age.

It could well be, therefore, that she was beginning to feel a certain panic about her future. She had very little money — indeed, by the standards of other stars both of her time and since — she had never really earned vast amounts of money. And if her main assets were beginning to decline what would become of her in three, five or ten years' time?

Whether such thoughts bothered her or not, she was in a very bad mental and emotional state by the time *The Misfits* was completed in November 1960. With the film over she officially announced her separation from Arthur Miller and once again left Hollywood and took an apartment near the East River in New York, where she was continually hounded by the Press who were anxious to find traces of another man in her life.

In the midst of all that she learned, to her great distress, that her co-star Clark Gable, whom she had very much admired, had died of a heart attack. So by the time she went to Mexico in January 1961 for her divorce from Miller she was already in a state of near-nervous exhaustion and it was really no great surprise that on her return to New York she collapsed under the combined burden of emotional stress and far too many barbiturates.

Nor was that the end of her problems because, for some unaccountable reason, she was taken to a hospital for the mentally disordered where, to nobody's astonishment, far from improving, her condition continued to decline. From this awful place she was rescued by the faithful Joe diMaggio, to whom she had turned not as a lover but as a friend when it was obvious that her marriage to Miller was breaking up. DiMaggio took her to a much less frightening hospital where she stayed for three weeks and later that year, after she had recuperated, she went back to California.

By then she was dependent both on her pills and the regular ministrations of a psychiatrist but nevertheless she made an attempt to restore some kind of order to her life. With the help of the ever-faithful diMaggio, whose devotion to her extended throughout her life and beyond it, she bought a fairly modest house, the first she had ever owned, in Hollywood. And then, in April 1962, she returned to Fox to make a film called *Something's Got to Give*, an ironic title because finally it was Monroe who gave.

She signed for the film because contractually she was obliged to do so but Whitey Snyder was convinced that she never wanted to make it. "She kept putting it off and putting it off and finally the studio forced her to start." The plot involved her in a nude bathing scene and she was willing, perhaps eager to do it, possibly because she had been getting herself back into trim, physical shape and was anxious to prove to any doubters who might be around that the famous body was still in good nick.

But, Snyder said, "She was never healthy. I don't think that her body was very strong. She was physically sick lots of times. I think that was because of the pills and not eating right. Some days she just couldn't show up and finally they dropped her after five or six weeks of off and on, hit or miss situation. The studio dropped her; they shut the picture down."

Snyder, who worked with Monroe for years, watched the pill habit developing. She would go straight home after a day's shooting, he said, and take a sleeping pill because "she wanted to look good in the morning; she wanted to get to sleep right away. But then," he said, "she'd probably wake up at nine thirty at night or something and take a couple more pills. Well, they'd put her down again for a while but after midnight she'd wake up again and take some more. It's like a drunk — you don't know when to stop. I'd say to her, 'Marilyn, you're going to kill yourself, you're going to mess up,' and she'd say 'I know,' but she'd go right on doing it. A lot of times she'd come to work and you couldn't get her awake for an hour and a half.''

In view of the way she died this testimony is rather significant but, on the other hand, if the drugs were making her too ill to report for work on time or even report for work at all, it becomes easier to understand the apparent callousness of Fox in dismissing her from the film, though it would have been hard to persuade Monroe of that.

When she was finally given her cards she was, according to her housekeeper, Mrs. Eunice Blackmer, "deeply hurt" but it's difficult to sympathise with her too much because one weekend in May, while she was apparently too ill to work, she flew to New York at the invitation of Peter Lawford to sing "Happy Birthday" to President John F. Kennedy at a massive celebration of said birthday at Madison Square Garden. She looked superb and sang prettily and the studio, which had already incurred excess costs of around one million dollars on the film because of her erratic behaviour, was furious with her.

She was able to work on about six more days during the next two weeks and on June 1st, her thirty-sixth birthday, the crew gave her a party. But a few days later she was fired. Lee Remick was signed to replace her but when Dean Martin walked off the film on the grounds that he had agreed to co-star with Monroe and only Monroe, the whole enterprise was dropped with writs fluttering about like confetti. In a statement issued through her secretary Monroe said: "It's time some of the studio heads realised what they're doing. If there's anything wrong with Hollywood it starts at the top. It seems to me it's time they stopped knocking their assets around.''

And she did indeed have a point. If her own behaviour had been less than admirable, Fox could hardly claim that they had been surprised by it. From the start they had known what they were taking on because by then her emotional and psychiatric problems and her drug addiction were no secret in Hollywood. Besides which, they were not exactly granting any favours by way of salary, for her fee for the picture was only 100,000 dollars — less than £50,000 — which, considering her stature, was truly a pittance.

Although there was talk around the end of June of the studio re-instating her and an alternative film project was discussed, nothing ever came of it. The few scenes she shot for *Something's Got to Give* were the last in which she ever appeared on film.

On the night of Saturday, August 4th, 1962, Marilyn Monroe was found dead at her home. How she died and what precisely had happened to her between her dismissal from the picture and her death have since become the subject of so much speculation that the truth is impossible to determine.

It has been suggested that at this time she was having an affair with the US Attorney-General, Robert Kennedy, the brother of the President. It has also been alleged that, as a result of this, she went into hospital in July to have an abortion; that the affair on his part was merely casual and on her part so serious that she believed he would leave his wife and marry her.

There is, however, no real evidence either to support or refute any of these claims. Frederick Guiles, author of *Norma Jean*, the best and least sensational of her biographies, sets out both the affair and the abortion as facts; Norman Mailer, whose copiously illustrated biography *Marilyn* appeared much later, is not so sure.

There's no doubt, though, that she knew both Jack and Robert Kennedy well. Whitey Snyder remembered driving her to a party at Peter Lawford's house for dinner one night when both men were there and Eunice Murray Blackmer was present on one occasion when Robert Kennedy visited Monroe at home. "I think she appreciated having him as one of her admirers," said Mrs. Blackmer, "but I don't know more than that."

The strongest evidence to support Guiles's theory that an affair took place between Monroe and Bobby Kennedy — evidence, as a matter of fact, to which Guiles was not privy — came from Inez Melson, Monroe's business manager. What she told me, she said, was something she had never publicly revealed before, although she would have revealed it if Bobby Kennedy had been nominated for President.

"Naturally," she said, "I felt very badly when he was assassinated but I didn't want him to be President, because I felt that a man who was father to ten or eleven children didn't have any right to be fooling around.

"Now I didn't know that he was [fooling around] excepting for the fact that in going through Marilyn's possessions after her death I found a letter that Kennedy's sister, Jean Smith, had written to her in response to a letter Marilyn had written extending her sympathy over the old man's [Joseph Kennedy's] stroke. In this Jean Smith said, 'We understand that you and Bobby are an item and we hope that when he comes back you will come with him.' Well, I just didn't think that was nice, you know. I was really angry about that because I could understand why Marilyn would be attracted to somebody who was a great personality and you don't criticise somebody for having admiration but I just didn't feel the family should approve of it . . . I didn't like the idea that 'We understand you and Bobby are an item'. It's just like she was a sort of concubine."

Unfortunately the letter from Jean Smith no longer exists. Mrs. Melson destroyed it just as, in her capacity as executrix of Monroe's will, she destroyed most of the papers she found in Monroe's house after her death, including letters from Arthur Miller — all of them, incidentally, signed "Pa".

She destroyed those papers, she said, to avert any danger of them falling into the wrong hands — the hands, for instance, of the Press, who were making sensation enough out of the sex goddess's demise — and she also destroyed the drugs she found in the house. There were "bottles and bottles and bottles of them and we emptied them all down the toilet".

Why had she done that?

"I don't know. What would you do with a lot of sleeping tablets? What motivated me at the time is that I knew there would be reporters and photographers around there and I didn't want them to see all those pills."

And that brings us to the second mystery of Monroe's last days: the mystery of how she died. Again the stories about that night are legion. Certainly her psychiatrist had visited her during the day and it has been rumoured that Bobby Kennedy did, too, and that she had dinner with him. But Mrs. Blackmer, who was with her all day, who was the last person to see her alive and who, indeed, discovered her body, denied that.

"I didn't really see much of her that day," she said. "She was in her robe and very much in her room and just wandering around in the garden. It was a quiet day." At one point Monroe's Press agent, Pat Newcombe, arrived. "Marilyn came into the room where we were talking and joined us but she seemed a little distracted." Then later, after Newcombe had gone, "Marilyn came to me and asked if we had any liquid oxygen in the house and I didn't know what she was talking about and she turned and walked away." At this point Mrs. Blackmer, slightly disturbed but not too much so for Monroe's behaviour was never predictable, called the psychiatrist, a frequent visitor to the house in any event, and he arrived about 4 p.m. and talked to Monroe in her room. He did not, however, stay very long and when he left Monroe and Mrs. Blackmer were alone in the house.

"Marilyn went to her room and then there was a telephone call from Joe diMaggio's son — he was one of those she would talk to at any time; she was very fond of him — and she talked to him in a loud, happy, gay, wonderful voice."

Up to this point then it had been a fairly normal day by Monroe's standards. She had been a little restless and there was, apparently, a certain amount of tension between her and Pat Newcombe but none of this was unusual. The psychiatrist, Mrs. Blackmer learned later, had suggested to Monroe that she should go for a drive in the evening to relax her but after the phone call she returned to her room and "She stood at the doorway and said, 'Well, we won't go for that ride after all', and then she said 'Goodnight' and closed the door."

That was the last time Mrs. Blackmer saw her alive. What happened after that not even she knows but it seems likely that at some time during the early part of the night Monroe either made or received a phone call, although nobody has ever come forward to admit having talked to her.

Mrs. Blackmer awoke, for no particular reason that she could think of, around midnight. "I opened my bedroom door, which was right next to hers, and I was aware of the telephone cord going into her room. And this was the alarm for me because she never slept with the telephone in her room because it might waken her if she had got to sleep. So I immediately called the doctor."

In normal circumstances that might seem a curious thing to do. If she were concerned, why call the doctor? Why not knock on Monroe's door and see if she was all right? The circumstances in Monroe's house, however, were not what other people might call normal. Mrs. Blackmer's reasoning was that if Monroe was asleep it would be a shame to waken her. But because she was concerned and needed reassurance from somebody she felt the doctor — by which she meant the psychiatrist — was as good as anyone: he, after all, was in fairly constant attendance on Monroe.

On his advice Mrs. Blackmer went outside the house and peered through the bedroom window. "The light was on and Marilyn was lying, without any covers, on her bed. So, of course, I ran back to the telephone and the rest is history."

In fact, everything happened in a considerable rush thereafter. Monroe's medical doctor was summoned and so, for some inscrutable reason, was the fire brigade. The Press arrived fairly swiftly, too — no doubt tipped off by the firemen. While chaos ensued outside, Mrs. Blackmer and various doctors went into Monroe's bedroom.

"The phone was under her. She was lying on her face and the phone was right there, caught in her arm and her hand." She was naked except for her brassière but this again was not unusual. Monroe never wore a nightdress and the only time she wore a bra was in bed, her argument being that she needed the uplift more at night than during the day.

It was some time before the police were called and a sinister interpretation has been put upon this but again, bearing in mind the total confusion of the situation, it is perhaps understandable. What with the Press and the baffling presence of the fire brigade and the necessity to keep photographers out of the bedroom it would not be altogether surprising if the idea of summoning the police only occurred as an afterthought.

But as a result of the confused events of that night all manner of theories have sprung up around Monroe's death. The first, which I think can be swiftly discounted, is that she was murdered either in an attempt to extricate the Kennedy family from a scandal (Monroe, the argument goes, was about to announce her love affair with Bobby) or, conversely, to implicate them in a scandal. (The reasoning behind the latter is a bit hard to fathom.) But either way no evidence of, and no really plausible motive for, murder has ever come to light and Mrs. Blackmer, who said she was accused by innuendo of being one of the murderers, treated the whole suggestion with scorn.

The second theory is that Monroe deliberately killed herself and indeed the coroner's report attributed her death to "probable suicide". But this is based on circumstantial, rather than irrefutable, evidence, the circumstances being that she had certainly taken a massive overdose of sleeping pills. But what motive would she have had for that?

No suicide note was ever found and when I asked whether Monroe had, that previous day, been in the mood of someone who might even possibly be contemplating taking her own life, Mrs. Blackmer said: "I doubt that very much. She had told me — one of the very first things she warned me about — that if she took sedation, which was every night, she was apt to forget and would take a second dose too soon. This was what she had to be careful about, so the first thing I was concerned about after she died was that this was what had probably happened."

What confounds the mystery, of course, is the unexplained presence of the telephone in her room. This has been used to reinforce the suicide theory, the argument running that Monroe, realising that Bobby Kennedy had no intention of destroying his marriage and ruining his political career in order to marry her, had deliberately taken an overdose of drugs and then, regretting it or possibly wanting him to know what she had done and why, had phoned to tell him so. The only fact available to back up this theory is that Kennedy was indeed in town that night. (In fact, he flew off the next day in a great hurry as soon as her death was announced. But that action on his part was not necessarily sinister. Whether he had had an affair with her or not — and I'm strongly inclined to believe he had — he had certainly been seen in her company and his rapid disappearance from the scene was probably due to the natural, though perhaps ignoble, self-protective urge of an aspiring politician to put as much distance as possible between himself and a potential source of embarrassment and scandal.)

The third theory is that Monroe died of accidental overdose and this is the one that is held by her closest friends. All of them had warned her at one time or another that she was taking far too many pills, and that one day she would forget how many she had taken and swallow one dose too many. Rupert Allan, for example, had spoken to her about this when "I caught her opening up the capsules and putting the contents in water to get the action faster". Whitey Snyder had talked to her about it; Monroe herself had warned Mrs. Blackmer that she was aware of the dangers of overdosing.

So the possibility of accidental death is very strong and it is supported by her friends with arguments that are perhaps not as trivial as they may seem. Inez Melson, for instance, refuses to believe that she committed suicide because "she wouldn't hurt people. She wouldn't hurt a fly," and she knew that by killing herself she would bring pain to "millions of people who adored her".

Rupert Allan said: "I'm positive she didn't kill herself on purpose. People who saw her body afterwards said that her hair needed a dye job very badly. She also needed a pedicure. Marilyn would never have gone out and let people see her when she didn't look great, her best. Never. No way."

Both lines of reasoning seem odd but who knows? If it was not her character to hurt people or to allow herself to be seen except at her best would she step out of character when she prepared to kill herself?

Or is suicide out of character anyway for anyone? And does a suicide really care whether her hair needs attention and her toenails are not at their prettiest? The argument simply goes round and round although, perhaps significantly, Rupert Allan recalled that Monroe had once contemplated suicide by jumping from a high building. When telling him about it she said she had changed her mind because there was a woman standing right below and she was frightened of landing on that woman and killing her, too. But what she had also told him was that she had been wearing a green tweed suit on that occasion and the story would seem to indicate (a) that she didn't wish to hurt others and (b) that she was conscious of her dress and grooming on what was intended to be her positively last appearance.

One other person who believes firmly that Monroe's death was simply a tragic accident is Jim Dougherty, her first husband. He said: "If Marilyn, or Norma Jean, had intended to commit suicide she would have written a note to someone; she would have told them why. She loved to write letters. There's no doubt in my mind that it was an accident."

Again, of course, this is merely a personal conviction but it's not unimportant that, at the time of Monroe's death, Dougherty was a member of the Los Angeles Police Department.

True, he was not personally involved in the enquiry into the circumstances of her death but as far as the murder theory is concerned he said: "The finest police department in the world investigated it and they came up with nothing and that's enough for me." And on the suicide theory he said: "I asked the man who investigated it what he thought happened and he said, 'Well, she just took an overdose,' and that was it. She was taking them to go to sleep and she was taking them to wake up and she just took too many."

I believe — perhaps because I want to believe, perhaps simply because it's kinder to believe — that Dougherty was right: that she took sleeping pills before she went to bed and that she woke up — once, twice, who can tell? — and in her fuddled state took more pills, too many more pills.

Marilyn Monroe was buried in Westwood Village Cemetery, just off Wilshire Boulevard. Her crypt is modest and only a few yards away from the din of constant traffic. But upon it each week without fail are placed four red roses. They are put there on the instructions of Joe diMaggio, whose love for her was so constant that, greatly eligible though he is, he has remained single since their divorce.

Both diMaggio and Miller seem strange partners for her but though, in most ways, the two men were very different they also had quite a lot in common.

They were both, in their own fields, the best: diMaggio the best baseball player, Miller in his time the best American playwright. And they were both highly moral and rather solemn men, a great deal older than Monroe. They were more surrogate fathers perhaps than husbands and that's an uneasy role to fill, especially when you are married to a woman who needs a father *and* a husband, a lover *and* a friend, who needs constant reassurance and respect and, above all, unswerving affection. Monroe sought these things from all manner of people, including her theatrical gurus, and never really found them.

It has been said that Hollywood killed her but that's too glib and too simple. Hollywood didn't kill her: it just failed to understand her, to understand the pain and the effort it took her to be what she was and to be as good as she was. In Hollywood she was often treated as something of a joke, a walking fantasy figure. It was acceptable to like her but not to admire her because "for Chrissake, she's just a dumb blonde, you know what I mean?"

What Hollywood quite overlooked, because such qualities are rare in the film business, is that there was about her an innocence and a sweetness that no other actress ever shared. During her association with Robert Kennedy she asked an educated friend to draw up a list of topics that she might discuss with him and a list of questions she might ask him. Hollywood would have pointed to this as evidence of her stupidity but in fact it was evidence of her sensitivity. She admired the man greatly, she was probably in love with him and she simply didn't want to bore him.

The irony of her death is that it was both tragic and, in an awful way, timely. She was thirty-six — not by any means old by normal standards but dangerously old for a sex goddess. Norman Rosten, the poet and her friend, said: "Where would she have gone from there? I mean, she couldn't continue to play the girl with the figure for ever and she knew it."

Billy Wilder said: "I knew it wasn't going to be a simple third act curtain for her. I just could not visualise Monroe in a rocking chair or in the Motion Picture Relief Home or married to somebody who was a pilot for United Airlines."

And, perhaps most brutally, but also most honestly, Joe Mankiewicz said: "Marilyn's death, coming at the time it did, was probably the very easiest and best and gentlest thing that could have happened to her. What everyone forgets is that Marilyn's career was finished: she wasn't about to get another film; she didn't have much money; the studio didn't want her and the men who wanted her were going to get increasingly lower in level. She was thirty-six and I put it to you, as a Queen's Counsel might say, imagine Marilyn alive today — very fat, boozing it up. I think she'd have been a pitiful, dreadful mess and nobody would be able to remember what they do remember, which is this incredible, off-beat, zany, wonderful, dizzy blonde. That's the way we should remember her and her death was the best thing that could have happened to her."

As an actress she was consistently underrated and sometimes cordially hated by her directors. After each of the two films he made with her Billy Wilder swore he would never work with her again. But nearly two decades after her death he told me that "never a week passes when I don't wish she was still around".

In an even higher tribute Joshua Logan described her as being "as close to genius as any actress I've ever known". That may be pitching it a little high but Logan's opinion is at least to be respected. What she certainly was, and what she proved herself to be time and again, was a most wonderfully gifted comedienne, a woman whose combination of abundant physical charms — a positive cornucopia of femininity — and wistful shyness made you at once want to laugh at her and yearn for her and protect her. Nobody since has come even remotely close to matching her. She was confused, yes; she was insecure, yes; she was demanding of more love and devotion and loyalty than any one person could reasonably be expected to give, yes. But when you look at her background none of this is surprising. She had a surfeit of all those warm and desirable qualities which myth and the movies instruct us that all American blondes ought to have — but only she had them. And yet, when you stand back and examine her life, she was doomed from the start: there's a dreadful, ruthless logic to the way she lived and the way she died.

If only, you think, if only someone had given her a great big hug when she was still a little girl and said, "Hey, listen, I love you," then maybe everything would have been different. But in that case she probably would never have become Marilyn Monroe and the world would have been the poorer for it because Marilyn Monroe was something rather special.

As Billy Wilder said: "She had no handle on life but, by God, she had some other things that if you knew what they were you could sell the patent to DuPont and they'd manufacture it. You would think that it's not difficult to make another Monroe; it should be easy — a blonde, a small girl with a sweet face, my God there should be thousands of them, they should come from all over the world."

But they don't. You can take every possible identifiable ingredient that she had and put them together and multiply them and add in the date and the number you first thought of and at the end of it all you've got is a blonde, a small girl with a sweet face and a remarkably voluptuous body. But you still haven't got another Marilyn Monroe.

Peter
Finch
Newly-arrived from
Australia and soon to be
discovered in Daphne
Laureloa.

above : With third wife, Eletha, who claims to have fallen in love with Finchie's feet.

opposite above : With Tamara, his first wife, and their baby daughter.

opposite below : Finch with his second wife, Yolande (whom he met, as he met all his wives, on a beach) with their children, Charles and Samantha.

Finch at the time of The Red Tent *(1969) when his career was going through one of its regular periods of decline.*

*The final triumph — Finch, as Howard Beale, winning his Academy
Award in* Network.

For a little while after Peter Finch died his widow Eletha, the young Jamaican girl who was in fact his third wife, used to visit his grave in Los Angeles and read *The Hollywood Reporter* to him. She would pick out the items of particular interest about what was currently going on in the film industry and then, putting the paper aside, would say: "Well, you haven't missed much. You're still the greatest."

Finch was not, of course, the greatest but a certain amount of exaggeration may be excused in a young widow. He was unique in that he was the first person (and at the time of writing the only person) ever to be awarded posthumously the Oscar for Best Actor and at the time of his death, at the age of sixty, he was firmly headed towards the ranks of the greatest. Indeed, if he had taken a little more care in his career and perhaps in his personal life he would have ranked among them already, but he was never a man to take much care.

In what might almost have served as Finch's epitaph, the British director Alexander Mackendrick once said: "If ever anyone set out to bugger up his career, Peter did." It doesn't quite serve as an epitaph because, at the very end, he had stopped buggering it up but until that point Mackendrick's assessment was sadly accurate. Over a period of forty-one years Finch had made fifty-one feature films, some of them excellent, some of them appalling. At times, as he reeled recklessly from one picture to another, it almost seemed as if he didn't know the difference between a good script and a bad one. And yet he did.

Olive Harding, his agent and in many ways a kind of surrogate mother to him, could always tell when Finch was playing a part that he didn't really want and in which he had no faith. "He sulked his way through it," she said. "He made not the slightest effort." Ultimately, of course, this was self-defeating and caused Finch's reputation as an actor to go up and down like, in the words of one of his friends, "a harlot's knickers". But, as Olive Harding said, "He never saw that. He didn't want to see it. He managed to turn things off in the most remarkable way as if with a key."

And yet at the same time, he was an extremely gifted actor, with the ability when the spirit moved him to turn in a performance of pure gold. His work in *Sunday, Bloody Sunday* and *Network* (to name only the two films for which he was nominated for an Academy Award) could hardly have been bettered and he had, once again, the unique distinction of being the only actor to win the British equivalent of the Oscar five times. Why then should a man capable of producing excellence be also content to turn in dross?

The answer to that, perhaps, lies in his extraordinary childhood, which was so strange that on those rare occasions when he described it to his friends they tended to disbelieve him since all of them accepted him, with the utmost affection, as a chronic liar. Only since his death have most of them come, with great astonishment, to accept his tales as the truth.

It's fairly typical of Peter Finch that the still unsolved mystery of his actual nationality is only a minor point of interest when set against the whole narrative of his early days. In Australia he is proudly claimed as an Australian and indeed he spent most of his formative years there. But the chances are that there was no drop of Australian blood in him at all.

He was born in London (in South Kensington, to be precise) on December 28th, 1916. His mother was Alicia Gladys Ingle-Finch who, although orphaned at the age of nine, was well-connected enough and eligible enough to have married George Ingle-Finch, a notable mountaineer and the son of an eminent lawyer in New South Wales. The marriage took place just over a year before Peter's birth, when George was serving in the Army and on the point of being sent to fight in Salonika. While he was away his young bride fell in love with Major Jock Campbell, a Highlander in the Black Watch, and her son was born some time later and on a date that could have made either man his father.

Peter never really knew George Ingle-Finch or Jock Campbell, though he met them both many years later and, depending upon his prevailing mood, he would claim either one of them as his parent. And, after all, this was only reasonable because either man, his mother's husband or his mother's friend (who after the dissolution of her marriage to George also became her husband) could have been responsible for his conception.

The matter was never really resolved because Alicia —the only person in possession of all the facts — never came forward with the definitive version. Her daughter and Peter's half sister, Mrs. Flavia Magwood, told me that Alicia had kept the secret even from her own children; though against that both of Finch's excellent biographers, Trader Faulkner, author of *Peter Finch — A Biography*, and Elaine Dundy, author of *Finch, Bloody Finch*, seem convinced that the actual father was Jock Campbell, the Scotsman, and not George Ingle-Finch, the Australian.

Nevertheless, George Ingle-Finch, being the incumbent of the marital bed at the time Alicia gave birth, was formally accepted as the father and, despite being aware of his wife's relationship with Major Campbell, may well have believed that he had indeed served in this office, for when his son (or at the very least his wife's son) was hardly more than two years old, George kidnapped him from his pram in the garden of Alicia's home in Sussex. By then the marriage existed in name only and there was a certain amount of hostility between husband and wife.

The kidnapping successfully accomplished, young Peter was taken to stay with his putative grandmother, Laura Ingle-Finch, in Paris and more than thirty years were to pass before his mother saw him again.

Flavia Magwood explained this inordinate lapse of time by saying: "The only thing Mother ever said was that in those days to have a divorce was not like it is today, when everybody does it and thinks nothing of it. George told her that if she intervened in any way or tried to get the child back he would make such a stink about the divorce that she would never be able to hold her head up again anywhere. She said she did try, she did make several attempts to get him back but they were unsuccessful and she realised there was no way she could do it. After that she just cut the whole business right out of her life. There was nothing she could do and that was that."

In any event, and whatever the feelings of his mother, the infant Finch found himself in Paris without benefit of either parent, for George, too, vanished from his life not to crop up again for more than three decades. Young Peter was not, however, altogether unhappy with his *soi-disant* grandmother. According to Trader Faulkner, who was both Finch's biographer and his friend, "he wasn't sent to bed early like other children. He was allowed to stay up late and I remember him telling me there was a marvellous girl who came one night and danced practically naked and that was Isadora Duncan. Then there was a guy who played the piano and, so Finchie said, he was a little guy with a bald head and a beaky nose and very thick glasses and he turned out to be Igor Stravinsky. Another night Nijinsky came and danced and jumped so high he nearly hit the ceiling. And that was the ambience in which Peter grew up."

The young Finch continued in this Bohemian atmosphere until he was nine, at which point his grandmother — clearly one of the great eccentrics of her age — became deeply interested in "spiritualism and theosophy and comparative religions and decided they should go to Madras to the congress of the Theosophical Society where Krishnamurti was supposed to make his great speech about being the Messiah".

In Madras Peter was allowed to run wild until one day he disappeared. Now there are two versions of what exactly happened at this time, the first being Finch's own, which he once recounted to me, and the other being slightly less romantic and therefore perhaps more plausible. What Finch said was: "My grandmother gave me to a Buddhist monk, I suppose as a sort of acolyte, and I lived in a room with this chap for about ten days, I think. I had my hair shaved off and I wore the saffron robe. I didn't know what he was talking about and he didn't know what I was talking about. Then eventually the British Raj got to hear of it and I can vaguely remember policemen and Army officers coming to get me."

The latter part of this is probably true; it's also probably true that Finch and the monk went out on the streets together with begging bowls. What is almost certainly not true is that his grandmother actually gave him to the Buddhist, the far more likely explanation being that Finch had wandered off from the European living quarters and been found by the monk who looked after him as an act of kindness until the whereabouts of his parents or guardians could be discovered.

It's also much more probable that he spent only two or three days, and not ten, in the Buddhist's company. It is, however, undeniable that the incident gave him an interest in Zen Buddhism which was to recur at odd intervals throughout his life and it's also fairly clear that it was largely because of this episode that his grandmother, who wished to go off alone to Darjeeling, put him in the care of her fellow-Theosophists. And they, understandably not wishing to be lumbered with a child who was likely to disappear at any moment and knowing he had a grandfather (Laura's husband) in Sydney, sent him off to Australia.

Peter Finch arrived in Sydney aged ten and with a cheque for £12 representing his entire worldly goods to stay not with his grandfather but with his Aunt Dorothy (once more only his putative aunt unless you accept George Ingle-Finch as his father). But Aunt Dorothy didn't want him and he ended up living with the Theosophists in the suburb of Mosman. He was contented enough there until Charles Ingle-Finch, the grandfather, decided to take him away. Now at this point Finch was still a very small boy but already he had been more or less mislaid by his mother, unwanted by his father and virtually abandoned in India by his grandmother.

As he said later: "I changed hands more often than a dud pound note."

What happened after he left the Theosophists was that he was taken to stay with an elderly maiden aunt in the genteel Sydney suburb of Greenwich Point.

This maiden aunt had little experience of small boys, didn't seem to like them very much and subjected the unfortunate child to very strict discipline, something to which he had never been accustomed before. Of course it might be thought that when he turned up at her door firmly stamped "Reject" what he needed rather more than strict discipline was constant loving care but unfortunately there was never very much of that about during Finch's childhood.

Paul Brickhill, the Australian writer and a boyhood friend of Finch, said: "He didn't really have a home life. He wasn't exactly a welcome guest there, more of an unpaid servant. He didn't get out very much. He had to check in at home and carry on with the housework. And even when he was away from there he always had a little bit of reserve about him; he was a bit on the defensive because he'd been pushed around so much and for so long. He kept most of his emotions inside him; he had a sort of self-imposed insulation around him."

Thus, remote and withdrawn, Finch stayed with his aunt until he was about sixteen when, on leaving school, he became a copy boy on the *Sydney Sun*. Later, dramatising his life as was his wont, he claimed to have been a reporter but he was never that. He wasn't even a copy boy for very long. Within a few months he settled a difference of opinion with his news editor by emptying a jug of water over the latter's head, a practice generally frowned upon in newspaper offices. Finding himself consequently unemployed he left the home of his stern aunt never to return and settled down to a temporary career as a drifter.

As he said much later to me: "I worked on a cattle station and jumped the rattler — which is jumping trains — and I was a hobo and chopped wood. I did anything like that; I had so many jobs I can't remember them. And then one period back in Sydney I was at the Salvation Army dosshouse and I really was at the very bottom of the barrel."

It was at about this stage — or perhaps a little later when, having moved up in the world a bit, he had a room in the red-light district at King's Cross — that he decided to become an actor. There is no definitive reason why anybody decides to become an actor: those who find their way into that profession approach it from a multitude of different directions. Trader Faulkner believed that Finch determined upon this career for himself out of loneliness. "He was always alone and therefore lived greatly in his imagination. Way back in the very early days in Paris, according to Peter himself, he used to people his world with imaginary characters and I think it became compulsive. He was a compulsive actor and also he loathed reality. His world of the imagination was his perfect world and he realised the truth of himself from the characters that he created within himself."

It's a most plausible explanation and the only point with which those who knew him well (including indeed, in retrospect, Trader Faulkner himself) would be inclined to take issue is the assumption that he ever "realised the truth of himself". One of the more remarkable aspects of Peter Finch is the unanimity with which his friends agreed that they could never fully understand him and that he never learned to understand himself.

He had an innate ability to inspire deep affection, even love, in his friends — but never comprehension. Tony Britton, the actor, who knew him as well as anybody, said: "He was an enigma, an amazing, wonderful, extraordinary man but a total enigma. I don't think that Finchie ever really knew who he was and I'm quite certain that none of us who were his friends ever knew who he was. I always used to liken him to an onion: you could peel off layer after layer after layer but you never got down to the real core of the matter, to the essence of who and what he really was. He was the most extraordinary un-get-at-able person."

Jack Lee, the director who worked with Finch on *A Town Like Alice* and *Robbery Under Arms*, said: "He really belonged nowhere and that was one of his troubles. He didn't know where he was as a child, he didn't know how he had started, didn't know his antecedents and he was a drifter. He didn't have any roots and that, I think, was one of the great tragedies of his life."

Then, too, there is Paul Brickhill: "No one ever knew the real Peter Finch. I'm sure he really didn't know himself." And Bill Kerr, the Australian actor: "He's a broken jigsaw puzzle. I don't think anybody will ever put him together because he was too complex a man. If you try to fit the pieces together I think you will get so far and then there will be a lot that will never be explained about him."

His childhood, said Trader Faulkner, had the most profound effect on him. "He was a self-seeker, seeking for his own identity."

What is remarkable about all these statements is that they were made by people who hardly knew each other or did not know each other at all. Certainly they had had no opportunity to discuss Finch among themselves and yet each of them had come independently to the same conclusion about him. He was an elusive, enigmatic character, mysterious even to himself, who had been so moulded by his bizarre childhood that the capacity to "bugger up" his acting career was firmly established within him even before that career had actually begun.

It started, in fact, in an extremely modest way when he lied his way into the theatre by convincing the manager of a Sydney music-hall (who must have been a remarkably gullible fellow) that he had had stage experience in London. So at the age of eighteen Finch found himself working as a chorus boy in vaudeville.

From there it was but a small step to playing straight man to a Jewish comedian named Bert Le Blanc. Bill Kerr who knew him in those days said: "He was a very good straight man but he was always hard up. He had only one pair of trousers, which he used to keep under the mattress and he'd sleep all one day if necessary to get a crease in them so he could go to an audition next day."

The vaudeville experience led to walk-ons and small speaking parts and even to brief appearances in Australian films of very low budgets and even lower ambitions. Gradually on stage, screen and radio he began to be recognised as one of Australia's most promising young actors, though in truth the competition was not exactly fierce.

But in 1941 his career was rudely interrupted by the Second World War. Finch volunteered for the Army, served briefly in the Middle East and helped to defend Darwin against Japanese bombers as an anti-aircraft gunner. It was while on leave from this duty that he met a beautiful young Russian émigré and ballerina named Tamara Tchinarova. He met her, as a matter of fact, on a beach and thus established a pattern from which he never varied: he met each of his three wives on beaches.

Tamara remembered him as "very thin, a bit pathetic and very shell-shocked" from his experience in Darwin. This vulnerable, little-boy quality that, throughout his career and give or take the shell-shock, was to have a devastating effect upon women worked its charm on Tamara and within five months, in April 1943 when Finch was twenty-six, they were married.

From the start, deeply in love though the couple were, Finch was by no means a conventional or dependable husband, the kind who could be relied upon to report home at any pre-arranged time.

Instead, he was much given to drinking late into the evening at the Sydney Journalists' Club with friends from his brief newspaper days or, as Tamara said, "He would meet characters in the street or in the pub and he would be interested in them and perhaps bring them home or go with them to another pub". He was constant and loyal, she said, to whoever he was with — but only while he was actually with them. "The tremendous insecurity he had from childhood meant that he didn't believe in relation-ships. He could cut himself away very sharply and very cruelly. Even in his lesser relationships he would become friends with someone he had met somewhere and that person would imagine he had a friend for life but the next day Peter wouldn't be interested any more."

Nevertheless, the marriage prospered and so did Finch's acting career. He was still in the Army but by now transferred to the Entertainment Unit with whose consent he appeared on the stage, narrated the commentary for a documentary film, broadcast on the radio and played a leading part in the war picture, *Rats of Tobruk*.

Demobilisation came in November 1945, and in the next couple of years Finch won Australia's most significant acting award, helped to found the Mercury Theatre in Sydney, played a tiny part in his first British film, *Eureka Stockade*, and, most significantly of all, was discovered by Sir Laurence Olivier and his wife, Vivien Leigh.

These eminent visitors were touring Australia with the Old Vic at that time and one day, in their honour, a potted version of Molière's *Le Malade Imaginaire*, with Finch playing Argon, was put on at lunchtime at O'Brien's glassworks in one of the industrial suburbs of Sydney.

In recalling the occasion Finch said to me: "I remember I was so nervous. The other actors in the company swore that before the curtain went up I swallowed some of the phoney pills that we had as props. After the show the Oliviers came round backstage and they were enormously impressed with the acting and the company but mostly I think with our courage. And Larry said, 'Vivien, this is the real theatre. These are the street-corner actors. This is what our business is really all about.' And he offered me a sort of chance, you know. He said, 'When you come to England, come and see me.'"

Going to England was a move Finch had been vaguely considering for some time and fortunately he was supported in this notion by Tamara — fortunately because it was she who had been doing something constructive about it, like saving money. So in August 1948, Mr. and Mrs. Finch set sail for England, although it is doubtful whether he would have gone, even with the encouragement of the Oliviers, had it not been for his wife.

Tamara said: "I didn't consider him to be ambitious. I was much more ambitious for him because I could see this talent he had and I felt it had to be given scope. In many ways he was a weak man and let himself be led. He never did anything to get a particular role, he didn't sort of bow to the right people but his personality was such that his charisma really warmed people to him and those who worked with him always wanted to work with him again."

This charisma came in very handy when Finch arrived, aged thirty-two, in London. Olivier was as good as his word and indeed gave him his first opportunity on the West End stage but it took a while to find the right part and in the meantime it was lucky for Finch that Harry Watt, the director of *Eureka Stockade*, had remembered him and warmed to him enough to help him find a good role (as a killer) in the Ealing film, *Train of Events*.

When that was finished he signed a contract with Laurence Olivier Productions and in March 1949, he made his debut in the London theatre playing opposite Edith Evans in *Daphne Laureola*. The play was an immediate success and so, more importantly, was Finch. His reviews were so ecstatic as to convert him overnight from an unknown to a potential new star — a star, some said, who might one day be as lustrous as Olivier himself.

And yet it didn't happen. Something, somehow, went wrong and Finch never really capitalised on that impressive first appearance. Perhaps the fault lay with his contract, which had tied him exclusively to Olivier who was unable to find exactly the right follow-up part for his protégé. Perhaps Finch was misguided to accept comparatively insignificant roles in films like *The Wooden Horse* and *The Miniver Story*. Or perhaps, as Tamara said, he simply lacked the ambition and drive to push himself onwards.

True, during his first four years in London he appeared in six more plays, mostly for Laurence Olivier Productions, and among the parts he played were Mercutio at the Old Vic (with Alan Badel as Romeo and Claire Bloom as Juliet) and Iago in Orson Welles' famous (or, depending on your point of view, notorious) *Othello*. This was a notable production if only for the fact that Orson Welles, the director, so arranged matters for Orson Welles, the actor, that as far as dramatic impact was concerned Iago was virtually reduced to a walk-on part. In any event, it did little enough to further Finch's reputation as a coming star.

In the cinema *Train of Events* had won him a certain amount of applause but that, too, was in 1949, the year of *Daphne Laureola* and it was not until 1952, when he played the Sheriff of Nottingham in the Disney version of Robin Hood that he again attracted the attention of the film critics.

Indeed, at this time of stagnation, or at best of slow con-solidation, Finch's personal life was rather more dramatic than his career. In the autumn of 1949 he had become a father when his daughter, Anita, was born and at around the same time he had been reunited with both George Ingle-Finch and Alicia.

George had emerged first. Soon after Peter and Tamara arrived from Australia he called on them at their hotel in London. He was, Tamara recalled, "very dry, very tall, very good-looking but there was no rapport between them. He said, 'Mistakes have been made. You must get in touch with your mother.'" And that was about as far as he was prepared to be drawn on the matter. Furthermore, having made this brief and unhelpful statement, he withdrew from their lives again. Peter did not keep in touch with him because, Tamara said, "the meeting was not a friendly one. It was not directly unfriendly but there was no communication at all."

Disappointed but undeterred, Finch followed George's advice and contacted his mother whom he traced, with the aid of Somerset House, through three marriages to her home in Cornwall.

His arrival on the scene was a traumatic event for all concerned and not least for his half-sister Flavia, who was then in her early teens. When Peter first arrived in England Flavia had seen his photograph in the newspapers and, noticing that his surname was the same as her mother's had once been, wondered whether he might be a distant relative. "Well," Alicia replied, vaguely, "he may be a cousin."

Later, when his detective work had borne fruit and he had discovered his mother's whereabouts, Peter phoned her. Alicia was then in the rather awkward position of having to inform her daughter that this Australian "cousin" was actually a bit more closely related than that.

"She waited," Flavia said, "until I was in the bath and then she rushed down the corridor, beating on the door and said, 'That photograph you saw in the paper — it's your brother', and then she rushed back down the corridor again. I came out dripping wet — I thought she'd gone off her head — and asked her what she was talking about. And then she explained who he was and said he was coming down to Cornwall with Tamara to meet us."

The actual meeting, Flavia said, was "a little bit strange". She and her mother met Finch and Tamara at the railway station and took them home for tea where conversation was understandably somewhat strained. Matters were not helped by the almost immediate arrival on a racing bicycle of a complete stranger, an acquaintance apparently of Alicia's third husband, who had told him to drop in any time he was in the area. Alicia introduced him to her son, her daughter and her daughter-in-law and the man settled down in anticipation of a lengthy stay. In fact it turned out to be a very short one for the visitor swiftly grew uneasy and finally made an excuse and left when it became clear that no member of this happy family group had the faintest idea what any of the others had been doing for more than thirty years. His sudden departure, and the obvious bemusement that had caused it, served to break the ice a little but it was still not an easy reunion. "I think," said Flavia, "that Tamara particularly thought we weren't emotional enough as a family, she being Russian and not used to English reserve. Mother was charming but quite flippant."

Tamara, indeed, was hardly less bemused than the unfortunate stranger.

"For me," she said, "it was a scene out of a play. It did not appear to be emotional at all. Of course being Russian I am full of emotion and if I had found a son that I hadn't seen for thirty years I would be very, very affected by it. But the scene was very calm, very superficial. We talked about seagulls and the village life and there was nothing personal said at all. Peter was shattered. He was shaking with nerves, of course, and then when we went back to London there was a great feeling of let-down, of disappointment, because there had been no explanation about anything. We never talked about anything of significance."

The closest Alicia came to providing an explanation of the events of three decades before was to repeat the story she had told to Flavia, that Peter had been kidnapped by George Ingle-Finch and that she had made unsuccessful attempts to get him back. And that apparently was the end of the matter.

Nevertheless, Finch did keep in touch with his mother for the rest of his life. For a while during the 1950s Alicia kept house for him in London and Flavia acted as his secretary. "I think he needed a family," she said, "his own family, something that actually belonged to him, not just cousins and distant relations. And I think he did need Mother in a way. But she's not an easy person to get close to. She has her own sort of withdrawal thing. Peter wasn't easy to get close to, either. He would appear to be sometimes; you would think you were getting through, but, perhaps because of his childhood, there was always a withdrawn part, a bit of him that was private that you weren't allowed into."

Of course, at the time of that reunion with his mother, or anyway quite soon afterwards, Finch already had a family of his own: he had Tamara and he had Anita. But such domestic bliss as the three of them shared was destroyed in 1953 when he went to Ceylon to star in the film *Elephant Walk* and began his well-publicised love affair with Vivien Leigh.

Ironically, Finch's role, as a tea-planter, had originally been offered to Laurence Olivier, who didn't fancy it but generously suggested Finch as his replacement. And when the two co-stars flew off together to Ceylon to begin filming he asked Finch to take care of Vivien Leigh. This was no token request because Olivier was aware (though, to be fair to him, Finch was almost certainly not) that his wife was ill. She was a manic-depressive, a clinical condition that was solely responsible for her frequently erratic behaviour.

The love affair began almost as soon as they arrived on location, continued throughout the filming in Ceylon and was still flourishing when the unit went to California to shoot the interior scenes. But by this time Vivien Leigh's health had cracked, with the result that a positively bizarre situation arose in California.

Finch's agent, Olive Harding — aware of what had been happening in Ceylon — had arranged for Tamara to be flown to Hollywood in the hope that her presence would help bring the affair (an inconvenient affair, to say the least) to an end. But, in the event, Tamara found herself helping to take care of her rival.

"Vivien was very ill, of course," she said, "and very vulnerable too, and even I, who was the injured party, looked after her because one couldn't help it. The woman was very, very ill and besides we didn't know what was the matter with her and the manifestations of that illness are frightening." Even so it was a distinctly charitable act on Tamara's part because she learned of the love affair as soon as she reached California. "It was Vivien who told me and, of course, she did not take kindly to the fact that I had arrived in Hollywood. It accelerated her illness greatly."

When Tamara demanded, not unreasonably, an explanation

from her husband himself Finch told her that "he couldn't help it. It was Vivien who started it all. But he also said that before my arrival thay had split up because they didn't want to injure Laurence Olivier or myself. Peter decided that he would stay with me and that was very difficult for Vivien to accept."

Finch, Tamara believed, did make an effort to bring the matter to an end when Vivien Leigh's health deteriorated to such an extent that she had to withdraw from the film and was replaced by Elizabeth Taylor. After filming was completed, Tamara said, "We stayed in Hollywood much longer than scheduled. Then we took a slow boat back to England and went for a prolonged holiday in Spain. Peter didn't want to face the Oliviers. He felt very, very guilty. It was in the two years after that, when she had recovered, partly, that Vivien pursued him. And I may say that if Sir Laurence had pursued me with such force, perhaps I would have been weak, too."

Despite Finch's good intentions then, the affair continued intermittently into 1955. "It unbalanced him completely," Tamara said. "It was impossible for anyone, I think, to resist the charm and beauty of Vivien Leigh. She was like a tornado and she affected our lives drastically."

Trader Faulkner said: "I think it was the great love of Peter's life really. I think that he loved, deeply loved Tamara. I think that the marriage to Yolande (Finch's second wife) was a physically blinding experience, an infatuation. I think that he loved Eletha (his third wife) deeply. But Vivien Leigh was an experience that shattered him. It was traumatic. And also he had this great feeling of guilt. I always remember that he said Olivier was like a father to him and he was very deeply ashamed of what he had done."

That being so, it might well be wondered why Finch did not keep his resolution to end the affair when Vivien Leigh left the cast of *Elephant Walk*. Trader Faulkner's theory is that "Peter couldn't help himself. A lot of blame has been put on him over this and on Vivien Leigh, too, but what I think most people overlook is that they haven't had that temptation. She was just about the most beautiful woman in the world and I can well understand Peter falling in love with her."

The affair, begun romantically in Ceylon, interrupted dramatically in California, resumed fervently in London, ended on a note of dark farce at Notley Abbey, the Oliviers' country home in Buckinghamshire.

Olivier, who had been as patient and understanding as any

husband could be expected to be, decided finally that the matter must be resolved. To that end he invited Finch to Notley Abbey and what happened there, in the words of Trader Faulkner, was this: "They all sat down to dinner and then Vivien went out of the room while Laurence Olivier and Peter Finch tried to sort out what the future was to be. But, because they were embarrassed, over the port Olivier started to play the old, senile butler and Peter played the aristocratic, rather decadent lord. And they improvised this scene until they were both in hysterics because it was the only way they could get around a direct confrontation. And in the end Vivien Leigh opened the door and said, 'Well, which one of you is coming to bed with me now?' And that's exactly what happened. Peter told me the story and so did Vivien Leigh. That was the end of it, but he never got over Vivien. She left a deep mark on him because they reached each other. The newspapers have made out that it was a passionate, physical affair and so it was. But it was also very much an affair of the soul."

That it had left "a deep mark" on Finch rapidly became clear to Tamara. He began to stay away from home for weeks at a time, to return unexpectedly and then to go away again. "He wouldn't tell me what he was doing and he was a very unhappy man. It was impossible to talk to him about anything. He would either go to sleep or walk away and he didn't take very well to responsibilities."

This was also the time when he began to drink and to earn in the British Press a reputation that he never really deserved as a "hell-raiser". The facts of the matter now appear to be that Finch's whole life was in a turmoil. Understanding though Tamara had been over the Vivien Leigh episode, it was nevertheless clear that the marriage was over except in name. Furthermore, Finch's career was very much in decline. His stage career had more or less fizzled out and he had signed a long-term contract with the Rank Organisation. Immediately he did so he decided it was a mistake and was reluctant to accept any script that was offered to him. Unfortunately such right of script-veto as he enjoyed was necessarily limited and he found himself in the position of turning down two scripts which he didn't like only to be obliged to accept a third, which he liked even less.

Jack Lee, who worked with him on two of his Rank films — *A Town Like Alice*, which was a notable success, and *Robbery Under Arms*, which was not — said: "He loathed his contract with Rank. He hated all the decisions that were taken by people who, he said, didn't understand movies, didn't understand drama, didn't understand literature, didn't understand art or anything at all. But he was short of money; he always was. He never had any money."

These then were unhappy days, the drinking days, though he was never the souse legend made him out to be. Trader Faulkner said Finch was what is known in Australia as "a two-pot screamer" — after the second glass he was tipsy. "I don't think he was an alcoholic. I think he drank to numb the sort of sterility and materialism of life. Peter was not a materialist; materialism got him down." Faulkner also advanced the interesting theory that, far from using alcohol as a kind of release, Finch needed it "to earth him because he was so high on life itself".

Well, be that as it may, Finch, the Rank contract-artist, was also Finch, the drinker. (Although, said Jack Lee, he never allowed booze to interfere with his performance as an actor. "When he worked he worked. It's as simple as that. Then he had a jolly good time. He would say, 'I'm going to get pissed tonight; tomorrow I'll work.' And he did.") Furthermore, Finch the wandering gypsy now emerged.

In Australia in his shiftless days he had often followed the Aborigine habit of "going walkabout", vanishing for days or weeks into the outback, and he began to adopt the same practice in England. Bill Kerr said: "He was a wonderful gypsy. There was nobody like him. He didn't care about things like paying rent and living in houses and having mortgages, all those things that other people believe are important."

So, during the middle and late years of the 1950s he would wander off where and when the mood took him. To friends like Tony Britton he would say: "Well, I'm off, mate. I'm off to the wild wetters," and then he would suddenly disappear, to Spain, or Ibiza, or Ireland, wherever he could be alone. It was not until Finch was dead that Britton discovered the origin of the phrase "the wild wetters". And then he found it in Kipling's story "The Cat That Walked By Himself": the cat who "went back through the Wet Wild Woods, waving his wild tail, and walking by his wild lone. But he never told anybody." And, to Britton, that was the perfect description of his friend, Finch, a friend who was totally unreliable, who would let people down more often than not, who would vanish from their lives for months at a time and would then turn up again and resume the relationship as though nothing had happened and as though no explanation was necessary.

But, at the same time, "You always had to be there when Finch needed you," said Britton. "He'd go away and you wouldn't see him for a year, two years. You wouldn't hear from him. But the moment he was back in town he'd be on the telephone, usually at two o'clock in the morning and from some club, saying, 'Hello, mate. I need you, mate. Come on down and have a drink.' You'd say, 'But Finchie, it's two a.m.' And then 'Oh mate, I need you.' And there was this sad, appealing voice at the far end of the phone. An amazing man. And one went and it was never a crisis. It was simply that he needed companions; he needed somebody to have a drink with."

The loneliness, the need for companionship, were genuine but the danger for those who responded to such low-key cries for help was that they would find Finch, the two-pot screamer, deep in his cups and delivering some wildly romantic version of his life story. Jack Lee had a brisk method of dealing with this: "I'd say, 'Oh, come off it, Finchie,' when he was giving way to some of his more fantastic flights of romanticism because he was a great liar. He would make up all sorts of things — this was his Spanish night, this was his Buddhist night. 'I'm Australian this week . . . I'm French tonight . . . I'm English tonight . . . My father was this, my father was that . . . I was illegitimate . . .' These things would go on and you'd say, 'Come off it, Finchie. What's it going to be tonight?' "

Along with the expeditions to the wild wetters and the drinking and the romanticising went the womanising, although Jack Lee believed that this was an unjust description of what actually happened. "Peter wasn't a womaniser; women were Finchisers." From his early days in King's Cross, the red-light district of Sydney, women had always played a significant part in Finch's life because he liked them and they liked him, an arrangement perfectly agreeable to both sides. "He was a great charmer," said Jack Lee. "He could make women laugh and if you can make them laugh you're halfway there."

As his half-sister, Flavia Magwood could never quite understand Finch's attraction for women but from those days when he was, as it were, between marriages and she acted as his secretary she remembered a whole succession of girls passing through his house. "I don't know what basically he was looking for other than that they were usually attractive women and they had to have a sense of humour. He couldn't stand anybody without a sense of humour. Even the most beautiful woman, if she was humourless, was out."

Tamara acknowledged that her husband had a fatal weakness for women, to each of whom he was attractive and faithful while she was actually in his presence but not for much longer. "I think his life would have been happier if he had had fewer but more significant relationships."

Olive Harding believed the key to his romantic and sexual conquests were "those eyes of his. He only had to look at women and they melted." But the need for sexual conquest, she thought, was also a need "to prove his manhood". And perhaps that is not totally at odds with Trader Faulkner's assessment: "Peter adored women and I think the reason was that he never really had a mother." But, despite that, or just as probably because of that, "he behaved badly to every single one of them". Or, as Jack Lee put it with as much affection as candour, "He was a bastard. He would fall for them and he would let them down, one after the other."

While all these facets of his personality were emerging starkly during the turbulent years of the 1950s, Finch was also making renewed progress as an actor. In 1956 he had returned to Australia for the first time to star in *The Shiralee*, a film directed by my father, Leslie Norman, which Finch later told Trader Faulkner was his favourite of all the pictures he had made. Quite apart from the fact that it was (and admittedly I speak with some bias) a splendid film it is not difficult to see why it appealed to him, for in it he played a swagman who wandered around Australia with the burden or, as the Aborigines have it, the shiralee of his young daughter. For Finch it was virtually type-casting, playing a man who lived his life in "the wild wetters".

A year later he was back in Australia to make *Robbery Under Arms* but thereafter he never returned again, possibly because the indigenous film industry had little to offer at that time but also because he was deeply hurt at the reception he received in the country which, as far as any country could be so described, was his homeland. Australia received him with studied indifference as it greets any of its native sons who have gone elsewhere to make their names. As Trader Faulkner said, "Australia has a reputation for cutting down tall poppies", and Finch, as tall a poppy as the country's films or theatre had produced, resented being hacked off at the knees.

In his new, or perhaps original, homeland of Britain he was treated much better. Between *A Town Like Alice* in 1956 and *No Love For Johnny* in 1960 he made eleven pictures and won the British Film Academy Award for best actor on three occasions, *A Town Like Alice* bringing him the first of them, *The Trials of Oscar*

Wilde, which he had made on loan to another company producing the second and *No Love For Johnny*, his last picture under his Rank contract, providing the third.

In the same period his marriage to Tamara had ended in divorce and three weeks after this became final in June 1959, he had married Yolande Turnbull, a beautiful young South African girl whom he had met — inevitably on a beach — at Durban while he was on his way to Australia to film *The Shiralee*.

What immediately engaged his attention, apparently, were her legs which he, with all the enthusiasm of a true connoisseur, declared were the best he had ever seen. By all accounts, including both his and hers, their relationship was an extremely passionate affair and also an attraction of opposites. On the one hand there was Finch, the gypsy, with his genuine dislike of material possessions, pomp and formality; and on the other there was Yolande, a socialite and daughter of a wealthy South African family, who liked to give strictly formal dinner parties in her own, elegantly-furnished home. On reflection now, I suppose, it was never likely that the pair of them would journey through life together into old age like Darby and Joan but at the beginning they both tried to make a success of the marriage. At one time they settled down in a neo-Georgian home in Mill Hill, north-west of London, a place of ten rooms and five acres set in semi-rustic suburbia; the ideal place, in fact, in which to entertain politicians, writers, artists and the like. And Finch, predictably enough, hated it.

Jack Lee said: "It was a ridiculous episode. He decided that he was going to become a lord of the manor, bought this expensive house with Spanish servants and held elegant dinner parties. It didn't suit him at all. He was a rough roustabout, as they say in Australia, and it was no good him being an English country squire, particularly in Mill Hill. I went there several times — daunting experiences. He'd come to the door all dressed up and wearing gloves and things. Awful. It didn't take him long to get out."

To give him his due, Finch did try. Tony Britton remembered that he "had this big garden and started to cultivate it. He also decided to go in for chickens but they all became mangy and died, one after the other. I don't know, they must be very difficult to keep or something, but Finchie failed hopelessly and finally gave it up as a bad job."

As Olive Harding saw it: "Yo was a very social person and a very good hostess and she gave lovely parties. But Peter didn't like them. He didn't like dressing up and putting on a dinner jacket. He liked to wear a pair of old jeans and slop about in the garden so I don't think it was altogether easy for them both at that time. I remember on one occasion I was just going to bed and Peter arrived at my flat. I knew there was a dinner party going on at his home and he came in and said, 'I can't take any more.' He was just miserable and wanted to talk."

Sometimes he would turn up in similar circumstances at Tony Britton's house and stay the night, sleeping on the sofa. "And there he would be in the morning, all curled up like a baby. It was incredible. He always slept in the foetal position."

One way or another the early 1960s were not particularly good years for Finch. On the credit side he and Yolande had two children, Samantha and Charles; in 1960 he went to Spain to direct a film for the first and only time, a documentary called *The Day*, which won him a number of prizes at festivals; and as a screen actor he had reasonable success in *The Girl with Green Eyes* and *The Pumpkin Eater*.

But on the debit side there were other pictures that did nothing for him except keep his bank balance afloat and there was the fiasco of the multi-million dollar version of *Cleopatra* in which he was scheduled to play Julius Caesar until his co-star, Elizabeth Taylor, became seriously ill and production stopped; whereupon Finch was replaced in the role by Rex Harrison. Finch suffered a mild nervous breakdown as a result of this and more or less simultaneously his marriage, despite all Yolande's efforts to keep it alive, was suffering an irrevocable and total breakdown.

Finch had a notoriously celebrated affair with the singer Shirley Bassey, as a result of which each was cited in the other's divorce action and, in November 1965, Yolande was granted a decree nisi on the grounds of her husband's adultery. None of Finch's friends was particularly astonished at this turn of events.

"I was never surprised when anything of Peter's broke up," said Olive Harding. "I always said to him, 'Don't marry, Peter, you can't take the responsibility that goes with marriage, you don't want the running of houses, the paying for houses or anything like that. Just enjoy life, because that's what you want to do.' I always felt that Peter hadn't grown up at all. He was at prep school age really." During the many years in which she handled Finch's professional affairs, Miss Harding felt herself to be as much a substitute mother to him as an agent. "He always had to have a sort of Rock of Gibraltar on whom he could lean. He had to have somebody's shoulder to cry on."

During the years with Yolande at Mill Hill there was one event of some importance to Finch when Major Jock Campbell turned up at the house and announced: "I am your real father." Finch was then about forty-five years old and had never seen Major Campbell before. As Trader Faulkner said: "It was an extraordinary experience because Peter had become accustomed to the fact that he had a doubtful father who didn't want him and then suddenly there's this charming old bloke with a sense of humour who, Finchie said, was 'very like me but, unlike me, very respectable and presentable' and he turns up and says, 'I'm your dad.'"

It's not altogether surprising in the circumstances that with a remote mother and a bewildering multiplicity of fathers, Finch sought elsewhere for a shoulder to cry on. But there was a limit to what even Olive Harding could offer in that line and in 1965 the limit had been more or less reached.

Divorced again and ill with hepatitis Finch sold such possessions as he had and went to live in Jamaica, an island that he had first visited and fallen in love with in the company of Yolande. Henceforth he would invariably go there at low points in his life.

On this occasion, however, he was lured back to England by John Schlesinger to make *Far From the Madding Crowd* in which he played William Boldwood and did much to restore his now sagging reputation. In the last few years there had been too many films of too little merit, no matter how well he had performed in most of them.

Far From the Madding Crowd restored him to national, if not international, stardom and, refreshed by the experience, he returned to Jamaica where, at the age of fifty and on a beach once more, he met Eletha Barrett, a local girl twenty-seven years younger than himself.

Recalling this initial meeting Eletha said: "He was walking barefoot and for some reason I looked at his feet and thought, 'Oh, my God what strong, beautiful feet'. And then his eyes, I looked into them and it was just magic, you know, real magic."

Finch and Eletha lived together, mostly in Jamaica, without the benefit of wedlock for some years. Their daughter Diana was born in Rome in 1969, at which time Finch was trying to get his career going once again with *The Red Tent*, only his second film — the other being the forgettable *The Legend of Lylah Clare* — since he had made *Far From the Madding Crowd* in 1966.

Now, with Diana and Christopher, Eletha's son by an earlier liaison whom Finch later adopted, he had five children, rather more perhaps than his share, especially as he was never a particularly good father.

"That was the saddest thing of all," said Olive Harding. "I said to him one day, 'Why don't you see the children?' and he said, 'I can't. When I see them I cry and it makes them cry.'"

He would make a great fuss of his children when they were young and he was living with them. But later, when they were apart, it was a question of out of sight, out of mind. Tamara said: "He would phone Anita up and say, 'Let's go to a show' and then he wouldn't turn up. He was forgetful."

Flavia said: "He wasn't really a children's man, you know. He didn't get on all that well with them. He didn't dislike them, I just don't think he felt he had that much time to spare for them. Perhaps he didn't think it was necessary to spend a lot of time with them because nobody had ever spent a lot of time with him when he was a child."

The Red Tent, a sombre tale of General Nobile's failed attempt to reach the Arctic by dirigible, with Finch playing the part of the general, was less than successful but once more John Schlesinger came to the rescue. Ian Bannen, the original choice to play the homosexual Jewish doctor in *Sunday, Bloody Sunday*, had fallen ill and Finch was asked to take over. He did so grudgingly and with definite reservations, telling Olive Harding, "I can't play a poof."

Fortunately he could and he did and it may well be that his performance in *Sunday, Bloody Sunday* was the best he ever gave. It won him an Academy Award nomination for Best Actor and, for the fourth time, the British equivalent of the Oscar.

"He was a wonderful actor," said John Schlesinger. "He was a very internal actor who always had something in reserve. There was always something quite extraordinary going on underneath. And yet he was uncertain of himself. He would hardly wait for the take to finish, for me to say 'Cut' before asking, 'Was that okay? Do you think that was all right?'"

With the Academy Award nomination, *Sunday, Bloody Sunday* brought Finch firmly to the attention of Hollywood. This had happened before, though to a lesser extent, with films like *The Nun's Story* and *The Flight of the Phoenix* but somehow he had never quite grasped the opportunities that were offered as a result or perhaps the opportunities themselves were not really worthy of him. This again was the case now. *Sunday, Bloody Sunday* was followed by two British films — *Something to Hide* and *England Made Me*, neither of which made any impression on the international market — and then by the ludicrous musical version of *Lost Horizon* which, despite the presence in the cast of Finch, Liv Ullmann and Sir John Gielgud, made a perfectly ghastly impression.

Bequest to the Nation, an adaptation of Terence Rattigan's play about Nelson with Finch playing the admiral, hardly fared much better after Glenda Jackson's honest and quite accurate confession on British television that she had been hopelessly miscast as Lady Hamilton.

All of which gave an unintentional touch of irony to Finch's remark to me, made while he was in Italy filming *The Abdication* opposite Liv Ullmann that, "the only reason you want to be well known and successful in this business is that it gives you choice". Finch was certainly well known, less certainly successful and if he had choice in the roles he played he appeared quite wilfully to be exercising it in totally the wrong direction. *The Abdication* did little to help him and indeed the best thing that happened while he was making the picture was that he married Eletha Barrett. The wedding took place in Rome late in 1973 when Finch was fifty-seven and Eletha was thirty.

For some inscrutable reason they applied first to a Roman Catholic church for a marriage certificate. Finch said: "The priest gave us the traditional talk about marriage and hoped that we were serious about it and said the purpose of it was to have children. It was a little ironical seeing that our two children [Diana and Christopher] were downstairs waiting. I didn't have the courage to take them upstairs. Anyway, I sat straight-faced through this lecture and said, 'Thank you very much.' And then he said: 'Have either of you been divorced?' And I said, 'Yes,' and he said, 'Oh, we can't do that sort of thing. You'd better try the Methodists.'" So they did. And the Methodists proved far more amenable.

After her husband's death Eletha said: "You know, if I had met him when he was younger I don't think I would have married him. He was the type of man who liked freedom of movement, to be on his own like an animal in the jungle."

Because Eletha, unlike Finch's previous wives, travelled with him wherever he went, there were those who suggested that she kept him on a leash, but she denied that vigorously. "No woman could keep Finchie on a leash. He kept you on a leash. He was a free human being. You had to mind your Ps and Qs with him because if you ever stepped out of line he would say, 'That's it. I'm off.'"

After the wedding and the completion of *The Abdication* Finch and Eletha returned to Jamaica with every intention on his part of retiring from acting. By now he was getting on for fifty-eight with three successive flops behind him and he was not at all a well man. He was already suffering from heart trouble and had been advised by his doctors to stop smoking and drinking, which advice he followed whenever he felt like it.

In Jamaica he bought a 107-acre banana plantation and settled down to the life of a working planter. Not for him the luxury of sitting on the verandah sipping a rum punch while others cultivated his land; he would toil beside them in the fields and for a year he devoted himself to this back-breaking labour with typical enthusiasm. But after that year the enthusiasm just as typically waned. It was unrewarding work in every sense, not least financially, and he grew bored with it.

So he sold the plantation and bought an eighteenth-century manor house with a handful of manageable acres a few miles away. His intention then was to become a kind of Jamaican version of the country squire he had failed to be in Mill Hill but as he was about to hurl himself into the role he was offered the part of Howard Beale, the apparently crazy but in fact unacceptably sane TV newscaster, in *Network*.

It was, as he told Eletha, the kind of role that comes to an actor perhaps only once in a lifetime and he seized it avidly. Once more his performance was such that he was nominated for the Oscar as Best Actor and this time there was no doubt that he wanted to win it. Though his heart was again giving him trouble he undertook exhausting publicity tours around America to boost the picture and himself and simultaneously he was playing Yitzak Rabin in *Raid on Entebbe*, a film made for TV in America and for cinema distribution elsewhere.

Inevitably the strain began to tell and he was advised by his doctor to have heart surgery but this advice he chose to ignore completely. Eletha said: "One day I got mad at him and said, 'Please, let's go to this doctor now. Have the operation,' and he said, 'You look after your life and let me look after mine.' He was a strong man and he said a man should die like a man." She was sure, she said, that he knew he was dying and that some time before the event he "had made peace with himself".

On January 13th, 1977, while on his way to join the director Sidney Lumet for yet another television appearance to promote *Network*, Peter Finch collapsed in the foyer of the Beverly Hills Hotel in Hollywood. He was rushed to hospital and underwent emergency open-heart surgery but to no avail. He died without regaining consciousness. He was sixty years old.

In April of that year he was posthumously awarded the Oscar for his role in *Network* and later the same film won him his fifth British Academy Award.

Looking back over the somewhat ragged patchwork quilt of his career one has both a sense of waste and the feeling that the best was yet to come. The sense of waste stems from the fact that too often he made the wrong films simply because he needed the money. Jack Lee described him as "the best actor I ever worked with"; Schlesinger and Lumet admired him enormously but there were times, as he "sulked" his way through some indifferent movie, when the enormous talent he undoubtedly possessed was less than visible to the naked eye.

At the time of his death Finch, who was born in England, raised in Australia and emotionally attached to Jamaica, was on the point of becoming an American citizen. His home and work were in Hollywood and *Network* had finally made him a major star in the United States, which is where it counts most.

So I don't think it's too fanciful to suggest that the next five years of his life, had he been granted another five years, could have been the most productive of all and could have seen him occupying the niche left vacant by Spencer Tracy, for there were definite similarities between them: they shared the same kind of power and presence on screen and they were both splendid and versatile actors. Given that little extra time and the confidence that comes with acknowledged stardom, Finch might well have proved that he was indeed a great actor and not merely an actor who was capable on occasion of touching greatness.

Even as things are the very least that can be said of him is that he died at the top or, as Paul Brickhill put it: "Peter beat the lot of them by achieving the absolute pinnacle in *Network* and then suddenly dropping dead before the Oscar was announced. I think that's the most marvellous exit line I ever heard of. You can't beat that. He died in the act of reaching for a star."

Yes, but he had lived reaching for a star, too, though the unanswerable question is: what star? And what did he hope to find when he had reached it? Always to his closest friends he had given the impression that he was eternally searching for something and didn't know himself what it was.

"It was as if," said Tony Britton, "he heard a distant shout, a very, very far distant cry from somewhere and he didn't know what it was and he didn't know what it meant but he knew he had to follow it and he knew he had to try and find the source.''

But, of course, he never did find it; he never could. Whatever it was that Peter Finch was seeking, that caused him — never maliciously but often thoughtlessly — to neglect and abandon wives, friends and children, it surely wasn't to be found in wealth or fame or Oscars. Rather did it lie a long way back, hidden somewhere in his own strange and solitary childhood.

Groucho
Marx
Groucho, the leader of the Marx
Brothers, who "wore a large,
painted moustache and affected a
cigar".

above : With his first wife, Ruth, and their children, Arthur and Miriam.

opposite : Groucho and his henchmen, Harpo ("a mute harpist afflicted with satyriasis") and Chico ("a larcenous Italian").

above : Groucho, the venerable cult figure, with Erin Fleming, who revived his career.

opposite above : All Groucho's wives were much younger than he. Kay Gorcey was only twenty-four (and he was fifty-four) when they married in 1945.

opposite below : Groucho with his third wife, Eden, and daughter, Melinda.

One week during their regular tour of the humbler vaudeville houses in America's Mid-West the four young comedians, Leonard, Arthur, Julius and Milton, were obliged to share a dressing-room with a troupe of German acrobats. (This must have been either a very large or a very crowded dressing-room; probably the latter.) What these acrobats were like as acrobats nobody now knows but they couldn't have been terribly good or they wouldn't have been on the same bill as the four comedians.

What does appear to be known about the acrobats, though, is that they couldn't speak English very well. In fact their grasp of English was so poor that they were unable to remember the names of the young men who shared their room. So, in order to identify each from the others, the acrobats gave them nicknames instead. Leonard therefore became Chico because he was always chasing the chicks; Arthur was Harpo because he played the harp; Milton became Gummo because he invariably wore gumshoes and Julius ... well, Julius of the grave, unsmiling countenance was henceforth known as Groucho.

Of all the explanations of how the Marx Brothers acquired their stage names this must be quite the most unlikely. I mean, if these German acrobats knew so little English that they couldn't even cope with names like Milton and Julius, how come they knew about chicks and gumshoes and grouchiness?

Far more plausible is the story put forward by Arthur Marx, the son of Groucho, who, while agreeing that the names were indeed invented in a vaudeville dressing-room, makes no mention of German acrobats but claims the brothers were so dubbed by a fellow American — a comic monologuist called Art Fisher, whose comic monologues are long forgotten but who merits at least a small footnote in the history books if he really was the man who re-named the Marx Brothers.

Why then drag in all these German acrobats? Well, I do so only because that version was told to me shortly before he died in 1979 by Herbert Marx, who was not only the fifth of the brothers but, under the name of Zeppo, became a significant part of the act and thus at least deserves to be heard. On the other hand since he didn't even know how he got his own nickname (the most acceptable explanation — and that only barely acceptable — is that he was so called because he was born in the year the first Zeppelin was built) he can hardly be cited as an expert witness.

When you consider that three of the brothers — Groucho, Harpo and Chico — were to become internationally famous, and even idolised, as the most original and anarchic trio of comics in cinema history, it's at least mildly frustrating that how, why, when, where and by whom they were given their names is now lost to memory. The only thing of which we can be certain is that it must have happened before the First World War because Zeppo wasn't actually there at the time. (Zeppo, who only joined the act during the war, was the baby of the family and treated as such until he was the only one left. "You don't know what you're talking about," snapped Groucho one night when at dinner Zeppo, well into his seventies, was reminiscing about the early days. "You're far too young to remember that.")

Julius and company (later to be Groucho and company) were first brought together as an act around 1910 by their mother, Minnie, who was both the family's immovable object and irresistible force and mapped out her sons' careers before they were of an age to have any say in the matter. Not that there is anything at all unusual in that. If, especially in show business, there is any truth at all in the adage that behind every successful man there is a woman, the chances are she's his mother.

Minnie Marx had emigrated to America from Germany with her family in 1880, when she was fifteen. Her mother was a harpist and her father a magician and ventriloquist but since there was a singularly small demand for non-English speaking ventriloquist acts in America he never worked in show business after he reached the United States. Even so, Minnie came swiftly to the conclusion that show business represented the best way out of the ghetto for poor immigrants in New York and after she married Sam Marx, himself an immigrant (from Alsace Lorraine), and had a family of her own she began to plan her sons' futures.

Sam appears barely to have been consulted in any of this, having no particular aspirations himself. He was a tailor — and, if Groucho and Zeppo are to be believed, very possibly the worst tailor in the entire history of the world — but he was also a gifted cook and so, in an early example of role reversal, it was Sam who stayed at home and looked after the cave while Minnie, the huntress, went out hustling on behalf of her brood.

They did not, of course, actually live in a cave; they lived in various overcrowded apartments in the poorer parts of New York's East Side. Zeppo remembered that "we had a two-bedroom apartment and there were five boys and my uncle and my grandfather and my mother and father, of course, all living there. Five of us slept in one bed and we didn't sleep too well. Those times were very difficult because we had no income. But my father, who was a very bad tailor, found some people who were so stupid they would buy his clothes and he'd make a few dollars that way for food. Then Chico would get a job occasionally and Groucho would be singing in the choir some place and he'd get paid for it and so we'd get along. We always owed the rent, though."

Groucho told his biographer, Charlotte Chandler (author of *Hello, I Must be Going*) that "we were ten people in one toilet".

"They were poor but very happy," she said. "He always remembered those days with great fondness and I think much of the brothers' respect for each other and each other's privacy came from living so closely together. They were really poor, though. Groucho used to say, 'Even other people's garbage was better than ours.' "

It was in order to escape from this kind of environment that Minnie started to thrust her sons towards the stage. For a start, Chico was given piano lessons, much to Groucho's resentment. Arthur Marx believed that his father was always a little envious of his elder brother "because Chico was the first born and Chico was given the piano lessons and was kind of a mother's pet. My father always felt that he should have had the piano lessons because, he said, Chico had no ear at all for music and he did. So he always felt he was cheated in that respect and he always claimed Chico was a rotten piano player and had a very bad left hand." The original idea was that since the family could afford piano lessons only for one son, Chico should pass on his knowledge to the others but somehow he never got around to that.

Now the Marx Brothers' cast in order of appearance was as follows: first came Chico, born in 1887, and in the following year came Harpo. Groucho was born in 1890 and Gummo in 1897. Finally, in 1901, there appeared Zeppo. There was also, in fact, another brother, Manfred, who was born in 1885 and died at the age of three.

Of the survivors Groucho was the first into show business, ushered onto the vaudeville stage as an infant soprano at the age of five. The others were not far behind him. By 1909, Groucho, along with Harpo and Gummo and a non-member of the family named Leo Levin, were component parts of an act known as the Four Nightingales and so-called because, according to Groucho, "none of the four of us could sing".

But from this inglorious start the inaptly-named Nightingales evolved into the Marx Brothers. The outsider, Leo Levin, vanished to be replaced by Chico and Minnie moved the family from New York to Chicago and there, in 1910, pitched her sons into the hard graft of the small-time vaudeville circuit.

Of the maternal influence on their lives Zeppo said: "If it wasn't for Minnie I don't know where the hell we would have been. Yet she had no talent herself — she was awful: couldn't sing, couldn't dance, couldn't act, couldn't do a damn thing. But we were very close to our folks. There was a lot of love there."

In later years, said Charlotte Chandler, "Groucho didn't let a day pass without talking about Minnie. Her picture was in his bedroom and whenever something happened in his life — something good or something bad — whenever there was a great moment to share, at the end of the day he would stand there in the dark, very quietly, in front of her picture and share the moment with her. He always said the boys would never have been anything without her."

Against that, however, Arthur Marx told me: "I don't think my father was as close to her as the others were or as he may have claimed later in life. The legend of Minnie simply grew. He used to tell me that she lived in Little Neck and he said he used to pass her house every day, coming in from New York, and he said he never stopped to see her. I think he was giving me a lesson, like 'You'd better stop and see me when I grow old and grey'. But I don't think he really had much interest in her. Harpo had more and maybe Zep."

Whatever the extent, or limitations, of Groucho's filial devotion it was Minnie's devotion and ambition that kept the brothers on the road for several years, first as a singing act, then as a comedy act, playing one-night stands around the Middle West. As Groucho reported later to Charlotte Chandler, it was a hard life but "we didn't know it because we were young and when you're young nothing is really hard".

"All his stories," she said, "centred on chasing girls, which was of great interest to the Marx Brothers all the way through their lives, and on food. Groucho was much influenced by those days of living in boarding houses. When we ate at his house he always had all the food served on separate plates — the salad, the vegetables, the entree were all served separately — because he remembered when it was all dumped onto one plate in those boarding houses. And then the one thing he would never have for Thanksgiving Dinner at his own home was fish. He might have turkey or he might not but he never had fish because that's what the Marx

Brothers had in the boarding houses at Thanksgiving. They always had the least expensive rooms and they always got fish, while everyone else had turkey or something special."

Zeppo didn't remember the fish but he did recall the brothers performing their act five times a day and he most certainly remembered the girls. There seem to have been a great many girls and I asked him how the brothers managed to notch up their enviable record of conquest when they rarely spent more than one day in the same town. He said it was achieved by what he called "three-sheeting". The three-sheets were the posters with the brothers' names and pictures outside the theatre. "After the show we'd get dressed quickly and go out and stand by these three-sheets and when the girls passed by some of them recognised us and nodded and that was all that was necessary . . ."

In some towns, though, even this didn't work and then, he said, "We'd always wind up in a whorehouse and Chico played the piano and Harpo would do something and Groucho would sing and they loved us, these hookers. They just loved us and, er, usually for free."

At girl-chasing Chico was the acknowledged family champion because he worked at it (as he also worked at gambling) with an intense dedication that might have been better — or anyway more usefully — applied to his work. The writer, Norman Krasna, a long-time friend of Groucho's, claimed that sexually the rest of the brothers lived for years on Chico's cast-offs. As for Groucho . . . well, Zeppo said: "He couldn't run as fast as Chico and the rest of us but he had his share, of course. I never considered Groucho a very great lover. Chico was great and Harpo and Gummo, they were fine."

(On this occasion, presumably Zeppo was — unusually for him — too modest to mention that though he himself may not have been quite in Chico's class he was well up to par with the others.)

Groucho, though much inclined to talk salaciously of women and his conquests of them, was actually a romantic, which may help to explain why he was married three times. Norman Krasna insisted quite firmly that "he had less sex than your average business tycoon. Groucho was fairly inept with women as a matter of fact. He liked them but he was no chaser: I don't think he'd even pinch them, for God's sake. He was no lecher."

But, I said, bearing in mind that he talked about women and sex so often, wasn't it possible that he would have liked to go through life ricocheting from one woman to another? Krasna said: "I don't know whether he would have liked to or not. I *can* tell you that Groucho's normal life didn't consist of him having to do with lots of women. Now he had more possibilities than, say, you or I — that I believe. But he didn't come up to the possibilities and I'm certain of that. I wouldn't say he was adolescent but he was naive — he wasn't a real sophisticated fellow around girls. His approach to a girl was odd, I thought, coming from a fellow you would expect to be more assured. If he got stuck on a girl — and she was usually a lot younger than he was — he was never cynical about it: he'd actually write a poem to her.

"I believe he was a true romantic: he fell in love with the wives he married, each one of them, and other women that he couldn't marry for various reasons he was genuinely, seriously in love with. It almost didn't become a man as sophisticated as he was to be that bowled over that quickly."

Groucho's own version of his attitude towards women — as once related by him to Charlotte Chandler — was summed up by a chain he saw on the ankle of a starlet when he was quite young. On that anklet, apparently, were inscribed the words: "Heaven's Above." Miss Chandler, however, was not entirely convinced: "In reality," she said, "Groucho tended to put the women in his life on a pedestal and they kept leaping off and he didn't know why."

Going back to those early days of "three-sheeting" and the whorehouses, Zeppo put the difference of approach of the various brothers rather succinctly: "Groucho would get a girl and she'd be very stupid and he'd talk to her about, oh, Shakespeare and Gilbert and Sullivan and he'd sit there and discuss this stuff with this girl who'd never heard of any of it and he'd try to impress her that way. The rest of us would just get right to it. We didn't waste time with Shakespeare or Gilbert and Sullivan."

Zeppo joined the Marx Brothers' act in 1918 when America entered the war and, feeling that the Marx family should make at least some token contribution, Minnie insisted that Gummo should join up on the grounds that he was the most expendable member of the troupe.

No doubt as a piece of critical judgment her decision was faultless but, not altogether surprisingly, Gummo was distinctly offended and though he obeyed his mother's instructions he never rejoined the act.

With Zeppo's arrival, however, the Marx Brothers' act took on its now familiar shape. In the words of S. J. Perelman: "Their leader wore a large, painted moustache and his three henchmen impersonated a mute harpist afflicted with satyriasis, a larcenous Italian and a jaunty coxcomb who carried the love interest." (The painted moustache, incidentally, first made its appearance when the brothers were playing an engagement on what, I suppose, would now be called off-off-Broadway. One night Groucho was late arriving in the theatre and, having no time to stick on his false moustache, painted one on instead. The audience didn't notice or, if it did notice, it didn't care and Groucho continued to wear a painted moustache from then on.)

By the time Zeppo joined them the brothers had graduated to the big-time vaudeville circuits and in 1921 they made a silent film, *Humour Risk,* which they financed themselves but which has since been lost. The big-time, however, is relative and the true big-time, the big big-time, could only be achieved by success on Broadway. Such success, overnight success, indeed, came finally to the Marx Brothers in 1923 after a mere thirteen years or so of hawking their wares around the country.

The show responsible for this change in their fortunes was called *I'll Say She Is* and it was an amalgamation of the best scenes from their vaudeville act. In fact, though, the brothers' Broadway debut could easily have passed almost unnoticed for they were booked into an out-of-the-way theatre which the critics rarely bothered to visit. But an apparently more important and more easily accessible show than *I'll Say She Is,* which was due to open on the same night, was suddenly cancelled and the critics, left with nothing better to do, went to see the Marx Brothers instead. The reviews were ecstatic and the show ran for two years.

Now by the time the brothers arrived on Broadway Groucho was married and a father. He had married in 1920 when he was thirty and his bride, Ruth Johnson, was nineteen. A year later their son, Arthur, was born.

Ruth had been introduced to Groucho by Zeppo, who had met her in a pool room and immediately recruited her as his dancing partner in the act. As Zeppo remembered the occasion, "I saw this blonde, she was very pretty and I really got stuck on her just by seeing her. And I said, 'Jesus, I bet I could make a dancer out of her', so I talked to her. I said, 'Would you like to be in show business . . .?' "

The old, old story, of course, and it worked. What Zeppo had not allowed for, however, was that Groucho would fancy her, too. Ruth was only an adequate dancer, Zeppo said, but "I tolerated her because I was stuck on her. But in the meantime Groucho moved in and he beat me to it." Fortunately this caused hardly any resentment because Zeppo was always a philosophical soul. "I didn't spend too much time on any one girl," he said. "I felt I didn't have that much time to waste."

Ruth continued as his dancing partner after the marriage and indeed after she became pregnant, although this did make Zeppo's life difficult. When he originally signed her up she weighed around 125 pounds but with marriage (and pregnancy), he said, she got up to about 150 pounds and could hardly get her legs around his waist when he had to lift and spin her. "So one day," he said, "I spun her so hard she couldn't hold on and she flew out across the stage and into the orchestra pit and that finished her. She couldn't do that dance any more so I got another partner."

Meanwhile *I'll Say She Is* was followed by another Broadway success, *The Coconuts*, Groucho and Ruth settled down as householders in Great Neck, New Jersey, and in 1927 their daughter Miriam was born. The following year the brothers notched up their third successive stage hit with *Animal Crackers* and while that was still running they signed a three-picture deal with Paramount.

The first of these pictures, a cinema version of *The Coconuts*, was made at the Astoria Studios in New York and appears to have been a totally chaotic exercise. Chico, in whose estimation work came a very poor third to women and cards, would continually wander off in search of a girl or a pinochle game and the others would go away and look for him. Sometimes none of them came back at all. Nevertheless, the film was an immediate success, which was just as well because even while it was being made Groucho was being wiped out, financially, in the great Wall Street crash.

Alone of all the brothers — the rest being inveterate and largely unsuccessful gamblers like their father — he had carefully saved and invested his money until he was worth nearly a quarter of a million dollars. The Depression took every penny of it.

Arthur Marx said: "He was always nervous about money up until the Crash but at that time he thought he had it made. Then he lost it all and as a result he got terrible insomnia and never really could relax again. There was always a worry about money in our house when we were kids."

Charlotte Chandler said: "It really affected his whole life. Probably till the very last years, when he was so old and knew he had enough to last him, he was quite frugal."

In that same eventful year, 1929, Minnie Marx died. During the last week of rehearsals before the brothers took *Animal Crackers* out on tour, the whole family got together for dinner at Zeppo's apartment where, by all accounts, Minnie had such a good time that she suffered a stroke and died the same night. In an appreciation of her in *The New Yorker,* the critic Alexander Woollcott wrote: "She had done much more than bear her sons, bring them up and turn them into play actors. She had *invented* them. They were just comics she imagined for her own amusement."

Undoubtedly it was Minnie who had done most to keep the brothers together, for within a few years of her death they had drifted apart, at least as far as their social activities were concerned. This was not because they didn't get along well together; indeed they retained a close affection for each other until the end of their lives. But they were very different people with very different interests.

Chico and Zeppo, for instance, were womanisers and gamblers. Chico in fact was described to me by his nephew Arthur Marx as "a degenerate gambler". And Zeppo said: "Oh, Chico, he was wild — he was really wild. He didn't care about anything. All he wanted was gambling and women. I don't think there was a day in his life that he didn't gamble at something. He was in a poker game once and Harpo saw two fellows cheating him, so he went to the house phone and called him and said, 'Chico, you're being cheated.' Chico said, 'I know and I don't care. This is the only game in town.'" Chico was such an inveterate and compulsive gambler that sometimes, in desperation, he would give people money to play him at cards.

Arthur Marx said: "My father didn't approve of Chico's lifestyle. They'd be in a show on the road and waiting for Chico to come on stage and there'd be no Chico. He'd be fifty miles away in a whorehouse or some gamblers would have him backed into a closet, telling him they weren't going to let him out until he paid them what he owed them, because he never had the money to pay even half his gambling debts."

Harpo was, by contrast, in Zeppo's words "a love". Everybody seemed to love Harpo. Gummo once said that Harpo played exactly the right instrument — the harp — because "he was an angel". Even Groucho apparently agreed with that definition and went so far as to say that he wished he had had a marriage like Harpo's. Harpo married only once and he and his wife, Susan, adopted five children. Norman Krasna said of him: "He was just a famously well-loved man. He'd walk into a room and dogs and children would go to him. He adopted so many kids because he said his idea of great happiness was to come home from the studio and see a face in every window." He even wanted to adopt Shirley Temple, becoming so keen on the idea that he went so far as to offer to buy her from her parents but unfortunately for him they weren't interested in the deal. In his youth Harpo, too, was a considerable card player, an expert at bridge, but when he married he appeared to renounce all vices and settled down to a life of contented domesticity.

Gummo, the reluctant soldier, went into the rag trade in New York after the First World War and when that enterprise failed joined Zeppo in his agency business in Hollywood. He was the quietest of the brothers and later became Groucho's manager. He and Harpo were probably the two of whom Groucho was fondest.

As for Zeppo, Groucho believed that he was potentially the funniest of them all and it was his misfortune that he joined the act when it had already taken shape and there was no need for another funny man. At one time, after he had retired from acting, Zeppo was one of the most influential agents in Hollywood, though in all probability Gummo was the business brains of the outfit. Zeppo, in any case, was as fanatical a gambler as Chico. "In the beginning," Arthur Marx said, "he used to play cards with rich Texas oil men, who really weren't great card players, and he'd take them for thirty and forty grand a night. But then he got hooked into Las Vegas, because he bought a piece of the Flamingo Hotel, back in the days when Vegas was first starting up after World War Two and he got interested in that kind of gambling, casino gambling. One weekend he lost 65,000 dollars and he spent the next year trying to recoup, by which time he'd lost a million dollars and was broke again. It's horrifying. It's hard to believe he could be that brainless."

So, with Minnie dead, the brothers began to lead their separate, social lives although professionally they were still very much together. In 1931, after filming *Animal Crackers,* they all moved to Hollywood to make their third Paramount picture, *Monkey Business.* They may have been late getting there — Chico, Harpo and Groucho were already in their forties — but they were, after all, established stars. Even so the transition from filming in New York to filming in Hollywood was not easy for them because *Monkey Business* was the first picture they had made with a script which hadn't first been tried out on the stage.

"They were very worried about it," Charlotte Chandler said, "because they were used to working in front of a live audience and testing their jokes that way. What Groucho said all his life — his philosophy, or as much of a philosophy of humour as he had — was that if it gets a laugh, leave it in."

As with all their films, *Monkey Business* was put together by a multitude of scriptwriters. The brothers were never easy to write for, largely because they were individual characters who required individual bits of business, and Groucho was possibly the hardest of all to encapsulate in a few lines of dialogue. Simply to provide him with long speeches, full of non-sequiturs and puns, to be delivered at high speed, was not enough. As he himself said that was indeed his style but in capturing the style too many writers overlooked the need to be funny as well. Frequently it was Groucho who added the jokes and frequently there were rows and altercations.

The Marx Brothers cannot have been comfortable to work with. One of their most famous writers, S. J. Perelman, described them as "capricious, tricky beyond endurance and altogether unreliable. They were also megalomaniac to a degree which it is impossible to describe." As a footnote to that he added: "I did two films with them, which in a way is perhaps my greatest distinction in life because anyone who ever worked on any picture for the Marx Brothers said he would rather be chained to a galley oar and lashed at ten-minute intervals than ever work for those sons of bitches again."

Sometimes their directors, no less driven to distraction than the writers, would come up with desperate remedies for the brothers' lack of discipline. On one film, Zeppo said, "the director was going crazy. One of us would be over here, Groucho would be over there, somebody else would be someplace else. Chico would be in the dressing-room with some girl and the director would say, 'Okay, boys, we're ready to shoot' and there'd be nobody around. So he had four cells built on the set with four locks on them and there were cots inside and the minute the scene was over, whoever it was had been in the scene would have to be locked in his cell so they always knew where we were. It worked pretty good." Then he added thoughtfully: "But Chico got out of his cell quite often."

Monkey Business was followed by *Horse Feathers* and *Duck Soup,* the most satirical of all the brothers' films, wherein Groucho accidentally becomes president of Freedonia and wages war on the country's neighbour. Later on Groucho maintained that this was his favourite picture but such a judgment may have owed a lot to hindsight because it was delivered during the latter part of his life, after *Duck Soup* had been retrieved from obscurity, dusted down and re-appraised by a new generation of Marx Brothers enthusiasts. At the time it was made, in 1933, it had hardly any impact at the box office and, since *Horse Feathers* had done no better, Paramount did not offer to renew their contract.

At this point the Marx Brothers' future looked a good deal less than promising. They seemed to have worn out their welcome in the cinema and they were not much inclined to return to the harder graft of Broadway shows. But now, for once, Chico's gambling addiction brought them a stroke of luck. He had met Irving Thalberg of MGM in a card game, which is not entirely surprising. Where else did Chico meet anyone except in card games — or possibly in bedrooms? Anyway, Chico persuaded Thalberg that the brothers were still potentially a going concern and Thalberg agreed, swayed, according to the cynics, by the fact that inevitably Chico owed him a large sum of money and there was no possibility of getting it unless the brothers were employed. His first official meeting with the four of them was, however, to say the least, unconventional.

"They had an appointment and they were ushered into his office by his secretary," said one of their screenwriters, Morris Ryskind. "Thalberg wasn't there and the secretary said to wait — that he was out and he'd be back soon. Well, the boys got pretty sore waiting for him and when he finally came back and opened the door there was a fire going in the fireplace and the boys were all sitting round it, naked. That was his introduction to the Marx Brothers."

Undeterred, Thalberg went ahead with his plan to sign them up. Financially the move was good for them but artistically it involved a change of approach. At Paramount they had been iconoclastic and arrogant and sometimes in those early and more untidy pictures they seemed to be putting on a show simply to amuse themselves. At MGM their pictures were softer and more conventional, more deeply plotted. They were still very funny but they lacked that original hard edge. Thalberg was responsible for this. He believed that their box-office receipts had fallen off because hitherto they had appealed largely to men but his theory was that in most cases it was women who decided which films they and their menfolk would go to see. What women wanted, Thalberg argued, were big production numbers, musical scenes, romantic interest and a reasonably plausible storyline. All these things, plus far more generous budgets, he gave to the Marx Brothers. The purists regretted the change but economically it made sense and the brothers approved. As Groucho said: "The reason we stopped being anarchic in our humour and became semi-lovable instead was simply a matter of money."

In any event he had a great respect for Thalberg. "He was the best producer in Hollywood. He hated L. B. Mayer [the head of MGM] and so did I. I always had a capacity for hating anybody that my boss also hated."

Unfortunately, Groucho's dislike for Mayer, which he never made any attempt to conceal, had its repercussions later. After Thalberg died, Mayer, who seems never to have forgotten a slight whether real or imagined and could out-hate anybody, withdrew the studio's support from the Marx Brothers and allowed their career to go into decline again.

But before that happened they had their biggest popular successes with *A Night at the Opera* and *A Day at the Races,* both closely overseen by Thalberg himself and both consumer-tested on the stage in vaudeville before filming started. While *A Day at the Races* was still shooting, however, Thalberg died.

Arthur Marx said: "My father was really broken up, more shattered than I've ever seen anybody — not so much about Thalberg, I imagine, but for himself, feeling that his career was going down the drain again. He did like Thalberg personally and thought he was a genius but he saw it as a bad break for both of them. The problem was that Louis Mayer didn't like my father much because my father didn't treat him like a king and after Thalberg died he wouldn't let the brothers take their shows out on the road any more, he wouldn't pay money for first-class writers and he wouldn't give them the production facilities they'd had before. They really didn't make another good picture after that."

Nevertheless they kept busy. They were lent to RKO to make *Room Service* and then returned to MGM in 1939 for *At the Circus* and, the following year, *Go West,* both directed by Edward Buzzell. None of these films was up to their previous standard and at this time, with Thalberg gone, they had very little interest in pictures any more. Zeppo had left the act to become an agent and Groucho and Harpo were financially secure. Chico, however, was not and it was his plight that kept the three brothers together.

"When my father signed up for the last three pictures for MGM," said Arthur Marx, "he did so only on condition that

Chico would let him and Harpo take his money and put it in some kind of trust so he couldn't squander it all. My father said he was sick of making pictures and he was tired."

This was a laudably fraternal act on the part of Groucho and Harpo but it didn't really work because Chico got into trouble with the professional gamblers again and these impatient men having threatened — to no avail — to break his arms and his legs unless he paid them the money he owed, presented him with their final offer, namely that if he didn't come across with the cash they would have no recourse but to kill him *"pour encourager les autres"*. So Chico's money was taken out of trust, his debts were paid and he gambled away what was left. By then Groucho was so dispirited that when the MGM contract was completed (with the making of *The Big Store* in 1941) he did retire from films for five years.

It was probably a wise move because in the opinion of Ed Buzzell the brothers were already past their best when they made *At the Circus*.

"They didn't have any enthusiasm at all," he said. "It was just a case of money. They took the money and they made the picture and that's all there was to it. They ran around like little pixies but they weren't pixies any more — they were old men, trying to be pixies."

Casting his mind back, he added somewhat bitterly: "Groucho was tired all the time. He'd come in in the morning and before he'd start work he'd sit down and smoke a cigar. Do you know how long it takes to smoke a cigar? He took all the time he wanted and then he'd put the cigar down and say, 'Okay, I'm ready for work', every day for forty-five days."

Me: "Did he bring his own cigars?"

E.B.: "No, he didn't. He asked the property man to give him a cigar."

Me: "Why?"

E.B.: "Because he was cheap. He was really cheap. He liked to smoke the studio's cigars."

During the filming of *At the Circus* Groucho reached his fiftieth birthday and the studio gave a party for him. Everyone turned up except Groucho. Buzzell said: "He didn't like it. He was fifty years old and we had this party for him with a lot of goodies and he wouldn't come out of his dressing-room. He said, 'No, I'm an old man of fifty. I'm not coming out.' So we had the party without him."

The problem with the two films he made with them, Buzzell said (and it was a problem for which nobody thereafter ever found a solution) was that it was difficult, if not impossible, to think of anything new for them to do. "There was Harpo with his harp and Chico with his piano and Groucho with his talk and it was the same meat with different gravy in every picture. They couldn't change the formula because they were so steeped in their own method of working."

Of all the brothers Buzzell preferred Harpo: "He was a sweet man. Groucho was a vitriolic son of a bitch."

Me: "Did you not like him much?"

E.B.: "Oh, I liked him. You couldn't help liking him, but you feared him, too. He had a vitriolic tongue and you stayed away from him if you could. Socially, he wasn't very well liked. He had a few friends, good friends, but a very few."

And so in 1941, tired and no longer interested in the picture business, the brothers entered into retirement. A year later Groucho's marriage to Ruth Johnson ended in divorce after twenty-one years. It had not been a happy marriage for some time because Ruth had become an alcoholic.

Susan, Harpo's wife, said Groucho had driven her to it and in truth he cannot have been an easy man to live with.

Zeppo said: "He was very difficult because he'd put people down, especially a woman like Ruth, who was stupid. It was hard for Groucho to tolerate stupidity. He liked bright people. Also he was a cold man."

This seems to be a singularly harsh judgment both on Ruth and the marriage. Norman Krasna said that for a long time the couple appeared to be perfectly compatible. But as Groucho grew older he preferred to spend his evenings at home reading or playing the guitar, or listening to Gilbert and Sullivan to whom he was passionately devoted. Ruth, on the other hand, being eleven years younger than he, still liked to go out at night and, with Groucho's approval, friends like Krasna would take her dancing. But then, as her children grew up and Groucho was either working long hours at the studio or collapsing exhausted at home after a hard day, Ruth found consolation at her tennis club, in the bar more often than on the courts.

Arthur Marx said: "I think it was a good marriage until she started drinking. He liked her. She was pretty. I think the problem was that she always wanted to be in show business, which she was when he found her. But in later years in Hollywood when she was just somebody's wife and a kind of nobody she started to resent the fact that she'd quit the business. My father made her quit. Actually, he made all the wives quit. Chico's wife was in the act and Zeppo's first wife, Marion, was in the act and there was a lot of rivalry between the wives. So they made a rule that none of them could be in the act and of course that made all of them bitter. Twenty years later they were saying they could have been Marilyn Monroe.''

Fuelled then by mild resentment and the fact that her husband was becoming somewhat reclusive, Ruth began drinking for solace. Arthur Marx said: "It was kind of sad because I really think she loved him and he loved her. Of all the wives he had I really think he loved her the best.''

After the divorce, his film career apparently over, Groucho spent the rest of the war years entertaining the troops, as too did Harpo, while Chico formed a band and toured with it quite successfully. Groucho also tried his hand, not very notably, in radio and announced that he would henceforth remain a bachelor since, being disillusioned with marriage, he would not "get hooked a second time". In 1945, though, he did. He married Kay Gorcey, ex-wife of Leo Gorcey, one of the Bowery Boys. Groucho was fifty-five and Kay was twenty-four and a year after the wedding she gave birth to a daughter, Melinda.

In the same year Chico's band began to fail and, as usual, he was in desperate need of money. Once again, largely to rescue their wayward elder brother, Groucho and Harpo agreed to make another film, *A Night in Casablanca*. It was no better than all right and, apart from *The Story of Mankind* in 1957 in which the director, Irwin Allen, had the original — though hardly inspired — idea of putting the three of them in separate scenes in the same movie, it was the last time the Marx Brothers appeared together on film.

After *A Night in Casablanca* Groucho made six pictures without his brothers, none of them particularly successful. "The thing was," said Arthur Marx, "that he wanted to break away from Chico and he didn't want to be dependent on him and Harpo. He wanted to be on his own. He used to say straight acting was a cinch, anybody could do it. But the pictures were only fair. He wasn't a very good straight actor.''

In fact Groucho's career might very well have faded away by the end of the 1940s had it not been for a quiz show called *You Bet Your Life*. He was the compere, the quiz-master, the presenter and the resident comedian. The show began on radio in 1947 and later transferred to television where it rapidly became one of the most popular programmes on any network.

"Perhaps it was the chance it gave him to ad-lib that Groucho was proudest of," said Charlotte Chandler. "He loved to do that. He would say it was the best work he ever did. Also it used the character that Groucho had created and gave him the chance to reach a mass audience that he'd never really reached, to the same extent, in films."

Altogether *You Bet Your Life* lasted for fourteen years and while it was running Groucho changed wives yet again. He was divorced from Kay Gorcey in 1951 and three years later he married Eden Hertford. As he grew older his brides grew comparatively younger, for Groucho was sixty-four and Eden was only twenty.

Of Eden Zeppo said: "She was another girl who was not what you would call brilliant but she was nice and she was good for Groucho because he would insult her and she wouldn't understand it. He thought that was cute."

Groucho's view of women is very hard to pin down. He was married three times and indeed appears to have had a great respect for the institution of marriage but he always seemed to choose very young and very pretty girls who, through no fault of their own, could not keep up with him intellectually. According to Charlotte Chandler: "He was married for forty-seven years but to three different women and he said it was fun with all of them for a while. People said Groucho expected too much from his women but he had a good feeling towards all his wives. He said he had a few good years with each of them and maybe that was as much as anyone could expect."

Taking this philosophical view a little further he also attributed the eventual failure of all his marriages to the fact that he invariably chose his wives for their looks. And for their innocence, too, I imagine since they were all extremely youthful. Certainly he seemed to prefer innocence in women to sophistication, but innocence, alas, is a most perishable commodity and once it had perished his wives became a disappointment to him. It might have been better, or anyway less painful, for all concerned if he had simply had affairs with them, especially the last two and especially if you bear in mind the opinion of his son, Arthur, that "he was a born bachelor really. He just wanted a wife to have dinner with."

But beneath the womanising façade — the façade, indeed, when you consider the extreme youth of his wives, of a dirty old man —

there existed a most puritan conscience. To Charlotte Chandler he said: "I had to marry them. Chico didn't but I did."

"His values were very much marriage and family," said Miss Chandler. "He thought the greatest thing was the marriage of Minnie and Sam, his parents, and Gummo's marriage, which had lasted, and Harpo's marriage, which was a great one. He said, 'It's only fools like me who have to pay alimony.' "

His marriage to Eden lasted, in name at least, until 1969 and on the subject of alimony, about which he felt keenly, there is a story that some time after their very expensive [for him] divorce, he took her to a party. When somebody asked him why he had brought her, he replied: "Because I like to be close to my money."

While his marriages came and went Groucho carried on with his new, solo career in the radio and TV quiz show. The very last joint appearance of the Marx Brothers came in 1959 when Groucho, Harpo and Chico were brought together for an episode of a TV series, by which time Chico was seventy-two, Harpo was seventy-one and Groucho was sixty-nine. Two years later Chico died, a compulsive gambler to the end and, as usual, broke. Harpo lived on in retirement in Palm Springs until 1964 and when he died he left his harp to the State of Israel. Only Groucho of the five brothers remained in show business and so, very properly, he was the main recipient of all the kudos when the cult of the Marx Brothers was established, or re-established, in the early 1970s.

Before that happened, however, his third marriage had come and gone and in 1971, at the age of eighty-one, he met a young Canadian actress named Erin Fleming, who was to become his assistant and business manager and who was greatly to change his life.

At the time they met she was in her middle twenties and doing secretarial work between acting engagements and Groucho, in retirement once more, was in a somewhat depressed state of mind. "He seemed to have the feeling," said Miss Fleming, "that he was washed up in show business, which struck me as supremely absurd. He didn't think he could get a job, he didn't seem to recognise who he actually was and he was just a bit dilapidated."

Erin Fleming decided that this nonsense would have to stop. She encouraged him to get back to work, to appear for example on chat shows on TV, and so Groucho moved into the final phase of his career and in some ways into his greatest fame. Coincidentally, or perhaps not, soon after Erin Fleming began to take him in hand the Marx Brothers cult began. In New York in 1972 and in response to a petition signed by thousands of college students *Animal Crackers* was given a second premiere, forty-two years after it first opened, and Groucho was present at this gala occasion — indeed he was mobbed by his youthful admirers. It was by any standards a remarkable occasion, an act of homage to a little old man of eighty-two, a veteran of seventy-seven years in show business, who had become a hero — virtually a god — to a generation young enough to be his great-grandchildren.

Erin Fleming did not find it remarkable because, she said simply, "I believe he was a truly great man and a great comedian."

But to her he was much more than that: "He was like my little brother and he was my father and he was my husband in that he was the master of the household and the payer of the bills. And he was in many ways my child."

Charlotte Chandler said that "Groucho announced to all around and at all times that it wasn't a physical relationship, because he wanted to protect Erin's reputation. But he would also say, over and over, that if it weren't for Erin he would give up show business and for him that practically meant giving up living."

Groucho's sudden re-emergence as a star, almost in fact as a living legend, was not, however, appreciated by all. Some members of his family thought it was inappropriate and undignified at his age to be making public appearances and doing a sedentary comedy act on the chat shows. Zeppo, though, was not among those who held this view. To me he said: "I think Erin kept him alive the last seven or eight years. He was in love with her and she was in love with him. She took care of him."

Taking care of him cannot have been a simple task because the passing years didn't exactly turn him into a dear little old man. Erin Fleming said: "He woke up at six o'clock in the morning and he was a bear until lunch, a grizzly bear, he was just awful. He was a man of great routine; he liked to plan his day very precisely — eleven o'clock: haircut; twelve thirty: walk; one o'clock: lunch, and so on. From four until six every day we read together and from six till seven he would play the piano and at seven precisely we sat down to dinner."

His bad moods — when he was "a really crotchety old goat" — were often connected with money and the paying of it. Erin said: "He was the biggest tightwad who ever lived. He paid the bills at two o'clock on Friday afternoon and I attempted to be as far away from him as I could possibly get."

Throughout his life, or anyway since the Wall Street Crash of

1929, Groucho had a widespread reputation for stinginess, for being the kind of man who not only knew the value of a dollar but also had a marked reluctance to break into one. But as with many tightfisted people he could, in certain circumstances and when the mood was upon him, be generous. He was, Zeppo said, generous in his donations to charities and he was in fact also generous to Zeppo when the latter's gambling habits left him occasionally embarrassed for ready money.

Very likely it was, as Arthur Marx believed, the shock of having once been financially ruined that made Groucho ultra-cautious. Norman Krasna said: "He was careful in a strange way. For instance, he wouldn't take his hat from the car into a restaurant. He said: 'I'm not going to buy my own hat back all the time from the hat-check girl.' So we'd park the car some place and walk to the restaurant in the rain and this ten-thousand-dollars-a-week actor would catch cold and he'd lose his ten thousand that week. One of those colds cost him more than all the tips he might ever have paid for his hat.

"But he had a principle about it. Now, on that basis you'd say a man who doesn't want to tip hat-check girls is a stingy fellow — but when we did a play together one time he didn't like the way the leading actor was talking to the director so he turned to me and said, 'Let's close this.' I said, 'But we've got 26,000 dollars in this thing' and he said, 'What of it?' Now I don't like to think I'm a stingy fellow but I'm always tipping hat-check girls and never giving up 26,000 dollars and that was the difference between us."

Groucho, Krasna said, was not exactly a frugal man but neither was he extravagant; he lived well but could have afforded to live better. For a long time he did his own shopping to keep an eye on the bills and his talk often revolved round money.

When they were working on the play they wrote together Groucho would go to Krasna's house for script conferences and "He'd sit down, take the cigar out of his mouth and say, 'How much do you think pumpernickel costs?' and I'd know it was gonna be that kind of day."

The conversation would then develop as follows:

"I don't know. How much does pumpernickel cost?"

"Sixteen cents."

"That's good."

"Let me tell you something: I can remember when you couldn't lift sixteen cents' worth of pumpernickel."

"Really? Fine."

"I tell you something, young man — as pumpernickel goes, so goes the nation."

This was a serious conversation because Groucho was essentially a serious man — a dour man, Krasna said. ("His normal expression was not-smiling.") But along with that went a mischievous sense of humour. Krasna remembered being in a lift with him once in New York and on the way down they were joined by another man, a stranger, who — as is the way of people in lifts — pretended they were not there at all.

"Groucho says to me, in his normal voice, 'Where are you going tonight?' I say, 'I'm going to a play about Gilbert and Sullivan. It's closing in three nights but I want to see it.' He says, 'Well, all right if you want to but I heard it stinks unless . . .' and he turns towards this guy, this perfect stranger in the elevator, and says, 'unless this sucker wrote it, in which case it's great.' And the door opened and the guy just streaked out."

And then, of course, there are the famous Groucho stories, the story, for example, of Groucho resigning from the Friars Club on the grounds that he didn't want to belong to any club that would have him as a member. And, too, there was the time when he and Eden wanted to play golf at a club which barred Jews. He asked if they could play eighteen holes and when it was pointed out to him that Jews were not admitted, he said: "Well, can we play nine holes? My wife is a Gentile."

Zeppo vouched for the authenticity of both of those incidents and also for the occasion at another club with similar anti-Semitic rules, when Groucho asked if he and his daughter Melinda could use the swimming pool and was given the same answer he had received at the golf club and he replied: "Well, can my daughter go in up to her knees? She's only half Jewish."

Erin Fleming said: "He was ferocious. His tongue was a lethal weapon." He was indeed the master of the one-line putdown, a man who could be quite savagely rude to complete strangers for no reason at all. But as he grew older and the Groucho-cult spread, even his rudeness became a social asset, a part of the legend. People would travel miles to accost him in the hope that he would say something so memorably rude to them that they could go home and boast about it to their friends. This aggravated him quite a lot and he would complain that he wasn't even able to insult people any more, though he frequently wanted to. As Ed Buzzell said, he never mellowed with old age, "he just wasn't quite as brutal to everybody as he used to be".

In the latter years of his life various well-deserved and long–overdue honours came Groucho's way. In 1972 he received the French Légion d'Honneur, becoming a "Commandeur dans l'Ordre des Arts et des Lettres", the latter being an acknowledgment of the books he had written.

In 1974 he was given a special Oscar for services to the cinema and in the same year the Friends of the Cinémathèque Française presented him with a plaque which read: "To Groucho Marx, whose comedy is timeless; a gentleman and a gentle man; the master of the illogical, of the deflated platitude, of funny truths, of *reductio ad absurdum,*" and, with some reservations about the "gentle" man, this seemed to sum him up pretty accurately.

In 1975, on his eighty-fifth birthday, a Groucho Marx Day was declared by the Mayor of the city of Los Angeles and the following year Groucho made his last public appearance on the Bob Hope TV show.

Soon after that his health began to fade and the very end of his life was clouded by a protracted law suit between his son, Arthur, and Erin Fleming over the question of who was to be Groucho's conservator — in effect his personal, as opposed to his financial, guardian. Miss Fleming had been acting in that role but eventually and by mutual consent Groucho's grandson Andy, Arthur's son, was appointed by the court. It was a complicated and somewhat bitter lawsuit and perhaps the best thing to be said about it was that Groucho was very old and very ill and unaware that it was going on.

He died at the age of eighty-seven, some six months after the death of Gummo, on August 9th, 1977, leaving an estate estimated at between two and six million dollars, most of it in trust to his three children.

Some time earlier, just before his final illness, he had been talking about his life to Charlotte Chandler in the course of which conversation he made two remarks which, I feel, are worth quoting. When she asked him if he had any regrets at all about the women in his life and the wives in his life and asked what he would do differently if given the chance to live it all over again, he thought for a moment and then replied: "I'd try a few more positions."

And when she asked him to suggest an epitaph for himself, he said: "Here lies Groucho Marx — and lies and lies and lies. P.S. He never kissed an ugly girl."

The first part of that final statement seems to me to sum up his healthy irreverence for practically everything, including death and himself, and the second part to indicate that even to the end his priorities hadn't changed.

It's impossible wholly to separate Groucho from the rest of the Marx Brothers because together they created a new kind of comedy. They were the first, the originals and if today their films sometimes seem a little dated it's important to remember that this is because the Marx Brothers have been so often imitated — imitated but never equalled. Their targets were hypocrisy and pomposity; at their best they seemed to demand neither sympathy nor applause and didn't care whom they offended.

They were a superb trio of clowns and Groucho, their leader and public mouthpiece, was the cornerstone of the act; the essence of Groucho was the essence of the Marx Brothers; with or without the others he was a great comedian and a great wit. There has, quite simply, never been another like him.

Jack Hawkins

"The Male Britannia".

above : Hawkins as the page in Saint Joan *in 1924 when he was thirteen.*

opposite : At nineteen he was in New York, appearing in Journey's End, *learning how to make bathtub gin and losing his virginity.*

above : Hawkins in 1972 — only a few months before the ill-fated operation to restore his voice.

opposite above : Leaving for Hollywood with his wife, Doreen, in 1960. By then he had already had his first treatment for cancer.

opposite below : The Hawkins family (Andrew, Jack, Caroline and Nicholas) at play in the garden of their London home.

Jack Hawkins was not, I think, a great film actor. The voice of sentiment, or possibly of that cheaper emotion sentimentality, insists urgently that he should be remembered as such but sentiment and sentimentality are false advisers. The qualifications for greatness as an actor, either on screen or on stage, include versatility, a breadth of range and while Hawkins may well have possessed such qualities he is not widely remembered for them. The cinema itself is responsible for that: it typecast him too often, in the public memory if not in fact, for anything resembling versatility to impress itself upon the mind of the onlooker.

What he was instead of a great actor was a great movie star, not perhaps if judged by any international yardstick of stardom but in his own land and in his own time he was the biggest and most bankable star around. Earlier, of course, in the 1920s and 1930s he had been a stage actor of high promise and considerable virtuosity, one who could switch from Shakespeare to drawing-room comedy with enviable sureness of foot, but once he decided to make his career in films his range inevitably narrowed.

Cinema audiences expect the familiar from their movie stars and what they expected from Hawkins was manly emotion and a stiff upper lip, the essentially British qualities (or at least what we used to think of as essentially British qualities) of sincerity, integrity and courage and nobody ever presented these things to the world with greater conviction than Jack Hawkins.

His friend Peter O'Toole summed him up best when he described him, with immense respect and affection, as "the Male Britannia". Other actors, equally adept at playing war heroes, might have laid some claim to such a title, but Hawkins, with his belligerent jaw and square, sturdy frame, not only looked the part, he had a quite unwanted advantage over any challenger: at the height of his career he faced the appalling loss of his voice through cancer of the throat with the doggedness, fortitude and sheer pluck that one would expect of the Male Britannia.

What made the blow even harder to bear was the fact that until it fell he had known nothing but success. He was born into modest, middle-class affluence in Wood Green, London, on September 14th, 1910, the son of a local builder and was known to his family as "the afterthought" because he was the youngest by ten years of four children.

His early childhood was unremarkable: at five he joined the church school, at eight the church choir, at ten the local operatic society and at twelve he was playing Ruth, the maid-of-all-work, in *The Pirates of Penzance*. No sign of the Male Britannia there. In the normal, English middle-class course of events he would have gone on to public school, perhaps to university, and then into commerce, industry, a profession or, as his second wife Doreen believed, into some kind of academic career.

But at this point a perceptive friend of the family, whose daughter was a pupil at the Italia Conti drama school for children, drastically altered the normal course of events. With the practised eye of the stage mother she spotted a grain of talent in young Jack's performance as Ruth and suggested that he might audition for the Italia Conti's Christmas production of *Where the Rainbow Ends*. There would be, she said, at least a little pocket money in it for him.

So he auditioned and was accepted and, at the end of the run, was offered a regular place at the school. Nor was that the finish of it, for within a few weeks he was asked to try out for the role of the page boy in Shaw's *St. Joan*. Shaw himself, along with the stars of the production, Sybil Thorndike and Lewis Casson, attended this audition and found him acceptable. And thus, with no anguish, heartbreak, starving in garrets or beating on unyielding doors, did Hawkins' stage career begin.

The actor Sydney Bromley, a contemporary of his at the Italia Conti school, remembered him as "a natural. I don't recall him attending classes even. He didn't need to." They appeared together both in *Where the Rainbow Ends* and *St. Joan* and Bromley said: "He had this contact with the audience. He was aware of his position on the stage, of his ability and personality. He knew it was all working."

Hawkins stayed with the Casson-Thorndike company until he was seventeen, acquiring along the way this testimonial from James Agate, the leading theatre critic of his time: "It is possible that in Master Jack Hawkins we have a very fine actor in the making. I have certainly never seen a boy player of so much promise."

The difficulty for any boy (or come to that, girl) actor is, however, to make the transition to young adult and finally adult actor. Even that came easily and without any effort on his part to Jack Hawkins. Basil Dean, the director, cast him as the school prefect in *Young Woodley,* and at once he was accepted as a juvenile lead, a status in which he immediately confirmed himself, though admittedly the play was a flop, as the younger brother in *Beau*

Geste, Beau being played by another youthful actor of some promise, Laurence Olivier.

By now Hawkins' career was progressing so rapidly that at the age of eighteen he was offered the leading role in a New York production of *Journey's End.* He was ridiculously young for the part but it was nevertheless his until the producer, Gilbert Miller, who had been under the impression that Hawkins was actually a year or two older than he really was, discovered his true age. And then, arguing not unreasonably perhaps that he couldn't risk the success or failure of his production riding on the shoulders of a mere boy, he relegated Hawkins to the second lead.

The show opened in 1929, the age of prohibition and the eve of the Wall Street Crash. It was an exciting time for a young man to be in New York and much happened to young Hawkins. He learned how to make bathtub gin — a potentially lethal enterprise — and rather less dangerously he lost his virginity, a commodity to which hitherto, as he said later, he had been clinging with a tenacity that puzzled even himself. Furthermore he fell in love with a young British actress, who was appearing in another play on Broadway, and when she returned to London he left the cast of *Journey's End* and followed her to continue his ardent pursuit.

Ardour, however, often burns too fiercely to last and in this case it was swiftly doused in the less heady atmosphere of London and within six months he was even more deeply in love with somebody else, the actress Jessica Tandy whom he met when they appeared together in the West End production of *Autumn Crocus.* By the end of 1932, when they were both twenty-one, they were married.

Miss Tandy had in fact first seen him seven years earlier when he was playing the page in *St. Joan.* "I went away from that production in a trance, it was so marvellous. And I also remember feeling very jealous of that small boy, who was no older than I was, acting in a play in St. Martin's Lane. I really envied him a lot."

The older, maturer, twenty-one-year-old Hawkins, a man who had discarded the encumbrance of virginity and knew his way around bathtub gin, impressed her rather differently. "He was great fun to be with and a very fascinating young man too. All the girls were mad about him and I was very much in love with him. Well, when you're in love at that age, of course, you think it's going to be for ever and ever — the fairy tale come true."

It didn't quite work out like that, alas, but still the 1930s were good years for both of them. They had a daughter, Susan, and Hawkins' career continued to prosper. In 1933 the drama critic of the London *Evening News* nominated John Gielgud, Robert Donat and Ralph Richardson as stars of the future and added: "Perhaps they will all be outstripped in the end by Mr. Jack Hawkins, who is only twenty-three. Mr. Hawkins looks like training to be the irresistibly breezy, infectiously gay young hero — the most indubitable of matinee idols."

By that time the infectiously gay and indubitable young matinee idol had already appeared in his first film, *Birds of Prey,* a picture of such modest accomplishment that most reference books fail to mention it, as indeed did Hawkins himself in his autobiography. He preferred to remember *The Lodger,* directed by Maurice Elvey in 1932 (and not to be confused with the earlier, silent version made by Alfred Hitchcock) as his first film. From then onwards he was continuously busy, between stage appearances, in the cinema. Between 1932 and the time war broke out he appeared in fourteen pictures, none of them of any great merit as he was the first to agree. Compared with the theatre, he felt, the cinema was second rate and films were hardly more than a convenient means of raising money to pay his income tax.

Meanwhile, his stage reputation was increasing swiftly. He returned to New York to appear in *Dear Octopus* and in the West End of London moved smoothly between farce and the classics, appearing frequently with John Gielgud, who said: "I did a play called *The Maitlands,* a modern play in which he was much better than I was. Then he played Horatio to my *Hamlet* and was with me, as Algy, in *The Importance of Being Ernest.* Just before the war we went to Elsinore with another production of *Hamlet* in which he played the king and the ghost and he was jolly good. He was so versatile. He could play modern stuff most awfully well and he was a very good comedian. He played Edmund in *King Lear* with me in the first year of the war at the Old Vic. He was so alive — full of variety and tone and great virility and an awfully easy man to get on with."

But the beginning of the war brought an end to Hawkins' progress in the theatre and it also saw the beginning of the end of his marriage to Jessica Tandy. In 1940 she was offered work in America and it seemed sensible that she should accept it, especially as it meant an opportunity to take their daughter, Susan, who was then aged nine, away from the bombing in London. So the pair of them sailed for New York and Hawkins waved them goodbye, never realising (how could he have done?) that it would be ten years before he saw them again.

With his family safely out of the way he set about trying to join the Army, a less easy procedure than one might have thought at a time of national emergency. For some reason best known to itself the Army had decided that it didn't need any more volunteers and it took great determination on Hawkins' part to get himself accepted. Having succeeded in this he was sent to officers' training school and, on graduating as a second-lieutenant, was instructed by the War Office to appear in a propaganda film called *Next of Kin,* a picture most notable for the fact that it was the first of many in which he was to appear in some kind of uniform.

Around the time this was finished, 1942, Jessica Tandy announced in a letter from the USA that she had fallen in love with the Canadian actor, Hume Cronyn, and intended to marry him. Hawkins reacted as many a man has done in similar circumstances by going out and getting extremely drunk. The resulting hangover was monumental enough to take his mind off his grief at the impending destruction of his marriage and by the time he had recovered from his hangover he had received orders to proceed immediately to India where the Army, having first trained him fully in the techniques of jungle warfare, decided that he was now fit to run troop entertainments. (Military decisions such as this probably help to explain why Britain traditionally loses every battle except the last one — though how it ever manages to win the last one continues to remain a mystery.)

However, Hawkins was still too bewildered by the whirligig behaviour of fate to be excessively upset (and certainly he wasn't surprised) when, a year after her Dear John — or more accurately Dear Jack — letter, Miss Tandy announced that she had divorced him in Nevada.

Many years later she said she still wasn't entirely sure why the marriage had broken up. "I think, looking back on it from my advanced years now, we were obviously both too young. We weren't mature enough to be married and to understand what it meant. We expected it to be a matter of living happily ever after which, of course, even in the best marriages is not true. So when there were difficulties we were not able to cope with them and there was a rift which widened over the years. One of us probably disappointed the other in some way or there were sins of omission or sins of commission. He was an extremely kind man, a good man — but not for me. What I do think is significant, though, is that each of us, later, made good and lasting marriages so I think we both learned a lot from the disappointments of our own relationship."

Hawkins' second — and good and lasting — marriage was to another young actress, Doreen Lawrence, whom he met while running Army entertainments in India. They met, in fact, in Bombay whither she had come with a touring company. She said: "I remember it very well. I saw this very tall, very broad figure come in through the door and he was looking quite smashing. He always wore uniform well. He came over and said, 'How do you do, Miss Lawrence?' and as far as I recall we had dinner together that night. Within ten days we realised we'd fallen very much in love. In fact we were already talking about marriage."

It was his "positive personality" that had such a devastating effect upon her. "He was a tremendously powerful person with infectious gaiety and great humour and wit."

Marriage, however, had to wait while Miss Lawrence continued to do her bit to entertain the troops and Hawkins rose in the fullness of time to the rank of acting Colonel in charge of ENSA for the whole of South-East Asia, in which capacity he even brought Gielgud to India to play Hamlet. Gielgud said: "It was interesting to see him in uniform with a swagger stick being very much the sort of head boy. I think he rather enjoyed the authority."

It was 1946 before Hawkins returned, a civilian once more, to England. By then most of his contemporaries had re-established themselves in the theatre and he was worried about his own ability to do so. Like most actors, Doreen said, he was constantly in need of reassurance and worried that he might never get a job again. But in his case there was no need for concern. His passage back into the theatre was as remarkably smooth and troublefree as his original entry had been.

He was asked to play King Magnus in *The Applecart* by Shaw, then took on a theatrical tour of Europe on behalf of the British Council and when he returned to London to appear in *Othello* and Shaw's *Candida* he was seen by Sir Alexander Korda, at that time still the most distinguished of British film producers, who promptly offered him a three-year contract.

Hawkins was naturally delighted but also much surprised. He still remembered films from his pre-war days as simply a way to earn quick money and certainly not as a medium in which he could make a career. Apart from anything else he had been told often that he had entirely the wrong-shaped face for the screen. Doreen explained that by saying: "They cast him in all the wrong sort of roles in those early films. He was playing juvenile leads and Jack was never really a juvenile lead. If you see pictures of him when he was young you'll see that he was rather tall and slim with a strong jaw and rather thin face. But after the war when all that Army training and square-bashing had broadened him out he was a different sort of person in shape and stature and face. And he was more mature; he was thirty-seven years old, you see."

Korda, too, may well have pointed all this out to him. In any event Hawkins accepted the contract which, apart from any other benefits it might confer, did at least mean that he and Doreen could now afford to marry and this they did in October 1947, at the Chelsea Register Office. Immediately afterwards Korda set him briskly to work. In 1948 Hawkins played leading roles in three films, *Bonnie Prince Charlie, The Fallen Idol* and *The Small Back Room.* Then, with hardly a pause to draw breath, he went into *State Secret, The Black Rose* and *The Elusive Pimpernel,* a Korda spectacular which took so long to make that between the time Hawkins first began work on it at the end of 1948 and the time it was finished in 1950 he had twice become a father.

The Black Rose, which starred Tyrone Power and which Hawkins made during a hiatus in the filming of *The Elusive Pimpernel,* brought him into contact with his first Hollywood director, Henry Hathaway. Hathaway was suffering from cancer at the time, a fact which he kept very much to himself. And years later when he had happily recovered and Hawkins was stricken in his turn, Hathaway was the first person to offer him practical help.

By the end of 1951 Hawkins had made nine films in four years and had also taken time off to play Mercutio to Olivia de Havilland's Juliet in a Broadway production of *Romeo and Juliet.* It lasted only six weeks but, if nothing else, it gave him the opportunity to be reunited briefly with his ex-wife Jessica Tandy (who had become a Broadway star after playing Blanche to Marlon Brando's Stanley in *A Streetcar Named Desire*) and of course with his daughter, Susan, neither of whom he had seen since they left England in 1940.

Hawkins was now a popular leading man in British films and a reliable supporting actor in more international productions such as *The Black Rose* and *No Highway,* in which the main roles were played by James Stewart and Marlene Dietrich. From such a position to stardom in one's own right is a considerable step and one not often managed by an actor of forty-two. Hawkins, however, achieved it in the course of one year and with the help of three films.

First, there was *Angels One Five,* a nicely underplayed drama set on an RAF station during the Battle of Britain. Hawkins' role as a group captain put him back into contemporary military uniform for the first time since *Next of Kin.* And as he wrote in his autobiography, *Anything for a Quiet Life*: "Over the next few years I played enough senior officers to stock the whole Ministry of Defence . . ."

Secondly, there was *Mandy,* the story of a deaf and dumb child, in which Hawkins played the headmaster of the school where the child was taught. Alexander Mackendrick, the director, said that frankly he didn't think it was a particularly good role, certainly not for anyone anxious to become a movie star. "But I think that was the attractive thing about Jack. He thought the part was a good one and he wanted it for that reason, not because he was trying to build up a persona of a kind that would be appealing at the box office."

He remembered Hawkins as being "very much the successful West End theatre actor but he wasn't marked in any way by certain artificialities of the West End theatre. I think the thing that most intrigues me about Jack is illustrated in a story told me by another actor, who had worked with him in the theatre. He said that in one scene, where Jack was supposed to be angry, acting with him on stage was nerve-racking because you really thought he was out of control. He wasn't, of course. But he was able to perform with such urgency of belief that you thought he was out of control. It was something that I recognised in him later when I worked with him on *Mandy* — it's a capacity to immerse yourself so totally within a character that you don't act it, you are it. And Jack would do that. He could really absorb the personality of the character he was playing so that while he still appeared to be nothing but Hawkins he had in fact transformed himself."

Whatever transformation he effected in *Mandy* it was enough to persuade Charles Frend, like Mackendrick a director at Ealing Studios, that Hawkins was the ideal person to play the leading part of Captain Ericson in the film version of Nicholas Monsarrat's *The Cruel Sea.* It was this picture and Hawkins' performance in it that finally clinched his position among the top handful of stars in British films, for what he showed most memorably were the qualities with which he has ever since been associated in the public mind: power and rugged masculinity combined with an equally masculine ability to portray emotion and tears. The latter were seen most memorably in the scene in which Hawkins/Ericson breaks down after he has been obliged to drop a depth charge in the middle of a crowd of shipwrecked British sailors. The options open to him in the film were either to rescue the sailors or drop the depth charge because he was convinced, wrongly as it turned out, that a German U-boat was lurking beneath them.

Interestingly enough that scene was very nearly deleted from the finished picture. My father, Leslie Norman, who produced *The Cruel Sea,* as indeed he had *Mandy,* said that Michael (later Sir Michael) Balcon, the head of Ealing Studios, was unhappy with the sequence and "he said, 'We can't have our hero crying. You've got to do it again.' I pleaded with him and told him it was a great scene. But he said, 'No, you must do it again.' So we did, without showing Jack weeping. But when a representative of Universal Films came over from America to see the picture I told the editor to put the original scene back in. And at the end of it this bloke from Universal said, 'That's a great movie. It's got balls, especially that scene where Jack cries.'"

With its balls thus restored, *The Cruel Sea* persuaded the Rank Organisation to offer Hawkins a long-term contract at what he himself described as "a princely salary". Hitherto he had still been under contract to Korda who, for the most part, had simply been hiring him out to other companies. Korda was initially reluctant to let him go but in the end did so with some grace, parting from his star with this handsome testimonial: "Dear Jack, good luck. I am the man who had a golden sovereign in his pocket and did not know it."

But having changed hands the golden sovereign found himself being hired out just as before — albeit at a higher price — and quite often to American companies, though it was to be some years before he actually went to Hollywood to work. On the other hand he was never unemployed and between 1952 and 1960 he made fifteen films either in Britain or on location and by then he was earning £30,000 a picture — mere pocket money compared with the millions of dollars that are now offered to the likes of Robert Redford and Marlon Brando but very good money for the time.

Furthermore in 1954 — the year his daughter Caroline was born — and again in 1955 he was voted Britain's most popular male star and even, to his own considerable astonishment, was regarded as a kind of muscular sex symbol. In the now defunct *Sunday Graphic,* a columnist wrote: "Women fall like a ton of bricks for the strong, silent charm of Jack Hawkins. They have made him the biggest romantic idol in British films since the heyday of James Mason."

Hawkins was flattered by the interest of the women but not seduced by it — he was never a womaniser — and he was not really seduced by the often intoxicating delights of stardom either. His sons, Nicholas and Andrew, both felt that he enjoyed it a great deal though the whole family occasionally found it tiresome when he was mobbed in public but, said Andrew, he did like it enough "to feel that the price was worth paying". At the same time, as the writer and director Bryan Forbes put it, he didn't relish the trappings of stardom "in the boring sense of somebody who wants his trailer to be longer than anybody else's or takes out a tape measure to make sure he's got the biggest billing. Jack was above that sort of crap."

By 1959 then, Hawkins was well established at the top of his profession and had gained a respectable international reputation with his performance as the university don turned commando leader in *The Bridge on the River Kwai*. But now television was becoming a distinct threat to the cinema and money was becoming tighter. So he agreed to take a cut in salary to £20,000 against a percentage of the profits. In retrospect he believed this was a valuable move since it obliged him to take a greater interest in production and to recognise that TV was not simply a kind of fairground sideshow but an alarming and genuine competitor of the movies.

What's more he made a brief foray into television himself, appearing in *The Public Prosecutor* and then playing King Magnus in *The Applecart*. Later he became involved in the Edgar Wallace series, *The Four Just Men*, in which his co-stars were Vittorio de Sica, Richard Conte and Dan Dailey. For this he adopted his film-star policy and took a reduced salary and a share of the profits, which turned out to be rather a grave mistake because there weren't any profits. But, on the other hand, he was given valuable exposure in America and a reputation there was becoming increasingly important as the British film industry's circumstances grew ever more straitened.

In that year, 1959, Hawkins joined Richard Attenborough, Bryan Forbes and others to form Allied Film Makers, the purpose of which was to enable them to gain greater control over their own careers and to raise the backing to film *The League of Gentlemen* which Forbes had written specifically for Hawkins. In the story his familiar typecast image was neatly reversed: instead of playing a noble officer and gentleman he played an ex-officer and gentleman organising a spectacular bank robbery.

It was while he was making *The League of Gentlemen,* however, that Hawkins began to suffer serious problems with his throat. He had always, throughout his life, been subject to throat trouble. Sydney Bromley remembered him, even in the Italia Conti days, muffled up in scarves and saying that he had been to the doctor about his throat and Jessica Tandy, mixing her metaphors slightly, said his throat "was his Achilles' heel. Before I knew him, when he was in America, he had quite considerable throat trouble and that's where it would always strike him if he was ill."

But this time the throat trouble that struck him was far more serious. He had almost completed *The League of Gentlemen* and was rehearsing for a play he was to do in Manchester when his voice began to give out. Doreen said: "He seemed to have a cold or something and his voice was a bit gritty."

He went into hospital to have his vocal chords scraped, was advised not to attend rehearsals for the play and then, a few days later, was told by his specialist that he would have to undergo radium treatment for cancer. He was, Doreen said, understandably frightened. A threat to the voice is alarming for any actor but for Hawkins it was particularly so because he had a most distinctive voice, a voice that, more even than his appearance or his acting style, was his trademark.

The radium treatment lasted six weeks and though it caused him no pain the side effects took the form of deep depression. But this, too, passed after a lengthy holiday in Italy and when he went to Hollywood for the first time to co-star with Shirley MacLaine in *Two Loves* it seemed the cancer had been destroyed.

In fact he had six years' complete remission but throughout that time fear remained. "One never had any peace of mind," Doreen said. "One fell into the awful habit — at least I did — of listening to his voice. And I guess he listened to it himself and was very conscious of it. At times it would let him down a bit and we had some very hairy moments during those six years when we thought, 'Oh dear, something's happening . . .' "

Perhaps because of this Hawkins seemed to work harder than ever throughout the first half of the 1960s when there was a slight change in the emphasis of his career. He was now into his fifties and increasingly playing character roles — as in *Lawrence of Arabia* — as well as leading men. And it was while he was playing Allenby to Peter O'Toole's Lawrence that a lasting friendship was formed between them. It virtually began when David Lean, the director, asked them not to see each other off-set for fear that they would lead each other into bibulous habits.

O'Toole said: "We were nipping off in the middle of boring setups to have a light ale and keep the tonsils healthy. I've never seen Jack the worse for drink on set, mind you, though I have seen him taken drunk off-set. But he had a reputation and I had a reputation and none of it was ill-deserved."

On Christmas Eve, the shooting of the film still being in progress, Hawkins and O'Toole found themselves mournfully alone in an hotel in Seville. "The barman retired to bed," O'Toole said, "and we were serving each other drinks, very lonely. Then I had the bright idea of taking Jack to midnight Mass at the cathedral because there was nothing else to do really, other than go into an alcoholic coma . . . Now Jack had had his hair shaved for the part of Allenby and he was a bit of a vain man and wore a little toupee. Well, as the evening wore on it became less of a toupee and more of a sort of hair hat, which was balanced on the front of his head. And we were, I must confess, a little elevated. So we went to the cathedral and there was a gramophone playing Brahms and nobody singing at all. So we left and outside sitting on a couple of gargoyles were a make-up man and a hairdresser and we teamed up and went to a brothel. Now Jack thought it was a very posh restaurant, because it was a very elegant sort of brothel and he didn't know it was a brothel at all. He was sittting there and the toupee was falling over his eyebrows by this time and we were approached by a few little whores who Jack, in his courteous way, thought were nice ladies out celebrating Christmas Eve. And he said, 'Oh, how kind of you to join us. Do sit down.' At which point one of the ladies grabbed him in a particular erogenous zone and I remember the look of total astonishment on the Male Britannia's face and the hair hat slowly falling down over his eyes."

If this anecdote suggests that Hawkins was a toper, I must make it clear that he was not. He liked a drink and in particular he liked a drink in the atmosphere of an English pub but it appears to have been almost exclusively in the company of Mr. O'Toole that he fell resoundingly from grace. For there was another notable alcoholic occasion in 1965 when they were filming *Lord Jim* in the Far East and the pair of them, in company with the Irish actor Jack MacGowran, were delayed for a few hours in an Indian city.

"Well, it was a Muslim city," said O'Toole, "and it was dry, completely — not a drink to be got." Lesser men might reluctantly have accepted this unhappy situation but O'Toole saw it simply as a challenge. He insisted on Hawkins taking them to the British Embassy where they were told that the only people permitted to buy drinks in the city were licensed alcoholics.

"So MacGowran and I put our heads together and asked if the Embassy had a doctor, which indeed it did, so we finished up the three of us as licensed alcoholics and we went to a place called the Monopole or something like that where we could get this amazing paint remover, fire water in a label-less bottle and you carried it out in an anonymous little brown paper bag. So we finished up, with our three chits proving we were alcoholics, sitting in a park finishing this paint remover and Jack looked at his licence, his licence to be an alcoholic, and he said, 'If they catch you sober twice you get the fucking thing endorsed.' And that was the thing about Jack — he always had the pertinent remark. It wasn't always the wittiest but it was always pertinent."

In the six years after the radium treatment Hawkins made eleven films and mostly avoided his typecast military image. Then towards the end of 1965 he went to Hollywood again with a contract to appear in twenty-six episodes of the TV series *Dr. Kildare*; and the trouble with his throat recurred. Once again cancer was diagnosed and he decided to leave for London and return to the specialist who had treated him before. But this time it was not possible to use radium. Doreen said: "We both knew that the ultimate was facing us and that, unless some miracle occurred, he would have to have his larynx removed."

No miracle did occur and a date for the operation was set. Nicholas Hawkins recalled the moment when his father broke the news to the family. "We were all called into the sitting-room where he was standing with his back to the fireplace and he said he'd got cancer of the throat and if he didn't have the operation he would die. He wasn't emotional about it. He just made this statement."

But if emotion was not revealed it was there nevertheless. Doreen said: "It was absolutely dreadful for him because amputation would have been infinitely preferable. For an actor to lose his voice — and Jack's was really rather a good voice and of a special quality — well, there's just nothing to replace it. He didn't know what he was going to do: he went through all the degrees of despair. But he was so incredibly brave. He was always a man of great courage and he showed such enormous guts over this that one had to be strong, too. I guess we held each other up."

Nicholas, however, believed that if the only person affected by the decision had been himself Hawkins would have chosen not to have the operation at all. "He did actually say afterwards that if he hadn't had a wife and family he would have died rather than go through with it. Because as he saw it at the time an enormous part of his life was over."

As it was, on a Friday evening in February 1966, Doreen drove her husband to University College Hospital in London for the operation to remove his larynx and, to all intents and purposes, his career and his livelihood. On the way a car, shooting out of a side street, almost crashed into them. Hawkins wound down the window and yelled: "You bastard!" And that, he reported later in his autobiography, was his last public utterance in his own, natural voice.

To the extent that the malignant growth in the throat was totally removed the operation was a success but it left Hawkins altered mentally, as well as physically. "His attitude to life changed," Doreen said. "Some of the striving went out of him. I think he was amazed to find himself still alive and able to lead a very full life. He hadn't believed that would happen."

The first step towards leading the full life was to learn to speak again without benefit of a larynx. "He started talking within three weeks, which was quite incredible. He did it mainly on Guinness and champagne, I'm afraid. You see the oesophageal voice, which he now had to use, comes from the stomach, from a belch, and he found that if he drank Guinness and champagne it would produce the right sort of burp that started him talking."

Hawkins took a year off to recuperate and learn this new method of speech and at the end of that time he was as fully restored to health as it was possible to be. But he was still only fifty-six years old and though he had a comfortable home in London and a holiday villa in the South of France he was not a rich man because, unlike many other British stars, he had always refused to go into tax exile to protect his capital. In the past decade his earnings had been high — but so, too, had the income tax he had been obliged to pay. The problem that now faced him was how to continue to earn a living.

And at this point he discovered, as perhaps one only does in times of such adversity, who his true friends were. First Henry Hathaway sought his assistance in setting up a film to be made in East Africa. It was not much of a job — Hawkins merely acted as a go-between — but it helped to restore his confidence. And then Peter O'Toole offered him an acting role, the small part of the bumbling British ambassador, in his film *Great Catherine*. Hawkins, naturally, had misgivings about his ability to do it, even though he only had a few lines to deliver, but O'Toole was insistent. The role was for Hawkins, he said, and only for Hawkins.

O'Toole who, after the laryngectomy, had sent him a laconic two-word cable saying merely "Shut up", told me the offer was made out of "charity in the name of love, certainly; in the terms of a hand-out, no. Good God, he wouldn't have accepted that."

By an ironic coincidence my father has had the same operation as Hawkins and, like Hawkins, later returned to work, in his case as a TV director. "When this thing suddenly comes to you," he said, "you feel crushed, as if your world has gone. Well, I know I felt that way and I'm sure Jack must have done, too." That being so, I asked him what kind of courage it must have taken for Hawkins, an actor renowned for the quality of his voice, to go back onto the set to deliver lines in that oesophageal monotone, what he called his "Dalek voice". "A great deal," he said. "He must have had a lot of guts to do that."

In *Great Catherine* Hawkins did indeed speak his lines in his own oesophageal voice and though he rightly prided himself on the fact that he was probably the only actor ever to do so, it was not a success because the very effort of producing the requisite 'burp' means that the phrasing and the timing are wrong. But at least he had proved that in every way except vocally ("What I should like now," he said in a rare TV appearance, "is for some bright spark to invent silent pictures") he was still in business as an actor. And even the voice problem was partially solved when it was decided that henceforth he should be dubbed, either by Robert Rietty or Charles Gray, both distinguished actors themselves with voices not dissimilar to that of Hawkins.

The first time Charles Gray stood in, vocally, was on *Shalako*. "Jack loaded us up with Black Velvet, I remember, and we had a run at it but it wasn't entirely successful — a lot to do with the Black Velvet, I think — and we had to do it again. Part of the trouble was that Jack had been saying the lines in his own voice and therefore gulping. So we came to a sort of arrangement. I said, 'In future, could you possibly try not to vocalise but just to mime the words?' which is an awful thing to say to an actor. It's like, you know, telling a dog not to bark when it hears the doorbell go. But afterwards it was much easier because there weren't those unnatural lulls between words."

With this kind of assistance Hawkins continued to play small, supporting roles in films, a remarkable achievement in itself and one that would have satisfied most actors similarly afflicted. But as time went by he became more frustrated by his handicap. Sir John Gielgud appeared with him in a scene in *Oh What a Lovely War* and said: "He played the scene — he hardly spoke but he had to weep, which he did most beautifully — with great skill. He was absolutely master of his technique. But I could see that he was under tremendous strain."

Closer friends noticed a change in him, too. Peter O'Toole said: "He became isolated. He was a man who thrived on company and conversation and communication. He became introverted, perforce; isolated, perforce. He lost what he was on earth for, which was to act — well, you've heard that voice — and he became sad, really, and depressed."

Bryan Forbes said that "sometimes, after the operation, when he was telling a story — and he loved telling stories, dirty stories, funny stories — he'd get to the tag line and he'd run out of air and then you'd see a flash of anger but it was anger with himself, not with other people."

Nicholas Hawkins said: "He became shorter with everybody, which is difficult to do if you can't actually speak. But occasionally there would be a stamped foot or just a glare. Obviously, there was enormous frustration. If he'd repeated something a couple of times and people still didn't understand what he said he would stamp his foot and become angry."

Hawkins was not, essentially, an angry or bad-tempered man, though his sons and friends would often be shown flashes of controlled rage. But he was an impatient man and in the spring of 1973 when he had gone as far as he could in developing the oesophageal voice, his impatience and his frustration led him into the decision that was to cost him his life.

From America there had come news of a device called a "Voicebak", designed for people like himself, which — when inserted into the throat — would, it was claimed, restore normal powers of speech. On an impulse one weekend he decided to go to New York to look into the possibility of presenting himself as a candidate for a Voicebak.

"What drove Jack mad about the oesophageal voice," said Doreen, "was the flatness of it. Being an actor he'd been used to being able to use his voice. To have this flat tone with no inflection, he hated. And he hated having to gulp air, which ruined the timing of everything he said. And that apparently would have been obviated with the insertion of this implant."

So he went to New York to investigate and when Doreen phoned him a day or so later, he said: "It's marvellous. I've seen a film of the operation and I've heard all about it and I'm going to have it done." She urged him to wait but he told her he had already arranged to go into the Flower and Fifth Hospital on Fifth Avenue to have preliminary tests and that she was not to worry. By the time she was able to speak to him again he had already undergone the operation and had been fitted with a temporary Voicebak device and at this point she flew to New York to be near him.

(Bryan Forbes reported on a conversation he had once had with the late Michael Wilding, who had visited Hawkins in hospital while the temporary device was in his throat. "Mike said the voice was totally back as it had been. The operation did work. Suddenly in that hospital there was old Jack's voice, just as it had always been.")

If this were indeed so, it still worked, alas, only briefly. For the doctors discovered another growth in Hawkins' throat, this time in the pharynx, and they had to remove that and then wait for the wound to heal before they could set about fitting the Voicebak proper. But unfortunately that wound never did heal.

Hawkins and Doreen stayed in their friend Lauren Bacall's apartment while they waited until he was fit enough to return to the hospital but, "One night, the middle of the night, he had this terrible, terrible haemorrhage. It finally turned out that the carotid artery had broken down and he almost bled to death. It was quite desperate. He was carted off to hospital again and given blood transfusions. But that wasn't the end of it. He had another haemorrhage. So then they had to take a vein from his leg and put a new artery in his neck and, oh, it was a long, long story of nothing but horror. Then he started to become paralysed down one side because of lack of blood to the brain."

Nicholas, the elder son, flew to New York and between them he and his mother made the decision to take Hawkins back to England and the specialists who knew him best. But this time there was little even they could do.

"The same thing happened all over again," Doreen said. "Within a week he had another terrible haemorrhage and went into St. Stephen's Hospital where they fought and fought and fought for him. But unfortunately it was never any good. He'd contracted a huge infection in this aperture they'd made in New York, which caused the artery to break down constantly. But Jack was enormously brave. He never lost his sense of humour and I suppose that's really what kept us all going."

Hawkins' courage and optimism were such that he began, even while in hospital, to learn the lines for a role he had accepted in Blake Edwards' film *The Tamarind Seed* but by then it was obvious to his family that he was never going to recover and perhaps it was better that he should not. The death of anyone you love can never come wholly as a relief but Hawkins' death on July 23rd, 1973, in St. Stephen's Hospital where he was still haemorrhaging and half-paralysed by a stroke was as close to being a relief for his family as any such event can ever be.

Doreen said: "I can never forget the last time we talked together. He was in intensive care all the time and he hated it because it was down in the dark. But he was so marvellous that day. He was full of life and he said he'd like a drink. He had some orange juice there and I put a little vodka in it for him and he said, 'Now, when am I to start work again?' So I said, 'Well, you'd better hurry up because they're waiting to start in September' and I didn't tell him that they'd probably started already and he never would work again. He said, 'Oh Lord, I must get out of this place, mustn't I?' And, oh, we laughed and joked and he was in such good form that I left feeling very happy. And then, of course, the next time I went he was in a coma."

By then the end was inevitable — and almost welcome. "I loved him too much to wish him to carry on living the way he was and I think we all felt the same. He would never have been right again, would never have been able to lead a full life and it would have been dreadful for him. It had been just one long tale of horror. I can only describe it as a nightmare that one never seemed to come out of. And I know how frustrated he was anyway with life. I suppose that's why he took this enormous chance on the operation."

The Voicebak was a gamble, a fifty-fifty chance at best for somebody in his condition, and Hawkins almost certainly realised that. The compromise with which he had lived during the last few years of his life was simply not enough for him. It would be wrong to suggest that he had gone to New York virtually on a suicide mission: he was too full of hope for that. But I believe, and his close friends believe, that he had gone there prepared to stake — and if necessary lose — what he had in a bid to recover what he had had before.

Bryan Forbes said: "I think Jack finally thought, I can't go on like this; the odds aren't too good but it's worth the risk." And Peter O'Toole said: "He'd been warned by many of us that it was highly dangerous and I think it was probably a defiance, an 'Oh, the hell with it, it'll either work or it won't' and he put everything on one throw and he lost. He went into it, if you like, with the idea of being prepared to die, rather than go on in this crippled fashion."

Hawkins was sixty-two when he died. Before his laryngectomy he had made fifty-six films; after it he appeared in ten more but in truth those last ten films were more notable for the fact that he could do them at all than for what he achieved in them. At the time he lost his voice he was easing into a new phase of his career and, but for the appalling ill-luck of cancer, he would probably have gone on to become a highly distinguished character actor. It's quite possible that he would have been given the opportunity, more and more, to display the versatility which he had shown as a young man but which his position as a movie star had given him very little chance to reveal. A Jack Hawkins unhampered by cancer and still alive and active today would very likely now be Sir Jack Hawkins. Others with no greater claim to a title than he have been knighted since his death.

But in the event Hawkins' career really ended on the day his larynx was removed. He died leaving his property to his widow, a trust fund for his children and a gross estate of £13,019. In any list of the world's greatest movie stars Hawkins, largely by virtue of the fact that most of his films were made in Britain for essentially British audiences, would probably not rank very high. Even so his achievements were considerable and few stars have ever been remembered with as much affection and admiration as he is. On screen, and in the last few years of his life, he was and remains the archetypal English gentleman, the archetypal English warrior who regards overwhelming odds simply as odds that are there to be themselves overwhelmed.

And as an actor he was, as Peter O'Toole put it, the man who "gave a different interpretation of the cliché Englishman, all phlegmatic and stiff upper-lip. He, more than any other man, impressed the stamp of English acting at its most red-blooded and clear and passionate." Or, to put it another way, he was in every sense the Male Britannia.

Edward G. Robinson

Edward G. around the time of Little Caesar, already close to forty and an overnight success after seventeen years in the theatre.

above : With his first wife, Gladys, in the earlier, happier days before mental illness destroyed her and the marriage.

opposite : Edward G., the man about town. He may not have been handsome but he was never less than elegant.

above : Edward G. in his later years when he worked mostly to support his art collection.

opposite above : 1956, divorce from Gladys and — Hollywood-style — the Robinsons threw a party to celebrate.

opposite below : Robinson and his second wife, Jane, on their way to Moscow and a tribute to the arch-gangster of Hollywood from, I suppose, the gangsters of the Kremlin.

On the last day of April 1952, United States Congressman Francis Walter of Pennsylvania looked upon Edward G. Robinson with what one might reasonably assume was a degree of patronising sympathy and declared, literally for all the world to hear: "I think you are Number One on the sucker list in this country."

Incredible though it may now seem Edward G. Robinson, star of countless movies and, more than that, a highly cultured gentleman, both connoisseur and patron of the arts, was grateful to him. He may also have squirmed or even seethed with very proper indignation (and indeed I like to think he did) but mostly he was grateful. The title of the nation's leading sucker is not perhaps one that is ever likely to be much coveted but it was a thousand times better than some of the labels which American congressmen and senators, American newspapers and even the American public had been attaching to him over the last few years.

To be publicly proclaimed a fool or dupe is, on the whole, preferable to being publicly proclaimed a species of traitor, which had been Edward G. Robinson's lot during a lengthy period of persecution. And there was a certain irony in that, because he had come to America some fifty years previously to escape persecution, not to be embraced by it.

He had been born Emanuel Goldenberg in Bucharest, Romania, on Tuesday, December 12th, 1893, the fifth of six sons of Morris and Sarah Goldenberg. Morris was a builder and he was also a Jew and so he and his family lived in a Jewish compound. It was not a ghetto exactly, as the Romanians would no doubt have been careful to point out; it was just a compound — not that this made a great deal of difference because in Eastern Europe in 1893, just as today, persecuting Jews was a kind of national sport. In Bucharest, it is true, they could do almost anything they liked just as long as they didn't attempt to enrol at the public schools or enter any of the professions, the latter being a somewhat academic point since exclusion from the public schools meant in effect exclusion from education. If in the face of this some Jew became a little uppity, remarking perhaps that the system hardly seemed quite fair, he was very rightly put in his place by being beaten up by groups of outraged and non-Jewish citizens and this, indeed, is what happened to one of young Emanuel's older brothers who was stoned by a mob and received brain damage which later on caused him to spend most of his life in a mental institution.

In 1902 Morris Goldenberg decided that, even for Jews, life must have something better to offer than this so he took his family to America, land of the free and the sweatshops. They settled down first in a tenement on New York's lower East Side and then in the Bronx where Morris opened a junk shop and Emanuel, now aged nine, was at last permitted to go to public school.

He had one remarkable stroke of luck: the city at that time was teeming with newly-arrived immigrants and the class for non-English speaking children at Public School No. 137 was full. Thus Emanuel, whose speech was incomprehensible save to fellow-Romanians, was perforce obliged to enrol in a normal, English-speaking class where it rapidly transpired, fortunately for him, that he was a gifted and natural linguist. Within a year he was speaking fluent English, most importantly — considering his future career — without a trace of Romanian accent.

Not that originally he intended to be an actor at all. His first ambition, according to Sam Jaffe, his friend for nearly fifty years, was to become a lawyer because, probably with memories of Romania still fresh in his mind, he wished to defend the poor. Failing that, he thought he might be a rabbi, doubtless for similar reasons. These public-spirited aspirations, however, vanished at high school because there the possibilities of an acting career impressed him as suddenly and vividly as his first glimpse of a motor-car impressed Mr. Toad (whom, I suppose, physically Edward G. in many ways resembled).

At the age of eighteen Emanuel Goldenberg won a place at the American Academy of Dramatic Art in New York City and there he ceased to be Emanuel Goldenberg. It was suggested to him that his was no kind of a name for an actor. Today it's hard to see why: Emanuel Goldenberg is as good a name as any other. But in 1911, as Edward G. recalled later, it was considered too long, too foreign and — even in America, land of the free — rather too Jewish.

Thus he became Robinson, after the name of a butler in a play he had seen, and he became Edward because that was the name of the King of England and he argued, reasonably enough, that if Edward was good enough for a king it was good enough for him. But with this adoption of an acceptable, Gentile name came an onset of guilt. It was, he felt, a denial of his Jewish antecedents and so he inserted the G. between the Edward and the Robinson. Officially it stood for nothing but to him it always stood for Goldenberg. It was, he said, "my private treaty with my past".

His original name, however, was not his only handicap. There was also the fact that he was no more than 5 feet 5 inches tall, chunkily built and not even within nodding distance of being handsome. On the other hand he did, undeniably, have talent and though, in the early days after his graduation, work was never plentiful he managed to scrape a living, first in summer stock and then, from 1915 onwards, in small parts on Broadway. His approach to producers who, on first sight of him were somewhat deterred, was rather touching. "I may not look much," he said, "but I promise I'll deliver for you on stage." And obviously he was as good as his word because after 1915 the young Robinson was never again obliged to leave Broadway in search of theatre work, although there was a brief hiatus in his progress when, America having entered the First World War, he volunteered for the Navy with a lofty image of himself as the saviour of democracy.

At the beginning of the war in Europe he had been — again ironically in view of later events — pro-German, largely because Russia and Romania, the two countries most notorious for their ill-treatment of Jews, were lined up with Germany's enemies. But the sinking of the *Lusitania* caused a change of heart and mind and Edward G. Robinson went to war. More accurately, he was prepared to go to war but in the event he contracted a bad case of influenza and never actually left harbour. Democracy, to his chagrin, was therefore saved without any noticeable contribution from him.

Later he was to do a great deal more to save democracy and in the process nearly destroyed himself, which is how he came to wander abroad for a time bearing the title of the nation's Number One Sucker.

However, in 1918 peace returned to the world and with it Edward G. Robinson was returned to the theatre with ever-increasing success. He appeared thereafter in twenty-eight Broadway shows, specialising mostly in old men and foreigners since — being in his own estimation rather like "a little gargoyle" — he was never asked to play romantic leads. Possibly to counteract this, he affected a dapper and flamboyant image off-stage. His clothes were always immaculate and expensive and on pre-Broadway tours he stayed at the best hotels and ate at the best restaurants. In this he was following the advice of his father who had suggested to him that if he lived beyond his means he would force himself to become successful.

But this paternal advice was heeded only up to a point. As a busy and successful Broadway actor Robinson could have afforded to live almost anywhere, but until he was thirty-three he chose to live at home with his parents.

Leonard Spigelgass, his friend and co-author of Robinson's autobiography, explained that decision thus: "Well, you see, he had a Momma and you didn't do anything that Momma didn't want you to do and Momma didn't want him to spend a nickel. There he was, a star in New York, his name above the title, and still living in the Bronx. Every night he'd take a taxi home and get out of it three blocks away so his mother wouldn't know he was spending money for a cab."

Eventually Robinson acquired enough courage to hack through this umbilical cord and set up house in an apartment of his own. As it turned out, he would probably have been better off staying at home with Momma because soon after he had achieved independence he met, at one of his own parties, a young actress called Gladys Lloyd and fell instantly in love with her. They were, as he was to admit later, entirely unsuitable for each other. He was a Jew and she was the archetypal White Anglo-Saxon Protestant, a Daughter of the American Revolution no less and, what is more, a divorcee with a daughter of her own. She was almost certainly anti-Semitic as well. Nevertheless Robinson loved her and she, presumably, loved him because after a highly discreet two-year courtship they were married on January 21st, 1927.

It was probably the most serious mistake Edward G. Robinson ever made and perhaps he suspected this from the start because, again according to Spigelgass, he never told his father of the marriage. "She was a Quaker, she was divorced and she had a child. It was a hopeless proposition," said Spigelgass, "from his father's point of view."

Now it is true that the father died quite soon after the marriage of which he was kept in ignorance. But for a thirty-six-year-old man not to tell his father that he had taken unto himself a bride is distinctly odd. And it could be that Robinson decided upon this secretive course of action because almost at once he realised that there was something, let us say, unusual about his wife. Her moods were always unpredictable: she could be loving and lovable at one moment; cool and hateful the next. As the years went by her behaviour became even more eccentric but from the very beginning she showed herself to be a remote, elusive person, half-disposed to love her husband, half-disposed to despise him.

In those early days of marriage, however, Edward G. did his best for her. He was then a star member of the prestige-laden Theatre Guild of New York and loyally he found work for his wife with the company, whose survivors remember her still, though not with too much warmth. "She was," said one of them, "all right. I never seemed to be very much interested in Gladys. She was just a wife — you know? To me she wasn't a good actress and she was sort of in the background as long as I knew them." But at the same time the marriage seemed, to outsiders, to be comfortable enough; the traumas that were to destroy it more than a generation later were still incubating.

At the Theatre Guild Robinson was playing leading roles in Dostoevsky, Shaw, Pirandello, and the like. But while this was good for his reputation it did little for his bank balance. Both he and Gladys had expensive tastes — in his case because he had come to be interested in art and was already, modestly, collecting pictures. He asked the Guild for a fifty dollar a week rise in salary and was refused. So he left the company to take the leading role of an Al Capone-like gangster in a play called *The Racket*. It was a big success in New York, banned in Chicago (possibly because the local authorities did not wish to upset that upright citizen, Mr. Capone) and ended up on tour in Hollywood. Many years later, in an interview with the BBC, Robinson said: "The motion picture tycoons all came to see this play and so the first role they saw me in was that of a gangster. And later on when they wanted me for pictures and the gangster cycle began they thought of Eddie Robinson as a gangster."

Still the significance of this was not immediately apparent. When the tour of *The Racket* ended, Robinson returned to Broadway to more acclaim and eventually an offer from Paramount to star in a film called *The Hole in the Wall*. He played a crook and Claudette Colbert was cast, most improbably, as an ex-convict. It was, in fact, Robinson's second film because earlier, in 1923, he had appeared with Richard Barthelmass and Dorothy Gish in a silent picture called *The Bright Shawl*. He had played an old Spanish don and he never liked to talk about it much, probably because the main attraction for him was not the artistic merit of the role but the opportunity it afforded to go to Havana and buy some cheap cigars.

But in 1929, with *The Hole in the Wall* moderately well received, Robinson went again to Hollywood to play a gangster (for Universal) in *Night Ride* and a middle-aged man with a mail-order bride in *A Lady to Love* for MGM. In this, starring opposite Vilma Banky, he was sufficiently impressive for Irving Thalberg, the studio wunderkind, to offer him a three-year contract worth — on the face of it and as long as his options were renewed and his films made money and he didn't upset anybody — one million dollars, a desirable sum at any time and infinitely so in 1930.

Robinson, however, disliked Thalberg. Somehow he got the impression, simply from looking into the man's eyes, that he felt actors were beneath contempt. So he turned the offer down and was so taken aback by his own effrontery that he promptly went outside and threw up, reflecting perhaps that each convulsive heave represented umpteen thousand dollars lost. (To say nothing, of course, of his lunch.)

Anyway, Robinson himself thought *A Lady to Love* was a pretty lousy film, even though it did quite well at the box office, and he went back to Broadway to star in a play called *Mr. Samuel*. The notices were good but public reaction was not. After eight performances the play closed, greatly to Robinson's despair. What was the point, he asked himself, of remaining true to the stage if, after eighteen years of solid work, he hadn't built up enough of a following to keep himself gainfully employed for more than a week? He was still seeking an answer to this dismal rhetorical question when a certain Hal Wallis came backstage and provided one in the shape of a contract with Warner Brothers.

"Eddie had great presence," said Wallis, "great stage presence and I had him in mind for one of the parts in *Little Caesar*, though not actually Rico."

Robinson accepted the Warner Brothers' offer — greatly encouraged by Gladys, who saw an opportunity to row herself into the movies, too — to play, not in *Little Caesar* right off, but in three other pictures of comparatively little merit: *Outside the Law*, *East Is West* and *Widow from Chicago*. *Little Caesar* came along in the late summer of 1930 and still Robinson was not considered for the main role of Rico but for the minor part of Otero, one of Caesar's underlings. After reading the script Robinson thought very little of this and, in the correct belief that he had hardly anything to lose, he accosted Hal Wallis and said: "The only part I'll consider playing is Little Caesar."

Wallis was amused rather than annoyed, impressed by the cheek but still unconvinced. "I told him we hadn't considered him for the main role and he was a little unhappy about it. Some time later he came into the office dressed for the part in a long overcoat and a slouch hat and read a couple of speeches. And immediately we made the decision to put him into the lead."

For both parties this was an eminently sensible move. *Little*

Caesar was a great box-office success and against all the odds it made Robinson into a star. I say "against all the odds" because, by and large, movie stars do not tend to be short and squat and with a face that looks as if it had been squeezed into some rough approximation of shape by a careless, giant hand. But that's how Edward G. Robinson looked and *Little Caesar* made him into a star and he remained a star for the rest of his life.

He always retained a special regard for *Little Caesar*. Many years later he described it to his grand-daughter Francesca as a kind of Greek tragedy with Rico as a man of overweening ambition who is eventually mown down by the gods as much as by society. The brothers Warner, having been brought up on a less classical tradition, saw it merely as a thundering good gangster movie and very hot stuff at the box office. At the end, as Rico lies dying in the gutter having been mown down by the gods (or, for those of a more prosaic turn of mind, policemen) he delivers the immortal line: "Mother of Mercy, is this the end of Rico?"

Well, yes, it was as a matter of fact because in those days Hollywood was much in the business of perpetuating the myth that crime doesn't pay. But it was also the start of Edward G. Robinson.

In the years to come *Little Caesar* was to establish him firmly in the public mind as a screen gangster — though, in fact, he played surprisingly few gangster roles — and it more or less erased the memory of his earlier stardom in serious works on Broadway. That was on the debit side. But on the credit side it took him, at the age of thirty-seven (rather late to be starting a film career), immediately to the top of the heap and ensured that he would not again have to leave Hollywood except by his own choice and political intervention. This was important because he liked Hollywood. He liked the material richness of life there, the big houses with their swimming pools and tennis courts and butlers, the lavish hospitality. It was all, he thought, a little vulgar, certainly, but the pace of life was slower than in New York and more agreeable. And there is no doubt, too, that he enjoyed the money that a film star earned.

As Hal Wallis said: "He enjoyed it because it enabled him to indulge himself in his great passion for art. He would do a film and then he would go out and buy a Cézanne or a Renoir and at that time you could buy them for, like, 30,000 dollars. And he would take a good part of his salary and put it into art when we all thought he was a little crazy, buying pictures. But he knew what he was about and he ultimately acquired one of the great collections in the country."

Robinson himself said: "When I was in the theatre playing respectable roles in Shaw, Shakespeare and Sheridan I was content merely to look at beautiful paintings. It was only after the succession of sizzling electric chairs when I indulged in crime in motion pictures that I could afford to buy these paintings. So you see, I made pictures of a kind to have pictures on my walls."

This was both an explanation and an apology, an apology for his public image which, on the whole, he heartily disliked because it did not at all reflect his own personality. He may have looked like a gangster but he was actually a reserved, sensitive and very intelligent man, who had taught himself to speak several languages fluently and had an impeccable taste in art. His friend Vincent Price, another man with a sharp eye for a good picture, said: "He was the only person in Hollywood who really was a serious collector. There were a lot of people who had sort of 'stuff', you know? Decorative pictures and everything. But Eddie would buy a painting and study the artist and get to know him. And particularly in the field of French Impressionism he was marvellous. He was a very scholarly man."

As much as anything else it was Robinson's love of pictures — and he genuinely loved them for themselves and not for their investment value; indeed, given the choice (which eventually he was not) he would never have sold one of them — that kept him in Hollywood. Like many others before and after him he was caught in a trap, a most beguiling trap, thickly carpeted with dollar bills but a trap nevertheless. Leonard Spigelgass said: "When you start off you make 1,000 dollars a week and that seems like the most money anybody ever heard of. So you buy a car and then you buy a house and then you buy a car for your wife and now you have two cars and you need another servant. And then you have a son and you need a governess and by that time the 1,000 dollars a week is used up and so now you've got to make 2,000 dollars a week and then you buy a picture and you buy another picture and so you need 3,000 and then you need 5,000. And that's how Eddie was caught. He was caught by affluence."

I don't imagine there is very much need to shed tears for anyone who finds himself shackled, and shackled, after all, on his own volition, by wealth. But Robinson was slow to realise the dangers. Theoretically, his contract with Warner Brothers gave him unusual independence, allowing him twelve weeks off a year to appear in a play but in fact this clause was useless, twelve weeks being barely long enough to rehearse a play, try it out on tour and then bring it into New York. It certainly provided no time for a protracted run. Unfortunately, by the time this had dawned on him, Robinson was already needing his 3,000 dollars a week just to rub along in the style to which he had rapidly become accustomed. So for several years his stage career was abandoned while he consolidated his position in films.

Little Caesar was rapidly followed by a string of movies — ten in less than three years — in which Edward G. played a variety of roles, including a Chinese involved in Tong Wars in San Francisco (*Hatchet Man*), a journalist (*Five Star Final*), a fisherman (*Tiger Shark*) and a senator (*Silver Dollar*). But in several others — *Smart Money,* for instance, *Two Seconds, The Little Giant, Dark Hazard* — he was cast, inevitably, as some species of crook, gambler, killer or gangster. Few of the roles made him happy but they did make him fairly rich. He bought a mock-Tudor mansion in Beverly Hills, where he filled in the swimming pool because he couldn't swim and refused to be seen in a bathing costume and turned the badminton court into an art gallery.

The need for this new house, far more palatial than his previous residence, came about because Robinson had reached another stage in the Spigelgass scale of a movie star's evolution. In March 1933, Gladys gave birth to a son, Edward G. Robinson, Junior, an event which the delighted father celebrated by buying a Degas, a Monet and two Pissarros.

To counterbalance this parental joy, however, his career was beginning to flag. He was making a large number of films but they were not proving very successful. Robinson was bored with his gangster image and Warner Brothers had more or less run out of any other ideas for using him. What could he do? He might have abandoned films and gone back to Broadway but, like many actors who aspire to higher things than typecasting, he could no longer afford it. The Spigelgass Principle had struck again: he could have returned to the theatre to play Ibsen or Shaw for, say, 200 dollars a week but, as Spigelgass pointed out, it probably cost him 200 dollars a week to have his art collection dusted.

So, trapped by his own possessions, Robinson remained, unhappily, where he was, frequently arguing with the studio over the roles they offered him and finally — Warner Brothers being quite unable to find anything better to do with him — being loaned to Columbia to star in a comedy called *The Whole Town's Talking*.

As it turned out, this was the saving of him. The film, directed by John Ford, was a great critical and commercial success and Robinson, of whom so little had been thought that when Columbia asked for his services Jack Warner replied: "You're nuts. Edward G. Robinson is box-office poison", returned to his home studios in triumph to sign another long-term contract, this time at 7,000 dollars a week. He needed quite that much because, while making *Thunder in the City,* again on loan to Columbia, he had acquired a Renoir and a Berthe Morisot in London and then, on a trip to Paris, a Gauguin, a Daumier, another Berthe Morisot and another Renoir, a Cézanne and a Géricault. He couldn't actually afford them but, on the other hand, he couldn't bear not to possess them, so the offer of a renewed contract, especially at a much higher salary and with a modicum of script approval, was not entirely unwelcome.

By now, 1937, Robinson was forty-four years old and if he had been the kind of man who was inclined to stand back and survey his own achievements he might have decided that he had done pretty well. He was an international star with more than twenty films to his credit (well, mostly to his credit; a few of them were best forgotten), he had an enviable art collection, he was still married to the same wife (and in Hollywood that in itself was a considerable achievement) and he had a son.

Unfortunately, at this comparatively pleasant juncture, his troubles were only just about to begin.

Politically, he had become an active supporter of the Anti-Nazi League, an innocent and indeed commendable organisation that helped victims of Nazi Germany to escape from the country. He supported, in fact, any organisation opposed to Hitler; he attended meetings, gave money and lent his name to help publicity. Of course, a good many of the other people involved were pro-Russia as well as anti-Nazi and he was aware of it. But what, he argued, did that matter? At the time, to be sure, it mattered very little; later it was to become appallingly significant.

Meanwhile, domestically his life was in considerable turmoil. When they had first arrived in Hollywood Gladys had been bored and unhappy and so, to placate her, Robinson had arranged for her to play small parts in some of his early films. When that didn't work, and it swiftly became obvious that Gladys was never going to succeed as an actress, he bought her the large house and provided her with servants. But that didn't work either. Gladys was a difficult, indeed an impossible, person to placate because she was ill; a manic depressive. Jane, Edward G.'s second wife, said: "One year she would love Eddie very much and six months later she despised him and that went on for many years and it's a very difficult thing to live with."

Leonard Spigelgass said: "She was a marvellous hostess. She was perfectly beautiful, she dressed very well, she had superb taste. And every once in a while you thought, 'Why doesn't she like me? What have I done wrong? Did I spill something on the floor?' and then, as you grew older, you knew that she was a manic depressive. She would go through these terrible depressive states. I'm not a psychiatrist but I think she was paranoid. She hated no longer being an actress and she hated being a movie star's wife. She wanted to be the movie star; she'd have liked him to have been the movie star's husband. She didn't understand what was happening to her."

By this time, after ten years of marriage, Robinson was well accustomed to his wife's eccentricity, her incomprehensible changes of mood, and he tolerated them and continued to tolerate them because, as Jane Robinson said, "He was very much in love with her." Nevertheless, she was becoming increasingly unreasonable and unpredictable. Possibly he hoped that the birth of their son would improve matters but, if so, he was greatly mistaken. From a very early age the boy, too, showed signs of mental disturbance and most unusual behaviour. At three he was in the habit of raiding his father's liquor cabinet and drinking himself insensible. Now at three, of course, this could easily be attributed to childish curiosity or, at worst, mere naughtiness which, taken firmly in hand at an early stage, could swiftly be corrected.

But Robinson was not the man to take such a course of action. He doted on his son and spoiled him. "He loved this boy," said Jane Robinson. "He was a Jewish father. It was 'My son, my son' and he was the only child Eddie had. Eddie didn't have this child until he was in his forties and the boy was most meaningful to him. But, like his mother, he was ill and so you can't blame him. You can blame Eddie for not admitting the boy was ill at three but that's as far as you can go. He always blamed Junior's bad behaviour on everything else. The school was wrong, the nanny was wrong because it was 'My son, my son'. The child was his whole life."

As Sam Jaffe said: "He looked forward to a great deal from that boy, who became the cross of his life. It was very sad."

Robinson himself later admitted that he was grossly over-indulgent towards the child. If he wanted a bicycle he got the finest bicycle on the market. If he wanted a baseball glove he finished up with the kind of uniform the Brooklyn Dodgers could hardly afford. If he wanted a train set he was provided with something barely distinguishable from the Atchison, Topeka and the Sante Fe. Edward G.'s conclusion was that "I gave him everything except myself." And that most important gift, alas, he didn't know how to bestow; perhaps he had come to fatherhood too late.

Still, an unpredictable wife and an undisciplined son notwithstanding, Robinson continued to prosper. He was regularly employed in films which, though not altogether satisfactory to a former classical actor, were at least well received and in 1940 he made the picture that gave him his greatest artistic pleasure — *Dr. Ehrlich's Magic Bullet*. Warners probably agreed to let him do it in the belief that it was another gangster movie but, in fact, it was the story of the German scientist who discovered a cure for syphilis. Cunningly, the script managed to avoid any reference to the word "syphilis" until the very end (a pretty noteworthy achievement, really) but nevertheless Robinson considered it an eminently worthwhile film and was extremely disappointed that he was not at least nominated for an Academy Award. Furthermore, it had the additional merit of shaking off, if only for a little while, the gangster image that was still doggedly following him around.

How doggedly it pursued him was illustrated a few years later, when he was entertaining American troops abroad. On one occasion, addressing a vast audience of soldiers, he began by telling them how proud he was to meet the men who were fighting to defend the free world. This, doubtless sincere, pronouncement went down like the proverbial lead balloon and it was not until, in desperation, he lapsed into the argot of the Rico character from *Little Caesar* that the defenders of the free world began to applaud him. The familiar, squat little gangster delighted them as the earnest patriot had not but Robinson was heart-broken that he could not communicate with these men except on such a basic level.

Edward G. was forty-nine when America entered the war, far too old even to think of volunteering for active service. Nevertheless he worked tirelessly to help the allied cause in any way available to him. For five years he had been starring in a weekly radio drama programme which he now left because the sponsors refused to allow him to tackle contemporary problems, such as the German threat to democracy or the Nazi extermination of the Jews. They wanted him to continue playing a fearless gang-buster because stories about gangsters sold soap whereas stories about Nazis did not. Even so, when he quit the programme Robinson received a citation of honour from the American League of California in recognition of his "outstanding contributions to Americanism through his patriotic appeals on the programme". The splendid irony of this award was only to become apparent later on.

But at the time he became free of his weekly radio commitment he was recruited by the US Government to go to London, there to broadcast anti-German propaganda in several languages on the BBC World Service. It was an assignment he accepted with alacrity, not only because of its contribution to the war effort but also because it afforded a relief from the tensions of home life. Gladys' condition had become progressively worse and a course of shock treatment at a sanatorium in Pasadena, California, had brought only temporary improvement. She still veered between the manic and the depressive, alternately regarding her husband as a saint or as some escapee from Hades.

Luckily, when he returned from London early in 1943, she was going through a prolonged manic phase and together they gave lunches and dinners for visiting servicemen and carried on doing their bit for the war effort. By the time peace returned Robinson had given 100,000 dollars to various wartime appeal funds.

Professionally, though, he had by then gone into another decline. He had now entered his fifties, which should have been less of a problem to him than it was to most other movie stars. Most other stars, after all, had begun their careers as romantic leading men and, at fifty, had to adjust to becoming character actors. Robinson, however, had always been a character actor and so reaching the half-century mark should not have presented any great difficulties. Unfortunately, this was not so. He found himself cast in a succession of feeble propaganda efforts, mixing comedy with drama — films like *Mr. Winkle Goes to War* (the title itself, one might have thought, would have made him cringe) the story of an over-age inductee who overcomes meekness to become a war hero. "Robinson," said the *New York Herald Tribune* sternly, "never succeeds in being either mildly amusing or properly courageous."

Briefly he returned to the stage — or, more accurately, to Madison Square Garden — to join the likes of Paul Muni, Frank Sinatra and John Garfield, in a one-night memorial to Nazi-executed Jews called "We Shall Never Die", which played to an audience of 40,000 people, and then he went back to Hollywood to revive his career yet again in *Double Indemnity,* in which he played the insurance investigator who unmasked Fred MacMurray and Barbara Stanwyck as the double murderers of the latter's husband. "Robinson," said the *New York Times,* atoning for the earlier acerbity of the *Herald Tribune,* "is the only one you care two hoots for in the film."

It was just as well he had this success because since 1942 he had been a freelance, he and Warner Brothers having agreed to terminate their contract. The studio no longer needed him because Humphrey Bogart, who had been lying fallow on its books for years, had suddenly emerged as an important star with a phenomenally wide appeal. And, for his part, Edward G. had quite sufficient status to launch himself onto the freelance market, with the proviso that, as a freelance, he couldn't afford to lay too many eggs. *Double Indemnity* and *The Woman in the Window,* directed by Fritz Lang, kept his reputation high, although he found that making the latter film was an uncomfortable business. For the first time on set he became aware of violent anti-Communist talk among the crew and his fellow actors. At first Robinson, who had been a staunch supporter of Russian War Relief, defended himself and such friends as had also been involved. He spoke warmly of the strength and the will of the Russian people, of the heroic defence of Stalingrad. It was, remember, only 1945 and the war was barely over. Robinson, no doubt slow to catch on, still harboured the naive belief that Russia was an ally. After a while, however, he realised there was no point in joining in the arguments; it simply directed suspicion of Red sympathies towards himself. Nevertheless, at the time the prevailing mood on the set was no more than disturbing as far as he was concerned; he had no reason yet to believe that it was, in fact, menacing.

The full realisation of that came two years later, round about the time he was playing the last of his great gangster roles, that of the pathological Johnny Rocco, in *Key Largo.* It was an enjoyable film for Robinson, the first in which he had appeared with Humphrey Bogart since he left Warner Brothers. Their roles, now, of course, were very much reversed. In the old days Bogart, the supporting player, had been obliged, by reasons of contract and script, to die at least one reel before Robinson. But, in 1948, Bogart was the big Warner star and Robinson was simply a guest player. Contract and script therefore demanded that he should perish early enough to leave most of the last reel to Bogart. It is to Bogie's credit that he was sensitive to these altered circumstances and went to great lengths to make Robinson feel valued. He treated him not just as a guest star, which almost anybody could be, but as a star guest, which is subtly different. He refused, for example, to go on set until he was quite sure that "Mr. Robinson" was also ready and in the right frame of mind to proceed. Because of such courtesy Edward G. had happy memories of *Key Largo,* which was fortunate because in the years to come very few happy memories would be granted to him.

Long before the film was released America had been stricken by an epidemic of mental illness which took the form of rabid anti-Communism. The sufferers from this disease banded together and sought victims to persecute, a simple enough task because the Government was on the side of the persecutors and had set up the grandly-named House Un-American Activities Committee to assist them. To become a victim, one of the persecuted, it was not necessary actually to be a Communist; it was merely necessary to be known to be, or to have been, not anti-Communist.

Robinson was a natural victim. He had supported Russian War Relief; he had spoken the commentary for *Moscow Strikes Back,* a Soviet documentary made in 1942; and he had openly been opposed to the Nazis as long ago as 1937. Now there are some who might feel that this was to his credit. But in 1947 and the next few years, to have opposed the Nazis and therefore, by implication, to have supported Russia before it became briefly fashionable to do so was found to be clear evidence of subversive activity.

And so in 1947 the smear campaign against Edward G. Robinson began. The *New York Times* claimed that he was on the initiating committee of a civil rights group called Red Front and *Newsweek* magazine revealed that he was "persistently found in Communist fronts". All of this came as a considerable surprise to Edward G. Robinson. Certainly during the war he had joined and supported all manner of organisations that were opposed to Germany and in sympathy with the Russian war effort. Innocent that he was, he had supposed that, by doing so, he was merely revealing his patriotism.

Of this absurd belief he was swiftly disabused. In 1949 the Senate Fact-Finding Committee on un-American Activities named him in its report, describing him as "Edward G. Robinson: prominent actor, frequently involved in Communist fronts and causes." There followed a long list of fronts and causes in which he was undeniably involved and which, according to the Senate Fact-

Finding Committee, had all been deeply infiltrated by Communist sympathisers. Ergo, Robinson himself was a Communist sympathiser. The only flaw in this apparently impeccable logic was that it was entirely wrong.

"Eddie was never a Communist," said Jane Robinson. "But he was a liberal and he had signed all kinds of papers. He really didn't know what he was signing."

Certainly, a number of the causes Robinson had espoused did turn out to be Communist fronts but there was no way in which he could have known that. At no time did they advertise themselves as Communist fronts; instead, they masqueraded as charities or as organisations fighting for civil rights or in defence of the arts. As Frank Capra, the director and a friend of Robinson's, said: "He loved his country. To say he was anti-American hurt him no end. His generosity, I think, got him in more trouble than anything else because they (the Un-American Activities Committee) found he'd written cheques to this political party or this other outfit but it all went under the name of some kind of aid to children or aid to this or aid to that. For him it was all charity. Somebody needed something for some children or the like and he gave."

Such an argument carried very little weight, however, in 1949. This was the time of the black list and Robinson was on it — not perhaps to the extent of some suspected Communists who could find no work at all but at least to the extent that from 1948 until 1956 the work he was offered was mostly in inferior films, even B-films, and he took it because nothing better came along.

Furthermore, his fees went down — a suspected Communist being in no position to bargain — and he was largely ostracised by many of his so-called friends in Hollywood. Of this period in his life Sam Jaffe said: "It almost killed him. He was a sick man, you might say, mentally sick over the whole thing, because when you know you haven't done anything against your country, when you've always been loyal to your country, to be accused as someone who is trying to destroy it is a terrible, terrible blow."

Today, a quarter of a century after that whole unsavoury and hysterical episode in American history, it seems preposterous even to suggest that Edward G. Robinson was ever a Communist. But how do you prove you are not a Communist when nobody will believe what you say? Between 1950 and 1952 Robinson appeared three times, at his own request, before the House Un-American Activities Committee, that latterday Star Chamber, to insist that he was and always had been a true and loyal citizen. In October

1950, on his first appearance, he supplied the Committee with details of his war record and with a twelve-page list of 300 organisations to which he had contributed over a ten-year period. The Committee was not impressed. Two months later he appeared again with a statement in which he declared: "I think I have not only been a good citizen, I think I have been an extraordinarily good citizen . . . I know my Americanism is unblemished and fine and wonderful and I am proud of it . . ." The Committee was still unimpressed.

But humble and even ingratiating though this statement made him seem, Robinson was not without courage. Victimised and shunned, unable to find work that was worthy of his talent and unable even to travel because his passport had been withdrawn, he was yet brave enough to respond to a plea for help from Dalton Trumbo, the scriptwriter and one of "the Hollywood Ten" who had been jailed for contempt of Congress when he refused to answer charges of being a Communist. From prison Trumbo wrote to Edward G. and asked for a loan of 2,500 dollars because his family was in serious financial trouble. Robinson sent the money at once and openly — indeed a brave thing to do at a time when guilt by association was virtually the law of the land.

On April 30th, 1952, Robinson appeared for the third time before the HUAC and on this occasion, too dispirited and too worn out to fight any more, he did what he had sworn he would never do and crawled before his tormentors. Once again he presented his twelve-page contribution file and once again he reminded the Committee of his war record. But in addition he told them — though he never believed it to be true — that he had been an unwitting dupe of the Communists. And that was enough. That was precisely what the Committee wished to hear, never mind whether it was true or not. Generously it forgave him for all the subversive sins and crimes that he had never committed and Congressman Francis Walter of Pennsylvania, the chairman of the Committee, was good enough to say to him: "Well, this Committee has never had any evidence presented to indicate that you were anything more than a very choice sucker. I think you are Number One on the sucker list in the country."

A more official statement read: "According to the evidence of this Committee you are a good, loyal and intensely patriotic American citizen." For both statements Robinson was grateful — though more for the latter, I suspect, than for the former.

In the midst of all the controversy Robinson had returned once more to the stage, starring in 1951 in an adaptation of Arthur Koestler's *Darkness at Noon*. The play was strongly anti-Communist, which is possibly one reason why Edward G. chose it. He was not, however, asked to appear in it on Broadway; that distinction went to Claude Rains; Robinson took over when the production went out on a national tour which ended, coincidentally, about the same time as he was cleared by the HUAC and at this stage it might have been thought that, having been discharged of all suspicion of treachery, the nation's Number One sucker could now return to normal life.

But, alas, not. The anti-Communist disease still raged in America and back in Hollywood Robinson was treated as though the charges against him had been found simply not proven. The ultra-Right wing faction, which virtually controlled the film industry, still believed that there was no smoke without fire and the ultra-Left wing faction, which earlier had offered him sympathy (no doubt for reasons which had little to do with altruism), now withdrew it on the grounds that in some obscure way he had betrayed a cause that was never his own. "People in this town," said Jane Robinson, "just wouldn't give him jobs. The parts were less frequent (a) because he was older but (b) because he had a stigma and he had this stigma all his life."

So now we have Edward G. Robinson, the great film star, with his career in a kind of limbo, snatching generally underpaid work wherever he could find it and at the same time, just to add a little variety to his problems, his personal life was disintegrating rapidly. Gladys' mental illness was becoming ever more serious. She was continually being admitted to clinics for treatment and her behaviour was increasingly embarrassing to her husband. In 1949, at the height of the anti-Robinson smear campaign, for example, she announced that she was suing for divorce, on what grounds it wasn't quite clear — least of all to Edward G. who first learned that he was to be divorced when he read about it in the newspapers. This announcement by his wife didn't exactly help him a great deal in his efforts to persuade the American public that he was actually a very upright fellow. True, Gladys withdrew the divorce action but then she revived it several times over the next few years.

It is, of course, difficult to blame her. Whenever she went, on her doctor's advice, into another clinic for another spell of treatment she was under the impression that Robinson was trying to get rid of her, to have her committed for life. He wasn't; he was merely doing the best he could for her, but in her unbalanced state it was impossible to persuade her of this.

It could be argued that Robinson's life would have been made a great deal simpler and more pleasant if he had allowed Gladys to go through with one of her threatened divorce actions. But for years he refused to do that because, according to Sam Jaffe, of a sense of loyalty: "He hated to desert her because she wasn't well."

And, too, there still remained the fact that he loved her. Many years later, when Edward G. had long been married again, Gladys died, and he said to his grand-daughter, Francesca: "I understand what you're going through because I miss her too. I loved her very much."

But there are limits to what even love and loyalty can stand and in 1956 when, yet again, Gladys threatened him with divorce Robinson finally made no objection. The break-up of the marriage, however, brought the end of one form of pain only to replace it with another.

By way of a divorce settlement Gladys asked for and was awarded one half of his estate. "The only way he could raise the money to do that," said Jane Robinson, "was to sell his paintings."

Well, so what? After all, that's all they were — just paintings, inanimate objects decorating his walls. These days great paintings are simply another commodity, a hedge against inflation; rich men buy and sell them all the time with hardly a second thought. But to Robinson his collection was far more than just an investment. Jane Robinson said his paintings were like children to him. "They were the most important thing in the world to him. He loved them more than anything, other than his son. In times of trouble they were his only solace. He would come down in the middle of the night and go from room to room and just sit with his pictures."

He loved them indeed to such an extent that all his money had gone into acquiring them. Apart from his house he had no investments in property or land; he owned no stocks or shares or bonds; he didn't even have life insurance; he simply had paintings. So when he realised that to meet Gladys' financial demands he would have to sell his collection . . .

"He almost died," said Leonard Spigelgass. "He almost died. He went to everybody that you can imagine who had wealth and asked them to give him a loan." In this he was unsuccessful. In 1956 he was still Edward G. Robinson, the man with the stigma, the actor whose asking price had gone down and he needed three million dollars, a sizeable sum to borrow even if he had been at the peak of his career and his popularity. And so he sold his pictures and he sold his house to satisfy Gladys. He sold the bulk of his collection for three and a quarter million dollars to Stavros Niarchos, the shipping tycoon (and twenty years later, according to Vincent Price, it would have raised 250 million dollars without any trouble), and he shared the proceeds with his ex-wife.

"He didn't mind the money," said Jane Robinson, "but he did mind the paintings. He minded those till the day he died. But the only way she could get even with him was taking his pictures away."

Altogether Robinson sold fifty-six of his seventy-two paintings, including Gauguin's *Horseman on Beach* (which fetched 200,000 dollars), Renoir's *After the Ball* (60,000 dollars), Matisse's *Dinner Table* (70,000 dollars), Corot's *Italian Woman* (200,000 dollars), Seurat's *Le Crotoy* (185,000 dollars) and Cézanne's *Black Clock* (200,000 dollars). "Which of them," asked a journalist at the time of the sale, "was your favourite?"

"My favourite?" said Robinson. "They're all my favourite."

Meanwhile, as this was going on, Fate, clearly believing he wasn't having a bad enough time already, had prepared another little surprise for him. On the day Gladys went to court for her final divorce decree, their son, Edward G. Robinson, Junior, turned up there too. He had been involved in a car crash in which the girl travelling as his passenger was seriously injured. Edward G., Junior was charged with drunken driving and mother and son, escorted by a mob of Press photographers, met in the hallway of the court.

On the other hand, 1956 was not all bad for Robinson, for this was also the year when he was finally rehabilitated. The stain of "premature anti-fascism" — the splendid phrase used to describe the political attitude that had brought him so much trouble — was partially wiped away when he played Dathan, the evil overlord who, in defiance of Moses, persuaded the people to worship the golden calf in *The Ten Commandments*.

It wasn't the part that rehabilitated him but the fact that he was personally offered it by Cecil B. de Mille. In Hollywood nobody was more Right-wing and more anti-Communist than de Mille, though there were many who were no less Right-wing and anti-Communist, and it was generally recognised that if de Mille felt that Robinson should be returned to the fold then perhaps the time had come when bygones should be looked squarely in the eye and addressed as bygones.

Having been welcomed back, however, the prodigal promptly left Hollywood for a lengthy run in Paddy Chayevsky's play *Middle of the Night* and did not make another film for three years. The picture with which he marked his return was a comedy called *A Hole in the Head* and during the course of it Robinson nearly ruined his newly-recovered reputation as one of the good guys by threatening to walk out in a huff. This fit of temperament was caused by the fact that his co-star, Frank Sinatra, wouldn't rehearse their scenes together. Robinson was a firm believer in rehearsals; Sinatra would have no truck with them.

The director, Frank Capra, thereupon phoned Robinson's agent with a curt injunction to get over to his client's dressing-room and inform him that if he walked out at this stage the studio would hit him for the entire cost of the picture so far. This did the trick.

"I get a call," said Capra, "to go over to Mr. Robinson's room. He's in tears and he grabs me and he kisses me and he's so sorry. There's a maleness about this man, you know, that is so male that when he grabs you and you embrace each other the strength and power this man has all comes out. He says, 'How could I do this to my friends? Let's go back and do the scene.'"

There followed a moment of archetypal Hollywood sentimentality. Capra said: "When I came back with him we created quite a sensation. 'I said, first of all let's get a big close-up of Mr. Edward G. Robinson, one of the finest actors the world has ever seen.' Well, that of course brought on big applause from everybody and Frank Sinatra walks in and Robinson goes over and embraces him and everything's fine." And that is how movies are made.

At this point Robinson was by now re-married. His new wife was the former Jane Adler whom he had first met in 1952. They had, in fact, been introduced by Gladys. They were married in January 1958, when Robinson was sixty-four and his bride was thirty-eight. At their very first meeting Gladys had said to Jane: "I think you'll do better with Eddie than I will. You take him. You're a Jew and so is he. I'm a Gentile and I don't like Jews."

After the wedding Robinson bought his old house back again and started to rebuild his art collection. It never had quite the same meaning as his original collection, but even so he built it up energetically, financing it by taking almost any role that came along. He took a rather grandiose attitude towards his paintings, insisting that he didn't really own them but was merely acting as custodian of them during his lifetime but he was passionate enough about them, according to Jane, to remain in films, even after his interest and ambition as an actor had long waned, simply to earn enough money to acquire more pictures. He would sacrifice almost anything, she said, for a painting. And then she corrected herself and added: "Not almost anything — anything. His love for art was enormous. I think he loved me as much as he was able to love me. He certainly didn't marry me because he had to; there were quite a few other ladies who would have married him. I think he appreciated me but I also think he would probably have traded me in for a Cézanne."

With that fine point understood by them both, life with Robinson, she said, was very simple. "You did things his way and his was a very good way. He demanded nothing of you except honesty and some form of intelligence. He was easy to live with, very easy. He came down at one thirty, had his lunch and when he wasn't working went to his club and played cards. If he was working he'd be at the studios at six or seven a.m. and when I brought him his lunch he was most grateful. He was always grateful for everything you did for him."

He did not, however, fit easily into Hollywood society. Jane Robinson said: "He would go to parties under protest and he'd be very charming and turn off his hearing aid. Then he couldn't hear anything and never had to answer and so he was never uptight. I don't think he ever felt all that keenly about people. They were never meaningful to him, with the possible exception of Sam Jaffe and his son."

It was the son, still known significantly perhaps as Junior, who cast a blight over Robinson's life during his last ten years or so. It would seem now that the boy had almost certainly inherited some form of mental illness from his mother. When he was about ten years old, according to Sam Jaffe, he was sent to a school in St. Louis where he attacked one of the teachers with a pair of scissors, with which he was apparently intent on blinding her. And this kind of erratic and anti-social behaviour continued throughout his life.

"I tried to teach him a little bit," Jaffe said. "I lived with them, with Eddie and Gladys for about nine months, but the boy wouldn't take to anything. He must have had the feeling that he was the son of royalty, something like that, and that nothing could harm him, that he could do anything. He identified himself with his father but, of course, he had nothing that his father had."

Eddie Junior had, in fact, certain advantages that his father never had. He was, for instance, tall and good-looking and he had ambitions, which he never fully pursued, to be an actor. In this aim he was hampered, no doubt, by the fact that he was an alcoholic. The drunken driving case, heard on the same day as his mother had obtained her divorce, led to sixty days in jail and on another occasion he was accused of holding up a taxi driver and stealing eleven dollars. Before the charge was finally dropped it had cost his father 20,000 dollars in legal fees. Another time his mother bought him a 6,000-dollar car and he claimed soon afterwards that it had been stolen and collected the insurance money. A little later the car was discovered in his own garage. Once more Edward G., Senior reimbursed the money.

Indeed, Robinson steadfastly supported his son until his own death. Leonard Spigelgass believes that to some extent this paternal loyalty was inspired by guilt. "Eddie inflicted on his son the same kind of discipline that had been inflicted on him by his own mother and father. You had to get the highest grades in school, you had to behave very well. He had inhibited the boy, thinking this was the way to bring him up so that he wouldn't be just a movie star's child. When the boy began failing at school, for whatever reason — and I suspect it was because his intellect was not very good; you know there's no law that says everybody has to be Einstein — Eddie would blame the teachers and change the school. I can tell you stories of the last weeks of Eddie's life when I listened in on telephone conversations at Eddie's request in which the boy pleaded — boy? This was a man — pleaded with Eddie for his love and understanding and Eddie interpreted it as a plea for more money. He just couldn't bear it that this boy didn't turn out to be Jack Kennedy."

Whatever the rights and wrongs of the situation Junior's relationship with Senior was rarely less than turbulent. "He attacked his father with a knife," said Jane Robinson. "He broke down our front door. He would be drunk at all times of the day and night and there was nothing you could do about it because the boy was obviously mentally ill. And he did really try for periods of time to behave but there was no way he could do it. He could not stop drinking. If Junior had been allowed to sink down to the bottom he might have pulled himself up when he was young. But Eddie couldn't take that chance, so he continued to support him."

Robinson, indeed, continually lived in hopes that some miraculous change would eventually come over his son. Francesca, Junior's daughter by a marriage he had contracted at the age of eighteen, said: "My grandfather would often try to explain things to me about my father when he was disappointed in him. And I would say, 'But, Grandpa, you know you have to understand this . . .' so it was back and forth. We were always sort of encouraging each other about my father and when my father was doing fine and not drinking my grandfather had a smile from ear to ear. When they were together they were fine; you could see that they loved each other very much."

It is Francesca's belief that her father simply opted out, that he never felt himself to be a person in his own right, that all his life he had to live up to and be measured against the name of Edward G. Robinson. And when this proved to be more than he could cope with, he found it much easier to climb inside a bottle and forget the whole dreadful problem. Whether or not that was the case, no miracle ever occurred and at the end of Edward G.'s life, father and son were again estranged.

"And yet," said Francesca, "it was really like my grandfather was his life and when that life went away my father could not exist and he died thirteen months to the day after my grandfather's death."

Edward G. Robinson, Junior, died in fact in February 1974. He was forty years old. Not much more than a year earlier his father had told him: "All us Goldenbergs live to our eighties. You've got forty-one years more. Enjoy yourself but make it work for you."

As it happened, Edward G. himself didn't quite make it to his eighties. In his last twelve years or so he had appeared in twenty-one films, most of them chosen for the opportunities they afforded to travel and buy more paintings.

Among them were one or two — *The Cincinnati Kid,* for instance, in which he co-starred with Steve McQueen — which he regarded with a certain pride. And his last picture, *Soylent Green,* a pessimistic science fiction story wherein he played a cameo role, enabled him to end both career and life on a note of distinction. Of the character he played he said: "He's a kind of an anachronism — a hangover from the old days, who knew the richness of living as it had been. He saw all this desolation coming on and there's a certain sense of guilt that he feels that perhaps he hadn't shouted enough and hadn't tried hard enough to stop it. The story takes place in the year 2022 which I hope will never be, even though I'm not going to be around then."

It's easy, no doubt too easy, to see that as a description of the elderly Robinson himself: an anachronism who had seen the good days and the bad days of America in the twentieth century and who had benefited mightily from the former and known his share of suffering from the latter.

At the time he made *Soylent Green* Robinson was a sick man. His health had been fragile since 1965 when he suffered a heart attack in Africa while filming *Sammy Going South,* a British picture. Five years later he had treatment for cancer and though this was, at least temporarily, successful, the cancer ultimately returned and this time it was obvious he would not recover.

Almost unbelievably in forty-two years he had never even been nominated for an Oscar. At times Hollywood seemed to have been handing the things out with cornflake packets but never to him. Now, however, when it was too late to do him any good and motivated, one likes to think, by a proper sense of shame, the American Academy of Motion Picture Arts and Sciences decided to give him an honorary award in March 1973. But, realising that he might not live to receive it, they asked Leonard Spigelgass to deliver to him an unengraved Oscar at the hospital where he lay dying.

As Spigelgass recalled: "I went in alone, just the nurse and Eddie and me, and I said, 'Eddie, they've given you an honorary Oscar and here it is.' And he said, 'You're lying to me. They're doing it because I'm dying and you're trying to pretend.' I said, 'It's yours. It's the truth.' And he took it and he held it and he looked at me and he laughed and said, 'You know, I've always hated this. I always thought it was wrong to get one — but I love it so.' And then he got a crafty look in his eye and he said, 'Who's going to give it to me?' And I said, and my mind's going like crazy, 'Who's going to give it to you? Why Laurence Olivier.' Now it's a popular story that Olivier was coming over to give him the Oscar but Olivier had never heard of it; I made it up in the hospital room.

"So then Eddie dictated to me what he would say to Olivier when he won the Oscar and he said, 'Do you think they'd mind if I came in a wheelchair? I don't think I'm going to be able to walk.' Well, he wasn't able to walk. He just died."

He died on March 27th, 1973, and the Oscar was accepted on his behalf — though not from Laurence Olivier, the actor Robinson had admired above all others — by his widow, Jane. It was engraved: "To Edward G. Robinson, who achieved greatness as a player, a patron of the arts and a dedicated citizen . . . In sum a Renaissance man."

Jane Robinson read out the reply that her late husband had dictated: "It couldn't have come at a better time in a man's life. Had it come earlier it would have aroused deep feelings in me. Still, not so deep as now. I am so very grateful to my rich, warm, creative, talented intimate colleagues who have been my life's association. How much richer can you be?"

Several years later Jane Robinson, now remarried to the director George Stevens but still living in Robinson's house, surrounded by many of the paintings Robinson had acquired, said to me: "I really can't sum up Eddie because for me he's very much alive. He was probably the most remarkable man for knowledge, for warmth, for compassion I have ever known. You can't put him in a little category and say 'That's Eddie', because Eddie was really all things. He was a Renaissance man in the true sense."

It is, of course, hard to encapsulate any man's life or work in a few sentences but it can be said of Edward G. Robinson that he appeared in eighty-six films, nearly always as the star, and that though he only received the one Oscar, the sort of honorary award that Hollywood bestows on people as an afterthought and as a reward for having lived a very long time, he was without doubt one of the great stars. If he is remembered mostly for his gangster roles such as Rico in *Little Caesar* or as Johnny Rocco in *Key Largo,* it's because he was physically, though by no means intellectually, suited to such parts. Probably he deserved a better fate, for there are those in Hollywood who believe he was not just a great star but a great actor, too. Well, when he was given the chance — which wasn't often enough — he did tend to live up to that testimonial, although I have a feeling that this kind of assessment of his talent owes a great deal to the work he did in classical plays on Broadway, before his Hollywood days. In the cinema his performances were always interesting and often outstanding but the films themselves were frequently mere potboilers.

He was an actor, I think, who should have played far more classical roles. That he didn't was possibly because the opportunity rarely came along after he left New York for California, and possibly because he just didn't care enough. Acting was only part of his life: it was something that occupied him but never obsessed him. He cared just as deeply about books, about travel, about languages and above all about art, and very often he simply used his career to subsidise these passions.

By all accounts he was a decent, kind and honourable man. His posthumous Oscar and his widow describe him as "a Renaissance man". He wasn't quite that but perhaps he came as close as anyone living and working in America in the second half of the twentieth century can hope to do. And in the end he may well have believed that to be remembered as a kind of Renaissance man was just as good as being remembered as a great actor.

Robert
Donat

The Romantic star of the 1930s.

above : Donat and his first wife, Ella, in The Rivals *at the Cambridge Festival Theatre in 1929.*

below : The family man — with John and Joanna in 1936.

opposite page : As Guildenstern in Hamlet, *aged twenty or thereabouts.*

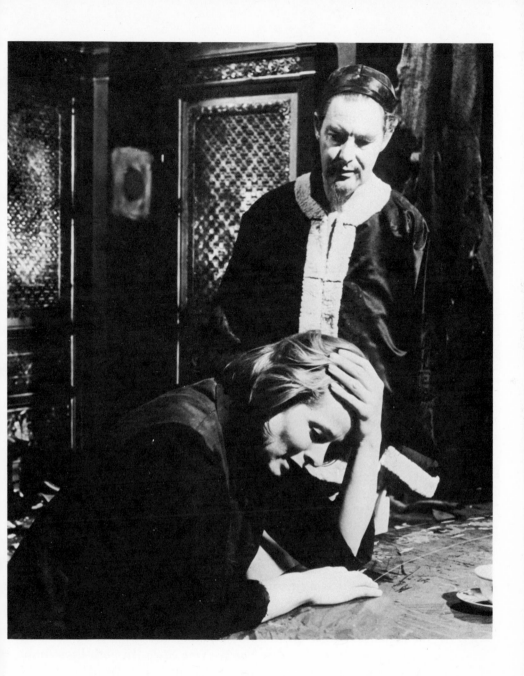

above : In his last role (with Ingrid Bergman) as the Mandarin in
The Inn of the Sixth Happiness. *His final line — "We shall not
meet each other again, I think" — was probably the most prophetic
ever spoken in the cinema.*

*opposite : With the second Mrs. Donat, Renee Asherson, whom he
met when they were filming* Cure for Love.

Robert Donat was the last of the romantic actors. The description is John Boulting's and is intended as a compliment, which is significant because, on the whole, John Boulting does not tend to be too complimentary towards Donat — certainly not towards Donat the man. On the only film they made together, *The Magic Box* (Donat starring, Boulting directing), they appear frequently to have been at loggerheads.

Still, that description: the last of the romantic actors. With a slight qualification, to make it "the last of the British romantic actors" it's a defensible argument, for nobody since Donat has revealed anything like the same combination of charm and good looks, beauty of voice and deftness of touch. Nevertheless, it's a description that he would have disliked intensely because he regarded himself as a character actor in the true sense. And if you take that to mean an actor of range and versatility who steadfastly refused to be typecast, that is precisely what he was. Indeed his most popular and probably best-remembered film performance was very much as a character actor: as, in fact, Mr. Chips. By and large he had scant regard for most of the films he made but for Chips he retained a considerable affection, partly because it won him an Oscar, but far more because it required him to age about fifty years, from a very young to a very old schoolteacher. To Donat the actor, as opposed to Donat the movie star (a role he never regarded very seriously anyway), that was both the attraction and the challenge.

It could be claimed, and is so claimed by that stern critic John Boulting, that the old Mr. Chips comes across as "a little bit of a burlesque"; that what one sees on the screen is less an old man than a young actor's impression of what an old man is like. But that is, perhaps, to forget that in the forty years since the film was made the techniques of the cinema (and not least the make-up techniques) have improved immeasurably.

In any event Donat's performance was a tour de force and a startling contrast to the more dashing and more truly romantic Donat of, let us say, *The Thirty-Nine Steps*. In both those films, and indeed in several others, he revealed an actor of remarkable gifts — gifts which, alas, were continually frustrated and at times literally stifled by chronic illness.

In his book *Robert Donat: A Biography*, J. C. Trewin described him as "a great actor lost". It's a shrewd summing-up, as accurate as John Boulting's and even more complimentary. What Donat achieved was notable enough; what he could and should have achieved, were it not for illness, would have been more notable still and would certainly have guaranteed his greatness rather than leaving it, as it is now, as a subject for conjecture. He was an actor of paradox, a film star — a romantic leading man as popular in his day as Clark Gable or Cary Grant — who infinitely preferred to work in the theatre. He was, too, renowned for the beauty of his voice and yet, after his death, a physician described him as "just about the worst asthmatic I've ever known". And he was essentially a gentle and reticent man who expressed his deepest feelings mainly in his letters: letters that were often full of pain and sometimes of quite violent anger.

His talent was extraordinary and yet, if you look at the quantity of his work, especially in the cinema, it comes to very little. In twenty-six years he made only nineteen films and in a lifetime in the theatre he appeared in hardly any of the great roles for which he was so admirably suited. Even so, Laurence Olivier thought so highly of him that he once said: "I believe that if he had not come upon such ill fortune in the way of health he would have had no peer throughout the world of acting."

Therein lies the key. Having bestowed upon Robert Donat a truly magnificent speaking voice nature, perversely and perhaps to ensure that he never became conceited about it, also inflicted upon him asthma of appalling savagery. And along with the asthma — the result or perhaps even the cause of it — went a measure of baffling self-doubt. "Robert was full of fear," said his first wife, Ella. "It was fear that absolutely messed up his life right the way through. He could not accept things as they were, for what they were. You know, when you have made a success of something and something has gone really well, you think you will never make it again; something will happen and you won't be able to go beyond it."

Donat was never intended to be an actor; with the exception of child stars, thrust into the limelight by parents generally trying to fulfil their own ambitions by proxy, very few people are. If all had gone according to plan he would probably have been a farmer in Canada; certainly his three elder brothers were despatched to Canada to become farmers at a very early age and no doubt Robert (or to give him both Christian names, Frederick Robert) would have followed them, had he not been a boy of delicate constitution and nervous disposition. Perhaps the farming careers mapped out for his sons and urged upon them whether they wanted them or not were Donat the father's way of achieving his own frustrated ambitions by proxy.

Ernst Emil Donat was a Pole, who had graduated at Leipzig University as a civil engineer, spoke six languages and on March 18th, 1905, the day Frederick Robert was born, he was working as a translator in a shipping office in Manchester. His youngest son described him later as a man "in whom early fires had cooled". He thought, in a vague sort of way, about emigrating somewhere and leading the rural life but, lacking the drive to do anything about it himself, he inflicted this rural life in a far-off land on his three elder sons.

Mrs. Donat was a Yorkshire girl, born Rose Alice Green, who appears to have been the dominant partner. It was she who decided that Robert was unfitted either by temperament or physique to be a farmer, so he alone of the four brothers stayed at home, being brought up for much of the time as, in effect, an only child, protected by his mother from the doubtless corrupting influences of the local lads with whom he was rarely allowed to play. It's quite likely, of course, that young Donat wouldn't have enjoyed playing with them anyway because although, like them, he had a strong Manchester accent he also, unlike them, had a pronounced stammer and was a long way from being sturdy — exactly the kind of boy, indeed, who would have been the natural butt of any local gang.

Still, when he was about twelve his parents, and certainly his mother, determined to do something about the accent and the stammer and sent him to a local elocution teacher, one James Bernard, who did his work so well that when both Manchester and stammer had been more or less banished from his pupil's speech he came to the conclusion that the boy might have potential as an actor. Consequently Robert took part in amateur dramatics and acquired a modest reputation for his ability as a reciter of poetry.

Even so, according to Donat's second wife and widow, the actress Renee Asherson, it wasn't Robert's own idea that he should seek a career on the stage, at least not so soon. She believes he felt that he had been pressured into it, pushed too early, although in retrospect, given James Bernard's opinion and Rose's endorsement of it, it's hard to see what else he could have been but an actor.

At the age of fourteen he had had a serious — and botched — operation on his nose and as a result of that, and the frail health that had caused it, he left school a year later without any qualifications at all. Since he was not strong enough for manual labour, even if his parents would have allowed him to consider it, the options that were open to him were very few and, all in all,

James Bernard's offer to make him his secretary was one he could hardly refuse.

In any event Bernard was obviously a good teacher. He taught Donat a great deal about the technique of acting, found him a few professional engagements and in 1924 encouraged him to go to London to take the entrance examination (for elocution teachers) at the Royal Academy of Music. There his acting ability attracted enough praise to persuade him to look more energetically for a job in the theatre and soon afterwards he was taken on by Frank Benson, a famous actor-manager of the era, who ran his own Shakespearian company. And in that, possibly for the first time in his life, Donat really felt that he belonged.

Renee Asherson said: "He always said that the happiest time of his life was when he was with Benson, when he was playing all sorts of parts and just being an actor in a company, learning his trade. I feel that had he gone on to be with a national company, like the Old Vic or something, that would have been his spiritual home."

Donat stayed with Benson for four years, starting with small parts in *Hamlet,* playing Guildenstern and what a local paper described to his own delight as "an amazingly gormless Second Gravedigger" but by 1928, when he was twenty-three and Benson was looking upon him benevolently as his heir-apparent, he had graduated to more important roles and had come to the conclusion that it was time to move on. His apprenticeship, he felt, was now over, so he left Benson and joined the Liverpool Playhouse.

By this time he was engaged to Ella Annesley Voysey, the daughter of a clergyman and the niece of a famous architect. They had first met when he was fifteen and she was an older woman of seventeen, an aspiring actress and dancer who introduced him to music and painting, both of which were in short supply in his own home. At that time, Ella recalled, the Donat family was quite poor and Robert was "very shy, very reserved". Poverty, or a close neighbour of it, were to recur from time to time throughout his life and he never really lost the shyness and reserve.

When he first met Ella he was already working for James Bernard and by then, she said, his ambitions — however he may have felt when first thrust onto the stage — were connected with the theatre. "There was never anything else," she said. And after Bernard there came the Benson Company and then Liverpool and later a stint at Cambridge working for Tyrone Guthrie.

All these, Ella said, were happy days, probably his happiest. He was unknown, anonymous even, merely one of a group: a man without very much responsibility at all. And his health at that time was, for him, pretty good.

He married Ella in August 1929, after a nine-year courtship and an engagement that was briefly interrupted because he had proposed to her during his summer holidays, quite forgetting in the heat of the moment that he was generally supposed to be deeply in love with a young actress in the Benson company. When he returned to the theatre to be greeted warmly by this actress, who had been confidently expecting a marriage proposal of her own, a certain degree of embarrassment was felt all round and Ella nobly withdrew from the triangle. But Donat's relationship with the young actress was never the same after that; possibly she felt, with some justification, that he wasn't entirely to be trusted out of her sight for too long. Besides, Donat and Ella remained in touch and met whenever their respective acting engagements allowed. After a time he began introducing her as "my sweetheart" and when Tyrone Guthrie invited them both to appear at the Cambridge Festival Theatre — Donat in leading roles; Ella in a humbler capacity — they decided to get married.

Flora (now Dame Flora) Robson was also at Cambridge with the Donats. She remembered him as highly professional, very good at comedy and at character parts and as a notorious "corpser".

"He was a terrible giggler," she said. "When we played *Rosmersholm* together we nearly ruined the play. It was unrelieved gloom for three acts and then at the end I said, 'I am going to kill myself. I am going to throw myself into the mill stream. Will you come with me?' And he held my hand and said, 'Gladly,' and he looked like the devil, trying not to laugh. Eventually we went off together to throw ourselves into the mill stream and as soon as we got outside the door, off stage, we rolled about in an agony of laughter."

On other occasions any mention of the word "bottoms" in a play was sufficient cause for outbreaks of uncontrolled mirth. As an anecdote Dame Flora's is not particularly riveting but at least it indicates that Donat did have mirth and laughter within him. And that was just as well because, on the testimony of his son John, it was this quality as much as anything else that carried him through the bleakest periods of his life.

Generally speaking, said Dame Flora, Donat "was heaven to work with. I have never acted with anybody who gave me more than he did." Tyrone Guthrie was impressed with him too, and believed he was at his best in low comedy. It was Guthrie's opinion that Donat's good looks and the beauty of his voice worked against him and persuaded people to cast him later in heroic, romantic roles when he was really a comedian.

A spell in Cambridge playing classical and semi-classical roles in repertory bred further ambition in Donat. He decided that what he needed now was success in London, the opportunity to display his wares in the West End theatre. He and Ella took a flat just off Shaftesbury Avenue and he began the rounds of auditions and agents' offices. But then, as always, theatrical London had a glut of ambitious and talented young actors and in his first twelve months there he worked for only eight weeks.

That first year, said Ella, was extremely difficult and his lack of progress worried her husband a great deal. It did not, however, worry her because "I had complete faith in his talent and his genius. I knew there was real quality there and had been right from the start." That quality showed itself, she thought, in his spontaneity: whatever the part, he spoke his lines as if he had just thought of them.

Gradually others, too, began to recognise that there was more to Donat than a handsome face, a musical voice and clarity of diction — not that such attributes are entirely negligible. God knows many stars have built up splendid careers with fewer raw materials than those. Still, by January 1931, word began to get around that Donat had possibilities and that year he appeared in eleven different plays, many in the West End, others on the fringe, a few at the Malvern Festival, and nearly all in repertory.

Fortunately 1932 was better and so was 1933 in that the plays he appeared in did tend to run long enough for the casts to find their way around backstage without the aid of a map. Indeed, early in 1932 Donat had a real success as Gideon Sarn in the adaptation of Mary Webb's novel *Precious Bane*. After the first night the audience chanted his name and the Press gave him enthusiastic notices. Paradoxically, though, work was less plentiful after this but the roles, when they did come his way, were better and more eye-catching.

Meanwhile, Donat had been making assiduous attempts to find employment in films. Whenever he heard that tests were being given he was there. In fact, he was there so often that he became known around the studios as "Screen-Test Donat", the man who never got the part. That he failed so consistently was not exactly his fault, since what he was asked to undergo were not so much tests as obstacle courses. Ella said: "They'd shoot him in evening dress at nine o'clock in the morning and all that nonsense. Or else he'd have to wait goodness knows how many hours all day and he probably had a drink and they said he was cross-eyed and, oh, they made all sorts of silly excuses."

But at last his persistence paid off. On his umpteenth test he was asked by the director to register mirth, rage and terror, very possibly in that order or quite likely all together. Donat did his best but then, understandably, fluffed a line and, said Ella: "He just sat back, roared with laughter and said, 'Oh my God, I've done it again.' " It was the laughter that did the trick for him. The test was shown to the Hungarian-born film producer, Alexander Korda, who watched it with every sign of boredom until Donat laughed, at which point Korda said: "Sign him up." Until that laugh — "the most spontaneous I had ever heard on the screen," Korda said later — the producer had, presumably, been under the mistaken impression, like everyone else, that Donat was cross-eyed.

So armed now with a three-year contract with Korda's London Film Productions, Donat made a modest beginning as a screen actor. He played a small part in a comedy-drama called *Men of Tomorrow,* another in *That Night in London* and a third in *Cash.* His first real opportunity came in his fourth film, *The Private Life of Henry VIII,* a film that established Korda's company on the international market, won an Oscar for Charles Laughton in the main role and effectively launched Donat into the movies in the part of Thomas Culpepper, the courtier who made the unfortunate error of cuckolding the king.

Henry VIII was a great success in America and success in America is no bad thing for an aspiring young movie star. It also served to jog the memory of Rowland Lee, who had been favourably impressed by Donat while directing *That Night in London.* Now, back in Hollywood whence he had come, Lee asked if he could borrow Korda's new contract star for a film version of *The Count of Monte Cristo.* Korda agreed and so did Donat, tempted no doubt by the offer of £250 a week, and thus he made his first, and only, working visit to Hollywood.

He hated the place immediately. He hated the lifestyle and the ostentation and, said Ella, "I think he hated the fact that you were either at the top or the bottom. He hated the callousness and the unreality of the approach there. It was all blown up, completely superficial." Well, he can hardly be blamed for that. Many another person of sensitivity and artistic integrity has come just as rapidly to the same conclusion.

Furthermore, he discovered on arrival that the studio, Reliance — one of the smaller companies — had very little interest in him and rather felt that he had been foisted upon them by Rowland Lee. Consequently, they had planned the film as a low-budget quickie to be shot in less than four weeks with a plot which, if you took away the title, would have given very little hint that it was inspired by the adventures of the Count of Monte Cristo. Donat fought spiritedly against this. He may not always have been quick to make up his mind about the parts he would play but, having agreed to a role, he always approached it with dedication and meticulous professionalism. The script he was now offered was not, he believed, worthy either of him or the book from which it had been taken, so he insisted on a full camera test to prove that he could play the count before, during and after the events at the Chateau d'If.

The studio was delighted by the result. It scrapped the footage already shot, doubled the budget and lengthened the schedule to turn the film into a spectacular epic.

The result was another critical and popular success and Donat left Hollywood a star. He left, however, never to return. Filming there, he said, had been such a gruelling and exhausting business that it left him no time for anything else. This, though, was something of an exaggeration because he did find time for a brief love affair with his leading lady, Elissa Landi. It was not much of an affair — although in view of later events it was not insignificant — and by the time he and Ella sailed for England he had virtually forgotten the lady.

Besides, he now had other problems on his mind for he was pursued on to the ship at New York by emissaries from Hollywood studios waving contracts and blank cheques at him, all of which he refused to sign. "They knew," said Ella, "that they'd got a good film . . . a whopping film and they were determined to sign him up and he wasn't having any. He said, 'No, I won't sign until the picture's been shown.' "

Donat's intention now, as it always had been even before he went to Hollywood, was to return to the London stage and furthermore, after the Monte Cristo experience, he was resolved to sign no more film contracts unless he was given script approval.

This latter decision led him into a legal altercation with Warner Brothers, who had announced a whole programme of movies for him, including *Captain Blood* and *Robin Hood*. Donat failed to turn up on the appointed day for the filming of *Captain Blood* and

Warners sued him for breach of contract, arguing that a letter he had signed some time previously bound him to them. Donat denied this, Warners took him to court and Donat won. It might also be argued that in terms of what Hollywood, though not he, would have called success (i.e. rapid international stardom), he also lost because the two roles he turned down instantly established another young actor, one Errol Flynn, as a very big star indeed. True, there was perhaps some artistic justification for Donat's attitude — even *Robin Hood*, splendid film though it turned out to be, wasn't exactly *Hamlet* — but throughout his life Donat ("that stubborn young guy", as a Warner Brothers executive described him) applied an idiosyncratic judgment to the parts he would, or would not accept.

At the time of the Warner Brothers law suit his attitude would have been easier to understand if, having declined commercial film offers, he had really pursued his ambition to play classic roles in the theatre. But he did not. He was invited to tour Britain with various Shakespearian productions, *Macbeth* among them, which would then be brought into London. He declined and in the event he never did play Macbeth, or Hamlet, or Lear, although he often spoke of doing all three and long had ambitions to make a film of *Hamlet*. Even Romeo, a part which in his young manhood seemed perfect for him, he only played once and then at a theatre festival outside London, though admittedly it was with the Old Vic Company and he was directed by Tyrone Guthrie.

Well, no doubt his health had much to do with his limited appearances in the great acting roles because, by the mid-1930s he was a chronic asthmatic. The asthma had first appeared in 1931, around about the time he and Ella had their first child, Joanna, and at the end of his long stretch of unemployment in London.

To what extent all these events were connected nobody was ever able to determine. Donat had always, of course, been delicate, always prone to chest infections. But asthma was something else again. Perhaps the worry of being out of work and the responsibility of having both a wife and child to support had brought it on. Whatever the causes, the effects were real and drastic enough but when I asked Ella whether she believed the illness was to some extent psychosomatic, she said: "Oh, very much so." And it was then that she described him as being "full of fear".

But fear of what? Failure, yes — but then that's fairly normal. Where Donat seemed to differ from others was that success appeared to frighten him too. *The Count of Monte Cristo* made him an international film star and the two pictures with which he followed it — Alfred Hitchcock's *The Thirty-Nine Steps* and the comedy *The Ghost Goes West,* directed by René Clair — simply confirmed his fame and popularity. At the age of thirty he was perhaps the cinema's leading romantic actor, one of the most sought-after young stars in the business.

But he was never able to adapt to that stardom. John Donat, his elder son, said: "He was a very private person and the public acclaim was something he found very, very hard to live with. He was not a star in that 'Hollywood' sense and he found it extraordinarily difficult to reconcile his need for privacy and to be himself with the fact that he was actually public property in a sense."

Sir John Mills, who acted with and was virtually discovered by Donat in the play *Red Knight* in 1936 (a period when the early excitement about Donat the movie star was at its height) said: "He went through a time, when he was an enormous star, of feeling that he had to hide away a bit . . . He had funny sort of ways of behaving at times. When we were playing in *Red Knight* in Southport he was recognised but, I mean, there weren't vast crowds around the hotel. But one morning I said, 'We've got to get him outside. He looks as white as a sheet.' So we went to see him and he was propped up in bed at eleven o'clock in the morning, the sun was streaming through the windows and we said, 'Bob, why don't you come for a walk, get a bit of air?' and the feeling was — I think it was his wife who said it — 'Do you think it will be all right?' And I said, 'What do you mean?' and she said, 'Well, being seen going out. Maybe we could slip through the back door.' And honestly he could have walked straight out of the foyer and along the front. Maybe a couple of people might have said 'Hullo' but that's all. I think he had that built-up feeling, which really wasn't quite necessary." It was the feeling perhaps of being built up into something that he wasn't and that he never wanted to be.

What he did want to be at this time — and the ambition frequently recurred later — was an actor-manager, like his mentor Frank Benson. *Red Knight,* a play set in the First World War, was his initial venture in that direction. Donat himself had the leading role, naturally, but the notices and applause on tour went to the young and unknown John Mills in a comedy role as a Cockney soldier called Sid Summers. The tour was not a great success, and Donat, who had backed the production with his own money, was strongly advised not to take it to London. He considered the matter carefully and then approached John Mills with his decision.

Mills said: "He asked me to have supper with him one night and he said, 'Have you heard the rumours that we're not taking the play in?' I said, 'Yes' and he said, 'Well, you know, you're terrific in the part and you must be very disappointed.' I said, 'Well, I am but I understand it, Bob.' And he said, 'Well, I've got news for you. We are taking the play in. That performance is far too good not to be seen in the West End.' And he took the play in against everybody's advice and the thing happened: he was nicely received and warmly received but Sid Summers stole the play. I think that's probably one of the most generous things I've ever known any actor to do, knowing what was going to happen and that he was going to come in playing second fiddle to a subsidiary part."

The play ran for about a month in London; Mills acquired a name for himself and Donat lost £5,000. In a sense he had come too far too fast. He was still only thirty-one but in the theatre he was already an actor-manager and in the cinema he was a star and obliged to live like one, which could be a very costly business. The trouble was that he had made only seven films and not very much money, so in 1936 financial worries brought on more asthma and another onset of uncertainty. Various ambitious stage projects were discussed and then shelved either because of ill health or simple indecision. Alfred Hitchcock wanted him to star in his film *Sabotage* at a fee of £30,000. The money would have solved Donat's problems but another savage attack of asthma and bronchitis caused him to cry off and in the end and in some desperation he agreed to co-star with Marlene Dietrich in Alexander Korda's *Knight Without Armour*. This was set in post-revolutionary Russia and had Commissar Donat charged with escorting Countess Dietrich to prison in Moscow. When all was decided asthma struck him down once again and for a time there was talk that he would be replaced by Laurence Olivier. Korda, however, remained loyal to Donat but when the star finally reported for duty, two months late, the film had slipped firmly under Miss Dietrich's control.

The balance of the roles had shifted: the countess was more important than the commissar and furthermore Donat and Dietrich didn't exactly hit it off together. Ella said he "hated" making the film and in the middle of it he had another fierce attack of asthma. There was one scene, Ella said, an emotional scene in which Miss Dietrich was disguised as a peasant, complete with shawl over her head: "Robert was going to take her hand affectionately. She said, 'You can't do that' and he discovered afterwards that her nails were gilded for the film premiere that she was going to that night with Douglas Fairbanks."

The picture opened in 1937 to hardly any acclaim at all and there followed a quiet time for Donat. He spent three months in Switzerland to recover his health and then, back in England, brought his own curious judgment to bear on plays that were offered to him. In the end he did none of them, turning down among other opportunities the chance to play Othello to Olivier's Iago at the Old Vic. And yet all the while he was protesting in letters to friends that he must get back to the stage before he became merely a film star. Ella said: "I don't know that his choice was really very good. He surrounded himself with a wall of fear — fear of not being able to succeed or not being on top. It was all very strange. But his standards were so high that anything less than the top, you see, was not enough."

In 1938 Donat signed a contract with MGM, the deal being for six films at a salary of £25,000 each to be made over an unspecified period of time. The latter clause was particularly attractive because there would be no pressure on him to work when his health was bad. Furthermore it was agreed that between each pair of films he would be free to return to the theatre for at least six months. Satisfied with such terms he played the leading role in *The Citadel,* an adaptation of A. J. Cronin's novel about an idealistic young doctor who becomes a well-heeled society quack in Harley Street. Donat, described by his director King Vidor as the finest and most co-operative actor he had worked with, won an Academy Award nomination, although on this occasion the Oscar finally went to Spencer Tracy for *Boys Town.*

When the filming was over Donat announced that he would go back to the stage. But again he did not follow through. He even turned down Tyrone Guthrie's suggestion that he should appear at the Old Vic playing either Hamlet or Romeo, whichever he fancied more. So again and again he declined opportunities that would have confirmed him unarguably as the great actor his friends and contemporaries believed him to be.

Instead of the stage he returned immediately to films to play Mr. Chips. Practically everyone he knew counselled him against it, predicting confidently that such a character, as opposed to romantic, role would ruin his box-office appeal and very probably his career as well. Instead, *Goodbye Mr. Chips* turned out to be the most popular and most enduring of his films and his performance at last won him the Oscar for best actor in 1940.

He did not, however, go to Hollywood to collect the award himself for there was a war raging on, under and above the Atlantic at the time. Spencer Tracy picked up the Oscar on his behalf and in doing so called him "the greatest actor I know". When the trophy eventually found its way to its rightful owner it was used, said John Donat, "as a door-stop for the loo, for which it was ideally suited. It's exactly the right weight and size." On the face of it this would seem to indicate a contemptuous attitude on Donat's part but John interpreted the matter otherwise: "Obviously to be named best actor was an honour and was certainly appreciated but the trappings of it were of no consequence to him."

The outbreak of the Second World War found Donat, still barely thirty-five, firmly established as the most important and most popular film actor in Britain; as a stage actor of vast talent, undoubted promise and, because of the opportunities missed through illness, disappointingly little achievement; and as a husband and father whose marriage was disintegrating. Soon after the war began Ella left him and took their three children, Joanna, John and Brian to California. It was not something she particularly wanted to do, even though she was anxious to take the children away from the bombs, but . . .

"Well, at that time," she said, "Robert was very much in love with somebody else. I just had a sudden realisation that he didn't need me any more and that probably the children did. So I went straight to London and booked my passage and went."

This was not, however, a case of a wife reacting, or even over-reacting, to one fall from grace on the part of her husband. "There were many people," she said, "roughly from 1936 onwards. And I accepted these friendships or love affairs, whatever you like to call them, because I felt that though I was the first one in his life I wasn't likely to be the last. After all, we all develop but we don't necessarily develop at the same rate." The marriage was not in fact dissolved until after the war but for all practical purposes it was over when Ella went to America.

Looking back on her life with Donat up until that point she said: "It had been a happy marriage, a wonderful experience. We never quarrelled, you know, and we enjoyed so much. But we really didn't bring out the best in each other. There was tension there all the time. The children always said we were different people when we were alone with them and not together. We were better apart. I always knew he was interested in other women. I think that from the time he was caught up in stardom — and I wasn't interested in stardom — his values changed. He had been blown up so quickly, too quickly, that he lost touch with real things."

There were other changes in him, too, that she had noted and that worried her. The asthma, for example, came upon him most violently when he was not working. "And I think I can explain that," she said. "Working as Robert did, he was completely involved in the character he was playing. When he came home from the set of *Chips* I would know what part of the film he had been doing. But now the picture is finished — *Chips* has gone. Who are you? I think that he was so taken over by what he did in his work that he lost himself and I think this was his tragedy and this is what he was afraid of. He couldn't find himself."

I said: "You mean that gradually Robert Donat was vanishing, that over the years you found you were living less and less with the man you married and more and more with the character from the play or film?"

She said: "Yes, there was no Robert. There was a picture taken of him in front of his book case with the most beautiful jacket and the handkerchief in just the right place and that face was quite blank, quite empty. I've always found that the most shattering picture of him."

An impression comes across of a man withdrawn into himself, of a man obsessed with his work and perhaps some element of that had been noted by his children. John Donat said: "He was a father I hardly met until I was a teenager." There was a photograph, John remembered, taken in the garden of himself when very young and his father with a model aeroplane they had made together and he said: "The reason that sticks so firmly in my memory and the reason the picture was taken was because it was so unusual. It was patently not a normal situation for Robert to be around playing with the kids. At the same time he loved his family and was in a sense a marvellous father but an absent one in that his career and, of course, from time to time his illness so very much took over his life."

With his family gone, Donat began the 1940s pretty much alone in London. His father had died, his mother and brothers were living in Canada and his love affair with a young British actress, the cause of his own family separation, ended when she went off and married somebody else. A new life was beginning for him and a less settled one than hitherto. In 1943 he wrote to Ella an affectionate, admiring and also very firm letter in which he said he was now "certain beyond any shadow of doubt" that they were unable to live happily together. And to complicate his life still further he became involved in litigation with MGM over the terms of his contract. Basically the studio was trying to prevent him from working for anybody else until he made another film for them. It was a complicated action that dragged on, sometimes quite bitterly, for a long time, although in 1941 MGM, rather grudgingly perhaps, relaxed its grip on him enough to allow him to make *The Young Mr. Pitt* for 20th Century Fox.

John Mills was with him in that film, as he had been in *Goodbye Mr. Chips* and was conscious, as ever, of Donat's remarkable professionalism. On the wall of his dressing-room, Mills said, he had a large chart. "It looked like an enormous temperature chart and it had the film from the word 'go' all charted emotionally. One scene would be up to 60 and the next one down to 54, then 87, then up to 92 and, although I knew what the answer was going to be I said, 'What's the idea of that?'

"He said something I've never forgotten: 'With a big emotional part in the theatre it's a piece of cake. The curtain goes up and you work your way through. It's a straightforward climb, emotionally. But with a very big emotional part on the screen it's a different thing altogether. You have to hit the high spot maybe in the first week. You shoot the end of the picture first, then you have a big lull and then another emotional high maybe six weeks later.' His idea, a marvellous idea, was to put down on paper how far he had gone emotionally in maybe the second or third week of shooting so that when he had to follow a scene four weeks later he knew what sort of peak he had reached. There was no haphazard acting with Robert."

After *The Young Mr. Pitt* Donat appeased MGM somewhat by playing a secret agent in *The Adventures of Tartu* for them and then, being clearly unfit for military service, he did his bit for the war effort by entertaining the troops on an ENSA tour of the North of England, after which he had another shot at actor-management in London. This turned out at first to be moderately successful, or at least not too unsuccessful, and while he was so engaged he also completed his MGM contract when he made *Perfect Strangers* with Deborah Kerr.

Then once more he returned to the stage, starring in his own production of Walter Greenwood's *The Cure for Love,* which again was moderately successful (and which was later to provide him with his second wife in the shape of his co-star Renee Asherson, who was fifteen years younger than himself). After three years, however, the ups and downs of actor-managership left him financially worse off than before, so in 1946 at the age of forty-one he was in fairly parlous shape: he had not made a film for two years; he had barely earned any money at all for eighteen months; his health was bad again and the need for some kind of success to re-establish himself merely heightened his fear of failure.

The sensible course, probably, would have been to make another film if only to bring a glow of health to his bank balance. But instead he made a further attempt at actor-management with, among other productions, Peter Ustinov's dramatic biography of Simon Bolivar, *The Man Behind the Statue*. This venture, however, failed too.

Ustinov remembered him as "terribly engaging, a very attractive personality. He was an extraordinarily good-looking man with a wonderful voice. It sounds awfully pretentious to say so, but it was like a viola. He had a great subtlety, a very emollient, consoling voice and this rather strange face — with a short nose and slightly plump cheeks."

Like almost everyone else who ever worked with Donat, Ustinov found himself on the receiving end of some quite irascible notes. In this instance the correspondence was one-sided and didn't last very long because Ustinov, being on his own admission the world's worst letter-writer, said, "I probably took away his vital supply of fuel because I didn't answer. I forgot."

Generally speaking, though, it was one of the more curious aspects of Donat's character that while he was, in person, a gentle and charming man he was also an inveterate writer of letters of barely-controlled fury which throughout his career he was in the habit of dispatching to writers, directors, producers and practical-ly anyone else who had upset him.

John Donat, who came to know his father well after the family returned from America, could not remember actually seeing him lose his temper but said: "He was a perfectionist in everything he did. He didn't suffer fools gladly and he was very, very easily upset. Now in that strange world of the theatre and cinema where the tensions are immense, both artistically and financially, Robert found a mode of expressing himself which was in total contrast to his nature. It became a kind of alter ego and he would dash home and write a letter that you would scarcely believe. This heat and anger, I think, was something he had never learned to express in his own personal life and in that sense the letter-writing was a way of externalising anger which must have been very deeply felt. On the other hand it must be pointed out that not all his letters were angry. Most of them were light and amusing and beautifully expressed."

Again there is the paradox: the brilliant, successful actor always afraid of failure; the gentle (in John's words "even humble") man capable of intense anger; the attractive, charming personality whom most people found extremely difficult to know. As John Donat said: "It's very strange. People loved him — the technicians, the cameramen, the guys who were there on the set with him had an extraordinarily deep affection for Robert. But I don't think one of them could say to you, 'I knew him'. Whether he put that distance between himself and others out of a natural shyness I don't know but it's a fact that he was a shy person and I think very few people got close to him. He was a lonely man."

As he grew older and his health worsened his loneliness increased. At times it seemed almost as though he were trying to isolate himself. In November 1946, he and Ella were divorced and he was almost broke again, having lost the £12,000 he had invested in the Ustinov play. Partly to make some money he appeared in the film *Captain Boycott* with Stewart Granger and then, in a much better role, revived his career considerably with one of his very best screen performances in *The Winslow Boy*. The following year, 1949, he starred in and — for the only time in his career — directed the film version of *The Cure for Love*. It did reasonably well at the box office but was generally dismissed by the critics.

This burst of creativity — three films in three years — was not to last. The 1950s began with Donat seriously ill and unable to work at all and it was not until New Year's Day 1951 that he was fit enough to return to the film studios to play William Friese-Greene, one of the pioneers of the cinema, a role coveted by most of the top stars of the time, in *The Magic Box*.

This had been planned as part of the celebrations for the Festival of Britain and Donat, the star, found himself surrounded by a veritable horde of equally starry names all playing cameo roles. Whether, in the uncertain state of his health and self-confidence, the presence of all this notable talent inhibited him it is difficult to say but certainly the director, John Boulting, discovered a very different Donat from the generous, giving actor whom Flora Robson and John Mills remembered with such affection.

Boulting said: "We were in constant conflict, which in a way is interesting because I think he's the only actor I worked with with whom I didn't have a very cordial and understanding relationship."

Things were made immediately difficult because, in the context of the script, Friese-Greene was a charming, attractive personality but also "a real bastard, a rascal, totally irresponsible". And Donat, according to John Boulting, didn't wish to show those aspects of the character. The argument, with Donat wanting only to portray Jekyll and Boulting insisting on a touch of Hyde as well, continued throughout the filming and neither of them really won.

Boulting said: "I think it was a drawn battle because there were things he did which met with my suggestions and there were one or two scenes when he licked me."

There was a particular occasion, he recalled, when Laurence Olivier was to play the policeman to whom Friese-Greene first showed his newly-invented moving pictures. Olivier was only available for two days, a Saturday and a Sunday, to shoot his scenes and Boulting, wary now of Donat, predicted to his producer, Ronald Neame, that there would be trouble. Donat had argued all along that the presence of an actor of Olivier's stature in such a small part would throw the whole scene out of balance.

Artistically it was by no means an untenable point of view, though the scene was so beautifully played by both stars that Donat was proved wrong. Boulting's premonition, however, was not. On the Friday before the Olivier sequence was to be shot Donat, who had been suffering badly with asthma throughout the filming, sent word that, though he was fit enough to work that day, he would not be able to come in over the weekend, which after all was the only time he had to rest after the exertions of the week and to recover from the asthma.

Boulting said: "Now he knew we only had Larry for that Saturday and Sunday, so I went to his dressing-room and found him sick, no question of that at all. He was really rough. I said, 'Bob, you'd better go home and go to bed.' He said, 'No, no. I'll play today but tomorrow and Sunday I can't. I'm not strong enough.'"

At this point Boulting said to him: "Bob, you don't work for a second today. We'll get a car to take you back to London but whatever happens you are going to work tomorrow and you're going to work on Sunday. If necessary I'll send an ambulance for you but you are going to work because as an artist you will kill yourself if you refuse to accept the challenge of acting this climactic scene with Larry Olivier. It will be interpreted by everybody as a kind of funk on your part.''

And then . . . . ''He just looked at me astounded — astounded that I should be so autocratic, so dictatorial. But he left the studio and that night I phoned him to find out how he was feeling. He indicated he was still pretty ill. But about an hour or two later I got a call from his agent who said, 'Bob has told me what transpired at the studio today. He'll be along tomorrow morning.' And he was and to his great credit, whatever his feelings about performing with Larry, he gave one of his best performances.''

Now this kind of behaviour sounds quite untypical and Boulting is prepared to concede that it was. He was careful to point out that this was the only time he ever worked with Donat, that it was towards the end of Donat's career and that Donat, continually surrounded on set by all the paraphernalia of the chronic asthmatic, was a genuinely sick man. But taking all that into account, Boulting's view of him is still decidedly cooler than that of most people.

He said: ''I don't think anybody really knew Robert Donat. He was the kind of man who was very elusive. He was one of the most withdrawn actors I have ever encountered. That smile and that lovely, mellow, gentle voice — those were his defences and they were very hard to penetrate. He wanted to be loved, of course, and that I think is the real key to Bob. I felt indeed a sense of pity for him. He was clearly a very complex character and I don't think he was a very happy man.''

John Boulting's experience may well have been unusual, one not shared by anybody else. But there would appear to have been some kind of metamorphosis in Donat's character around that time and once again the explanation probably lies in his ill-health and the treatments he was undergoing. Renee Asherson, who married him in 1953 after living with him for eight years, said that in his desperation to find a cure, or at least some alleviation, for his asthma he would try almost any new drug that came on the market.

She had first met him, she said, when he ''sent for me to play the part of Millie in *The Cure For Love* at the Westminster Theatre. I found him very charming and very sympathetic, not really as I'd imagined him — as I'd imagined a big film star: absolutely none of the glossy glamour that one associates with film stars. And, in a kind of way later on when I got to know him during the run, I was amazed to find that he was really a rather lonely person and very vulnerable and in need of people. And he was probably much more ill when I met him than I realised. He was extremely deceptive: if he'd had an attack he'd look absolutely awful, just as if he could die, and then something would enthuse him, and he'd smile, and look absolutely different, years younger, and you couldn't really tell (it was such a mysterious illness) you know, which was *him*? Was he like *that*, or was he really very ill? He loved people, was very warm — easily warmed towards them. This was the curious paradox about him. If one could have broken through that, and put him into this melting mood in which he was very genial and loved company — but there was another side that took over. . ."

Later, however, as the asthma became worse, she began to notice the change in him. "There was a part of Robert," she said, "that I didn't know, that perhaps nobody could know — the part that, in later years, was affected by the drugs the doctors so heavily prescribed for him and which quite altered his personality."

And John Donat said: "I couldn't list you the consultants and psychiatrists and hypnotists who had treated Robert over the years, or the hospitals and the nursing homes and the drugs."

In such circumstances any uncharacteristic behaviour, any apparent irascibility, would be perfectly understandable and it was doubtless John Boulting's misfortune that he should only have worked with Donat at such a time.

During the last few years illness became ever more the dominant factor in Donat's life. Apart from radio broadcasts and poetry recordings he worked very little after making *The Magic Box*. In 1953 he played (most memorably) Becket in *Murder in the Cathedral* for four weeks at the Old Vic and received a standing ovation every night.

And in 1954 he appeared as a clergyman with only a year to live in the film *Lease of Life*. But for every part he was able to accept he was forced to turn down several others on account of his health. Sometimes the choice was not even his.

Renee Asherson said : "One didn't know when the films were coming or whether he would be able to do them when they did. And then came the absolute horror, when money became tighter in the film world, of insurance tests. One had to face the insurance man and that, of course, was agony waiting for him to come round."

And if the insurance man — or, more accurately, I suppose, the insurance doctor — failed to pass him as fully fit the proffered role would be passed to somebody else. In three years Donat lost at least £50,000 worth of work that way. Indeed between 1954 and 1958 he hardly worked at all and when, at last, a film offer came his way and this time the doctor agreed that he was an insurable proposition, he and Renee were separated.

"I think," she said, "you just sometimes get to a state where you can't see the wood for the trees and it's better to be apart. We did intend to come together again, you know, and I waited for the crucial moment and waited until the last film in fact. The doctor said, 'Don't try and do anything until he has got through that,' because once he had done the film he would probably gain confidence. But by then, it was too late."

The last film was *The Inn of the Sixth Happiness,* which starred Ingrid Bergman as Gladys Aylward, the English missionary who went to China in the 1930s. Donat played an autocratic mandarin. When, before the picture started, he met the Press at a reception in London he said: "It is good to see life again. There have been times during the past years when I have been so desperate, so afraid, that I could not face anybody."

John Donat believed that among the reasons his father accepted the film — financial pressures, a longing simply to work again — the need to come back to life was most important. And perhaps that was recognised, too, by his fellow movie-makers for when he appeared on the set for the first time they gave him an ovation.

He was not however at all well from the very start of filming. Near the set, which was always closed to visitors when he was in front of the camera, he had a portable dressing-room with its own air-purifying unit and there he would rest between takes to regain his breath.

Almost at the end of the shooting schedule he had a brain haemorrhage and when he returned to work he was unable to remember his lines. Freddie Young, the lighting cameraman, recalled: "We had those idiot boards up all round the set, large boards with what he had to say on them. He would look, say, in Ingrid Bergman's direction and read this board and then he would look over there where there was another board. During the morning I went out of the studio to make a phone call in an outer office and I found Bob there, weeping. It distressed me very much and I said, 'What's the matter, Bob?' and he said, 'I'm so ashamed, Freddie, so ashamed of myself.' I sort of cheered him up but he was such a perfectionist, you see, that when he suddenly found he couldn't remember his lines and had to read them off an idiot board — something he'd never done in his life before — he was actually weeping in this little office outside the studio."

The last line Donat spoke in the film was to Ingrid Bergman — "We shall not meet each other again, I think. Farewell, Jen-Ai." It was just about the most prophetic last line ever uttered by any actor and all those around him seemed to realise it for, according to Dame Flora Robson, everyone on the set was in tears.

By then he was very gravely ill indeed and it can only have been determination and sheer courage that carried him through the film. Almost as soon as he left the set he collapsed and on May 19th, 1958, he was taken to the West End Hospital for Neurology and Neurosurgery and there, on the morning of June 9th, he suffered a stroke and died. He was only fifty-three years old and his total estate amounted precisely to the fee he was paid for *The Inn of the Sixth Happiness*.

Looking back, John Mills described Donat as "a tragic figure" and indeed there was a powerful element of tragedy in his life. From childhood onwards he fought bravely and with great fortitude against dreadful ill-health but for which, according to Peter Ustinov, "he could have been tremendously important. I mean, he was an important actor but he could have been much more consistently important. He could really have challenged all the others in the classical repertoire."

Donat left behind him an enviable reputation based on a surprisingly small record of work and achievement. It could be argued that because of the self-doubts to which he was prey, he shirked the larger challenges; the great classical roles which are the true yardstick by which an actor's work is measured. But surely the doubts were due, to a very large extent, to his knowledge that he didn't have the physical strength to be the actor he wanted to be and had the talent to be. Peter Ustinov said: "He may have been a person who was conscious of running on five cylinders all the time, conscious of the fact that he couldn't supply as much energy as other people and therefore tended to turn things down because in fact he was rationing himself in order to make it possible to do anything at all."

Talking to those who knew him well, one is left with an image of a hugely gifted man — but also of a frustrated and modest man who perhaps believed too little in himself. At the end of my conversation with her, his first wife, Ella, said: "He had given so much of himself to so many people — so much laughter, so much happiness — that it was sad that he should love himself so little."

And when I asked what exactly she meant by that, she said: "If he had loved himself, if he had understood himself a little more he wouldn't have been frightened and perhaps if he hadn't been frightened he wouldn't have had asthma."

I wonder, though, whether what he suffered was not so much a lack of self-love as a kind of self-anger. To know that you have been granted rare gifts but equally to know that, because of chronic ill-health, you will never be able to develop those gifts as you would wish must be a desperate thing.

Most actors, most stars, given a long life and perfect fitness, would be delighted to achieve what Donat achieved. But Donat was in a different league from most actors and even asthma, though it robbed him of what should have been a career of quite astonishing brilliance, could not disguise that fact. He may have been, as his biographer J. C. Trewin said, "A great actor lost" but I suspect that posterity may well accord him his rightful place as a great actor nevertheless.

Gracie
Fields

Our Gracie in the 1930s when she was only a little less popular than the Royal family.

*above : The Fields family recording a Christmas show. From the left,
Betty, Tommy, father, mother and Gracie.*

*opposite page : With her first husband, Archie Pitt — an acceptable
substitute for Svengali.*

*above : Gracie, aged seventy-one, and still pulling in the crowds at a
night club engagement in Yorkshire.*

*opposite above : Gracie with her second husband, Monty Banks,
whose Italian citizenship led to her wartime exile and accusations
that she was a traitor.*

*opposite below : With her third and last husband Boris Alperovici —
the self-styled "little grey man".*

When Gracie Fields died she was buried in Capri, her adoptive home, and beside her grave there's a small memorial tablet that says simply: "Our Gracie". And that is precisely what she was — not Capri's Gracie, of course (though they had an affectionately proprietorial attitude towards her even there) but Britain's Gracie, a kind of national institution.

More, perhaps, than any other popular entertainer this country has ever had, she seemed to belong to the people, to epitomise the cheerful, indomitable spirit that carried Britain through the Depression of the 1930s and the assorted nightmares of the Second World War. And yet she wasn't even in Britain for most of the war, was indeed branded a traitor by the Press because of her absence and spent nearly half of her eighty-one years living abroad.

Today, I suppose, she is best remembered for three songs, variously sentimental or comic and none of them particularly distinguished: "Sally", "Walter" and "The Biggest Aspidistra in the World". She wasn't, in fact, particularly fond of them and in any case they were only a minute fraction of the 400 songs she had in her repertoire, for she was a singer of remarkable range, whose voice was too good for most of her material.

In short this woman, Our Gracie, who was thought to be typically British, was perfectly untypical. She was unique, brimming with talent and the possessor of a personality so powerful and hypnotic that she could, according to her whim, reduce an audience of thousands to sentimental tears and, only seconds later, cause it to howl with mirth. At one time she was said to be earning a higher salary than anyone else in the world and in the late 1930s the position she held in the public's affection was second only to that of the King and Queen.

The story of this amazing woman began in Rochdale, a hard, damp and generally poor little mill town in Lancashire, on January 9th, 1898. She was born above her grandmother's chip shop in Molesworth Street, the eldest of the four children of Fred Stansfield, an unskilled labourer, and his wife, Jenny, and the fact that from these unlikely and penurious circumstances Grace Stansfield went on to become Dame Gracie Fields, millionairess, international star and a sort of public monument, was due almost entirely to the fierce drive and thwarted theatrical ambitions of her mother.

Jenny Stansfield, an orphan, had begun work in a cotton mill at the age of ten and had married Fred when she was eighteen because somehow she was under the impression that he was an actor and could therefore help in her determination to make a career for herself on the stage. By the time she discovered her mistake (he was actually a labourer at an engineering works) she was already pregnant with Grace and any prospect she may have had of becoming an actress or a singer or a music-hall artist, never much more tangible than a dream at the best of times, had gone.

Nevertheless, as Dame Gracie Fields said later: "My mother remained the most stage-struck woman I've ever met in my life." What happened, in fact, was that she simply shifted her ambitions from herself to her child. If she, Jenny, couldn't become a star then Gracie would. Now this is an easy enough plan to form but it's a great deal harder to carry out, especially when you live in poverty.

Tommy Fields, Gracie's younger brother and himself a popular and successful comedian, said: "We used to move every other week. It was a sort of moonlight flit because we couldn't pay the rent. My mother was so bad she used to forget to tell my father where she'd gone and he'd arrive home and find nobody there — everybody else had moved."

Most women, however stage-struck, might well have abandoned their ambitions when faced with this kind of daily struggle for mere survival but Jenny Stansfield seems to have thrived on setbacks. "She was a very, very strong character," said Mary Davey, who was Gracie's companion for more than forty years. "I was terrified of her, quite honestly. She frightened everybody, including Gracie when Gracie was a child and, of course, she was a tremendous influence on her children. Gracie's father was very easy-going and never wanted her to go into the theatre. He thought she'd be better off working in the mill, getting what he called 'a proper job'. But Jenny wasn't having that."

Almost from infancy young Gracie had it instilled into her that she was to make her career on the stage. To this end she was sent off, when she was still only a few years old, to the gallery at the Rochdale Hippodrome to watch the show and learn from the performers. "She was the only one who was allowed to go," said Tommy Fields, "because there wasn't enough money to send the rest of us. When she came back she had to tell us about all the acts and what they did and how the audience reacted and this way she became a very good mimic, even as a young girl. This was her beginning." It was also about as close to formal theatre training as she ever got because there was no money for stage or drama classes and, besides, her own career began when she was only seven and won an amateur talent contest at this same Rochdale Hippodrome.

She then left school after a formal education that had lasted little more than a year to play a tiny stooge in a music-hall act and by the time she was ten she was appearing in the first of a number of juvenile touring companies. It can't have been an altogether easy life because at thirteen she suffered a nervous breakdown and an attack of St. Vitus' Dance and, after six weeks in a convalescent home, retired from show business to become a cotton-winder in the local mill.

Left to herself that could well have been the end of all theatrical ambition for Gracie, but, of course, she wasn't left to herself. Minor setbacks like nervous breakdowns and St. Vitus' Dance were not going to deter Jenny and by 1912, aged fourteen, Gracie was back in show business with a troupe called Charburn's Young Stars. Now up to this point she was basically, indeed essentially, a singer but with Charburn's Young Stars she became a comedienne, too.

The quality of her voice caused a certain amount of jealousy and friction within the company. The others felt that she was always given the best songs and it wasn't fair. So, to keep the rest of them happy, the manager gave Gracie the worst song to sing. Tommy Fields said: "Well, this infuriated Gracie and after a time she got fed up with it and said, 'Right, I'm going to burlesque this song', which was a sad song. And the next minute she had the audience in stitches because she was pulling faces and all sorts of things and it was terribly funny." The management approved and told her to do it again and so comedy crept into her repertoire to be joined soon afterwards by mimicry, for she was an observant and accurate impersonator of the music-hall stars of her time. Her career as a mimic, however, did not last long.

Lilian Aza, who was later to become her agent, said: "She used to tour very small, very rough places in the beginning. She had quite a tough time in those little shows and at one place there was a woman who was billed above her — I think she had top billing — and one night Gracie came off after doing her impersonations, and she was a wonderful impersonator, and this woman said: 'Well, of course, anybody can earn a living doing other people's work and imitating other people. That's very simple.' People could squash Gracie very easily and she never did another impression from that night on. She couldn't take criticism, couldn't take it at all. A million people could tell her she was wonderful but if one person said she wasn't, that was the one she listened to."

In 1914 in a revue called *Yes, I Think So* Grace Stansfield, now known professionally as Gracie Fields, met a cockney comedian named Archie Pitt. He wasn't much of a comedian but he did have a sharp eye for talent and, spotting it immediately in the young Gracie, he persuaded her to join him in a revue of his own called *It's a Bargain*. On her sixteenth birthday he wrote in her autograph book, "To Gracie Fields — one day you are going to be a big star."

Despite such flattery Gracie didn't actually like Pitt very much but, egged on by Jennie who approved of anyone who approved of Gracie, she agreed to go with him and from that point Archie Pitt took over the task of promoting her career. Pitt was a remarkable and versatile man. He had been a shop assistant and a commercial traveller before turning his hand to comedy and he wrote the songs and sketches for *It's a Bargain* himself. But he was a promoter and a businessman rather than a performer and he swiftly realised that in Gracie Fields he had acquired a very considerable asset. So even though it was his own revue and, originally at least, a showcase for himself, he sacrificed himself and everybody else to establish Gracie as the star of it.

Lilian Aza, who was Archie Pitt's sister-in-law, said: "Archie definitely developed her talent. He didn't give her talent — nobody could have done that — but Archie developed it. He wrote wonderful scripts and sketches for her. Gracie was very funny and she came out with some wonderful, impromptu bits and pieces during the show. If she'd been with an ordinary comedian he'd have said to her, 'Listen, you do that again and I'll walk off the stage,' but Archie encouraged her. He'd take songs and sketches and pieces of business from anybody, he'd cut this person's act or that one's, to keep in anything that Gracie did. And this gave her great confidence."

For two and a half years Pitt toured his revue round the North of England, playing twice nightly and leading a hand-to-mouth existence. The audiences were small, the living and working conditions were rough but Gracie Fields was learning all the time. She played the soubrette and the comedienne, she stood in for the pianist when he was unwell, and she and Archie Pitt spent hours working on new bits of business for her to try out.

By the time *It's a Bargain* closed there was hardly anything she couldn't cope with on stage and very little she didn't know about manipulating an audience. Archie Pitt then exploited all this skill and experience in another revue, *Mr. Tower of London*, in which he and Gracie toured for more than six years with steadily increasing success. In 1923 and in the fifth year of this tour with Gracie, the now indubitable star of the show, Pitt decided to protect his investment by marrying her. He was forty-three and, as she said later, "a passable imitation of Svengali" and Gracie, an unsophisticated twenty-five, was ideally cast as Trilby. Since she was fourteen she had known nothing except the sheltered life of a company on tour; she had hardly spent more than a week or so at a time in any one place; she had met very few people apart from the other members of the troupe. At twenty-five, therefore, she was certainly old enough for marriage but she was not nearly experienced enough for it. But how could she say No to Archie Pitt, one of the two dominant influences in her life when Jenny, the other dominant influence, was urging her to say Yes?

"It was a business marriage as far as he was concerned," said Tommy Fields. "I don't think he ever really loved Grace and certainly she didn't love him. But this was a case of my mother's strong character coming back into the picture because she could see the potential Grace could have with this man and really she persuaded Grace to marry him, from that angle. And, of course, Grace never looked back from then on. She had a lot to thank Archie Pitt for as a manager and as an artist. But as a husband, no."

In later years Gracie herself said the marriage was "like a registered company: Archie was the brains, I was the asset". She also said that from the start, immediately after the wedding ceremony at Clapham Register Office, "I was a very, very unhappy woman." The best part of the honeymoon in Paris, she added, was when Archie suggested they should cut it short and get back to the show in England.

The position was hardly helped by the fact that the musical director of Pitt's revues, Annie Lipman, was also his mistress. She remained his mistress throughout the duration of his marriage to Gracie and only changed this status when, in the fullness of time, she became Mrs. Archie Pitt in her turn. Lilian Aza maintained that Gracie knew all about the set-up: "She knew about this at the time they got married. Gracie was never a wife in the accepted sense of the word. She had her work and her heart and soul were in her work. Archie was quite an ill person and had to have a special diet, and so on. Annie was the one who always prepared it for him and Gracie always told Annie to do it. So really it was Annie who took on the wifely duties."

Tommy Fields, on the other hand, presented a different version of the marriage, one in which Gracie was the neglected, rather than the negligent, wife. "Archie Pitt loved women and he loved money and that's what he got. It wasn't a happy marriage. But Gracie had her work and that alleviated the tensions and miseries."

Eighteen months after this uneasy, though financially convenient, matrimonial alliance had taken place *Mr. Tower of London* moved into the Alhambra Theatre in London and Gracie Fields became an immediate and sensational success. Both the critics and the public greeted her with ecstasy and she rapidly grew rich.

As the West End's newest star she was in constant demand: she began to make records; she would take time off between sketches in her Alhambra show to nip across the road and do a ten-minute solo act at the Coliseum for £100 a week (the most she had earned previously was £28 a week) and then, later on, she dropped the Coliseum act and instead took the straight role of Lady Weir opposite Sir Gerald du Maurier in the play *S.O.S.* She would appear only in the first act and then go to the Alhambra to do her stuff in the revue. What's more, lest anyone should accuse her of idleness, she would often finish the night with a cabaret stint at the Café de Paris.

Lilian Aza said there was only one word to explain this enormous popular demand for Gracie Fields — "magic".

"I've never seen another artist as magical as Gracie, never. She could change — she could change herself, she could change the atmosphere of the theatre. She could have an audience crying or so still you could hear a pin drop and the next moment they'd be screaming their heads off."

Gracie's brother, Tommy, said: "The public wasn't aware of it and neither was she but I think she literally hypnotised them. They were hypnotised by this colossal personality. If there were umpteen people on the stage they could still only look at Gracie Fields."

As her fame and success gathered momentum and the money rolled in in ever-increasing quantities, Archie Pitt built an enormous house called the Towers in Hampstead and, more altruistically, helped his wife to found the Gracie Fields Orphanage in Brighton. The Towers, a twenty-eight-roomed mansion with a gold lift, marble bathrooms, crystal chandeliers and a ballroom was not at all to Gracie's taste. It was far too grand, too ornate for her. Annie Lipman moved in as effective mistress of the house while the true mistress of the house, the one, after all, whose talent and efforts had paid for it all, remained mostly in her small sitting-room. She seemed, in any event, quite unaffected either by her riches or her fame.

"Gracie was the most unusual person in our business," said her brother. "I don't think she ever realised how popular she was. She was a simple person really, just a mill girl underneath it all."

And that, too, perhaps helps to explain her colossal popularity, for the Gracie Fields story could have been taken straight from the pages of the more purple-coloured women's fiction; it's the rags-to-riches tale of the little mill girl who conquered the world, married several times, earned a fortune and yet stayed firmly in touch with her roots. One of the many untypical things about Gracie Fields which the public chose to regard as typical was her genuine modesty.

In the early 1930s, however, the story of the little mill girl had reached one of many crisis points. The marriage of convenience to Archie Pitt was, not surprisingly, disintegrating fast and she thus found herself in a predicament that is by no means rare in the annals of show business: her professional life could hardly have been more successful; her private life could hardly have been less so. But at this decidedly low point her sister, Betty, introduced her to one John Flanagan, an Irishman and a painter of modest accomplishment who was to become the first, and very possibly the only, man with whom Gracie Fields fell quite passionately in love.

Flanagan was by all accounts a good-looking man and an erudite one. He introduced Gracie not only to art but also to literature and to what she regarded as the "bohemian lifestyle" enjoyed by himself and his friends. It was probably less bohemian than slightly hard-up but it made a pleasing contrast to the superficiality of the world of wealth and celebrity into which Archie was now doggedly thrusting her.

By this time she had left the cast of *Mr. Tower of London* and moved into an equally successful revue called *The Show's the Thing*. Contemporary London critics, marvelling at the range of her voice, were insisting that she could have sung Carmen, that she could have been the great coloratura soprano of the century. Gracie herself maintained that she was simply "a bathroom opera singer" and stuck steadfastly to the music-hall where she felt safe and confident.

The first few years of the 1930s, though, were to see her conquer another medium, film, and they were also to see the beginning and the end of her love affair with John Flanagan. The business with Flanagan was significant in several ways: it showed her, for a start, that there could be more to a relationship with a man than the financial arrangement she had with her husband, Archie Pitt, and it also introduced her to Capri.

She and Flanagan went there on holiday in the company of a mutual friend who, in that stricter age, was on hand as chaperon and Gracie fell in love with the place immediately. This was unusual in itself because in those days and on her own admission she felt homesick for Rochdale when she was no further away than London. Looking at Capri now — an expensive, over-developed, over-commercialised and overrated holiday resort — it's difficult to understand what she can ever have seen in it but no doubt it still retained a primitive charm fifty years ago and also, of course, she saw it first in the company of the man she loved.

In any event, within a year of that first visit she had bought herself a property on the south of the island and, because she had not hitherto been too careful with her money, it cost her just about everything she had, or at least everything she had bar £25. Initially, I suppose, she regarded Capri as a potential holiday home for herself and Flanagan but Flanagan, the lover, was soon, alas, to disappear from her life although to Flanagan the friend she remained steadfast until his death forty years later.

Ironically, it was her own fame and success that destroyed the romantic relationship. "John was very fond of her," said Lilian Aza, "but he couldn't accept the glamour and everything that went with it, or the fact that she could afford to buy things for him. He couldn't accept that at all. He didn't want it."

Tommy Fields said: "They had a tremendous amount of affection for each other but he knew nothing at all about the theatre. And, I'm afraid, Grace spoilt him. She just showered money on top of this poor fellow and he wasn't used to it. He'd never seen anything like this. So really and truly the break-up was her own fault for doing that. He said, 'I go around and I sell a picture for about £35 or £40 and then she comes home with two or three thousand pounds and chucks it on the bed. Well, where do you go from there?'"

Where they went, fairly swiftly, was towards separation. In every way perhaps Gracie was just too rich for Flanagan and for her own part, as Tommy Fields said, "I think she realised that they had nothing in common, outside of their lovely friendship, and Grace needed somebody with whom she had show business in common."

So, from her point of view, the gains from the relationship with

Flanagan were a brief but passionate romance, followed by a pleasant and gentle friendship and her introduction to Capri which, with or without her lover, continued to hold its enchantment for her and became the place to which she went to escape from pressure, to recuperate from illness and finally to live.

Meanwhile, despite his now precarious position as her husband, Archie Pitt, still acting on his own and Gracie's behalf, had started her off on what was to become an extremely lucrative, though never very satisfactory, film career. Her first picture, in 1931 when she was thirty-three years old, was a low-budget quickie called *Sally in Our Alley,* in which for the first time she sang what was henceforth to become her theme song.

The film was produced by Basil Dean and directed by Maurice Elvey and was designed with no loftier ambition than to cash in on her fame as a music-hall and recording artist. As in most of the subsequent films which Basil Dean directed, Gracie was a sort of Pagliacci figure, singing and clowning and losing the hero to the ingénue. Nevertheless, it was an enormous box-office success and launched Gracie on a secondary career which, by and large, she disliked intensely.

Lilian Aza said: "She didn't like films; she didn't like film work. She used to feel very closed in. She was what we used to call a 'one-take-Jo'. Whatever she had to do she did it right off and that first take was great. But sometimes she'd say to me, 'I'm going mad on this film. We've got twenty-take-Charlies and thirty-take-Freds and people who keep doing the same old line over and over again' and I think she got very bored with them."

Tommy Fields said: "She was never happy unless she had an audience in front of her and besides she was very conscious of the camera. She did the best she could with the films she worked in but I don't think she ever really made what I would call a good film and I think she felt that, too. She couldn't relax in front of the cameras."

Bearing that in mind and also bearing in mind the fact that in her whole career she only made fifteen films, mostly of very small merit indeed, it may be hard to see how she qualifies in any way for inclusion in a book about movie greats. And yet she does so for two reasons: in the first place, though the films themselves may have been, for the most part, trivial and banal, her own powerful and vibrant personality and her own vast and varied talents come across in every frame. And in the second place, Gracie Fields, both as stage and screen star, seemed somehow to represent the very spirit of Britain during the 1930s, the years of Depression and mass unemployment. She was tough, cheerful, optimistic and unbreakable — and the public responded with an outpouring of love that was quite extraordinary.

Her films and her stage shows played to packed houses. Furthermore, such is the illogical way of the movie industry, her reluctance to make films meant that producers chased her ever more ardently, waving increasingly fat cheques at her. By the mid-1930s she was the biggest female draw in the British cinema even though her pictures, mostly made by Basil Dean, were all pretty much the same. Dean was a respected film-maker but his appreciation of Gracie Fields was somewhat hampered by the fact that he had no discernible sense of humour. Gracie was aware of that but more or less resigned herself to the fact that there was little she could do to change the situation until Dean, by casting her opposite John Loder in *Love, Life and Laughter,* inadvertently did her a great favour, though it hardly turned out to his own advantage.

One day, as they waited between set-ups on that film, Gracie said: "John, how can I be funny with old Basil looking at me like that all the time?"

Loder replied: "You know, I've just done a film with a fellow called Monty Banks and he kept everybody in stitches of laughter."

"Then bring him down for lunch next Sunday," Gracie said and so it was arranged. The result of this casual conversation was that in Monty Banks she found both a new director for her next picture (*Queen of Hearts* co-starring John Loder) and also a new husband. The films she made with Banks may not have been a great deal better in content than their predecessors but at least they had style and humour, a pleasing lightness of touch. Furthermore, although by now she was in her late thirties, Banks created a more glamorous and romantic image for her.

He was an Italian, a fact that seemed unimportant at the time they met but one that was to have great significance for them both a few years later, and was himself a popular comedian and actor (in Italy, anyway) as well as a talented director.

He made Gracie laugh — which was a lot more than could be said for Archie Pitt, from whom she was now divorced — and very swiftly they became a great deal closer than just good friends. Banks, indeed, took over Archie Pitt's role as her guide and mentor and was deeply involved when Hollywood began to court her.

Hollywood, or more specifically MGM, had shown an interest some time earlier but had decided against making any kind of offer to her when the studio's representative in London compared her, rather shrewdly, with America's favourite crackerbarrel philosopher and comedian, Will Rogers. "Each of them," he said, "has a brand of humour which is strictly national," by which he meant that it didn't necessarily travel well. In the event, he was probably right at that. Gracie's humour certainly travelled well to what was then the British Empire but it was a taste that Americans never really acquired. Besides, she herself had qualms about Hollywood. "I've always been afraid," she said, "that they might make me sort of half and half and they might not use the right half either."

Nevertheless, Darryl F. Zanuck, head of 20th Century Fox, was eager to sign her and was able to attract her attention with the offer of a fee, somewhere around £200,000, which was even more than Mae West was getting and at that time Mae West was reputed to be the best-paid actress in America.

Gracie's was "the highest salary ever paid to a human being", according to the Fox publicity people — a most unlikely tale, of course, and almost certainly a lie. But, even so, £200,000 was a very considerable sum of money, especially in those days, and Gracie was in rather urgent need of a considerable sum of money because she had just been faced by an enormous tax bill from the Inland Revenue. Her income was immense but so were her outgoings and she had not then begun on the lucrative property investments that were to make her very rich later.

She also managed to get rid of a great deal of money through sheer generosity, especially to her family. "She gave us hundreds of pounds," Tommy Fields said. "I mean, it was embarrassing really at times. She didn't have to do it. We never wanted any money, we were all independent, all of us. But she thought nothing of giving us £500 each for Christmas. It was very nice but a bit embarrassing because what could we give her in return? What could we buy her? She had everything."

But still, even for a woman who has everything, £200,000 is a tidy sum and so Gracie duly went to Hollywood, though not before she had thoughtfully inserted in her contract a clause stipulating that all her films for Fox were to be made in England.

Eventually, then, her trip to California was mainly for the purpose of publicity and for what Fox regarded as the necessary process of grooming and glamorising. It was fairly typical of Hollywood that, having first been attracted by her naturalness and individuality, the studio promptly attempted to destroy these attributes by having her teeth either pulled out or capped and by changing her hairstyle and her clothes to bring her as close as possible to the current filmland stereotype. Gracie put up with this nonsense until she got back to England, whereupon she threw away the Hollywood gladrags and returned to her normal self.

Monty Banks had gone with her to California as part of the deal and it was he who directed her first Fox picture — shot in England, of course — *We're Going to be Rich*, in which her co-star was Victor McLaglen. It was an auspicious start to her contract, for the critic C. A. Lejeune said of it that it was "the first successful attempt to integrate her personality into a first-rate script and production". The film was made in 1938, in which year she also reached forty and was accorded two considerable honours. First she was awarded the CBE (and said to her mother after the investiture, "they should have pinned it on you") and secondly she was granted the Freedom of the City of Rochdale.

Of the two, it was the recognition by her home town that pleased her more.

She was now at the height of her popularity. She made two more films — *Keep Smiling* and *Shipyard Sally* — for Fox, her occasional stage appearances were to standing room only and her records were invariably best-sellers. But at this point she became dangerously ill with cancer of the cervix and was advised to have an immediate operation. The prognosis, however, was not good. The position, according to Tommy Fields, was that "if she didn't have the operation she would die within seven months and if she did have it there was slightly less than a fifty-fifty chance that she would survive. Anyhow, she decided to take a chance on that and thank God she did."

The operation took place at the Chelsea Women's Hospital in London and the public reaction to the news of her illness was simply phenomenal. It was as if the entire nation were waiting with baited breath for her to recover. Special prayers for her were offered up in churches all around the country; the *Daily Express* published a cartoon by Strube which showed a man standing under a window at the hospital and bore the simple caption "Our Gracie"; the Queen sent her a message of goodwill; Britain's leading politicians sent her flowers; and half a million people sent her letters and get-well cards.

Tommy Fields said: "I don't think it's ever been heard of before. I mean, the whole country was praying in church for her life. Such was the love for this woman that everybody felt as though she was a part of their own lives."

One result of the operation, of course, was that she had now lost any possible chance of having children, although to what extent that may have upset her is hard to say. Lilian Aza said: "She always said she'd have liked children of her own but I don't think she really took much interest. There were some wonderful kids at the orphanage that she could have taken under her wing and educated and looked after but she didn't."

By the time Gracie left hospital it was the summer of 1939. She was advised to rest for two years and after broadcasting a message of thanks to the nation (and a broadcast by Gracie was always a notable event. On one occasion an entry in Hansard read: "Gracie Fields is on the air tonight. It is obvious that the debate must end at an early hour.") she went to Capri with Monty Banks and Mary Davey to convalesce. This respite, however, was not to last long.

"It was obvious the war was going to start," said Mary Davey, "and she said, 'I must go back and do my bit' and we got back two days before war broke out actually. And right away, although she shouldn't have been working for two years, she decided she must go to France and do some concerts for the troops. We went out there in November and she was doing two or three concerts a day."

At this time she and Monty Banks decided to get married and to do so in California where Gracie's parents were now living and where she had already invested in a fair amount of property. After the honeymoon Mr. and Mrs. Banks returned to Europe, where she did another gruelling concert tour of France on behalf of the troops. But now Italy entered the war on the wrong side and Monty Banks, who had been born Mario Bianchi and was still an Italian citizen, became overnight an enemy alien. He was appraised of this fact while still in France and was also told that he faced internment if he went back to England. Choosing, wisely no doubt, to forego this doubtful privilege he nipped back instead across the Atlantic to America and Gracie went with him. To her mind it was the natural thing to do; he was her husband and her place was by his side.

The British Press, however, didn't see it quite like that. As soon as she had gone it began a smear campaign against her, calling her a traitor for abandoning England and accusing her, falsely, of having smuggled her fortune and her jewellery out of the country. Suddenly the woman everyone had loved and whose ill-health only a year or so ago had caused deep concern to the entire nation was presented as an object worthy of hatred and contempt.

"It was all so wrong," said Mary Davey, "it was all so untrue what they said and it really hurt her. She was really upset about it."

Not only were the Press stories wrong and untrue; they were also unfair. Admittedly, Gracie was living in sunshine and safety in Santa Monica and admittedly she found time to continue her film career in Hollywood during the war years. But she also did a considerable amount to raise money for Britain and to entertain the troops. One concert tour of Canada brought in £300,000 to help the war effort and twice, in 1941 and 1943, she returned to England for lengthy tours of factories, army camps, shipyards and munitions works. Her audiences, having read their newspapers, were at first wary and hostile, then warmly affectionate. Nevertheless, the Press continued its campaign against her, alleging that she visited the wrong places, that her tours were too short or that she short-changed the audience — this latter despite the fact that she would do three or four shows and sing as many as sixty songs in one day. She bore this most philosophically in the circumstances, saying that perhaps she had been built up too high, had become too much of an idol and that idols were invariably torn down in the end. Perhaps, though, the Press equated her with that other idol of the 1930s, Edward VIII, who, as the Prince of Wales, had been quite as popular as Gracie but who had then deserted his country by marrying Mrs. Simpson. The newspapers had turned against him too, though with a little more reserve, for fear of offending the royal family. In any event, the vilification of Gracie continued and was so fierce in one forces' paper, the *Eighth Army News,* that Winston Churchill himself finally intervened and told the editors to stop.

Meanwhile, Gracie's life in California was at least agreeable. She was certainly happier with Monty Banks than she had been with Archie Pitt, although this marriage, too, was very much a business arrangement. Banks had been in the film industry, both in England and America, since the early days of silent pictures and he, too, knew a good investment when he saw one. But he does appear to have provided his wife with cheerful company, if not passionate devotion, and there is general agreement that he was an amiable and likeable person to have around. On the other hand, he was also a compulsive gambler.

"He couldn't stop gambling," said Tommy Fields. "He liked to play cards and games like baccarat. And he was playing with the big boys in America, Zanuck and all that crowd, and he really didn't have the capital for that so he was certainly using a lot of Gracie's money as well."

Fortunately, she was earning quite a lot at that time, for between her second wartime tour of Britain in 1943 and the declaration of peace in 1945 she made four Hollywood films, the best of them being *Holy Matrimony,* in which she played a straight role opposite Monty Woolley and the last of them, known in Britain as *Madame Pimpernel* and in America as *Paris Underground,* a tale of two women carrying on resistance work in France during the Nazi occupation. Her co-star in this was Constance Bennett and it was not only the last picture Gracie made in Hollywood but the last she made anywhere.

Film-making was a career into which she had entered reluctantly and which she appears to have abandoned with no sign of regret. Nobody, not even Monty Banks really, though perhaps he came closest, and certainly not Fox, ever quite found the right way to use her in the cinema. Too often the roles she was given called only for a few songs and broad comedy; her acting ability, which indeed existed and which once caused James Agate to reflect that he would like to see her playing St. Joan, remained virtually untapped.

If she herself had cared more, then no doubt her pictures would have been better but she never did care much because film was a medium in which she always felt uncomfortable. She was an artist who responded to an audience; the warmer the audience the better she became. In the silence of a sound stage there was no reaction, nobody laughed, nobody wept, nobody cheered. In such an alien atmosphere her self-confidence waned and, besides, she was nervous in the company of other film stars, whom she regarded as "real film stars". Arthur Askey remembered her being in a state of total confusion because she was going to be introduced to Maurice Chevalier; Mary Davey recalled her being unable to bring herself to call Evelyn Laye anything but "Miss Laye" because "she's a very big star, you know". In the cinema even more than anywhere else she was, as her brother Tommy said, incapable of realising how extremely famous she was herself. And so, when she finished filming *Paris Underground* and her contract with Fox was over, she left the cinema for good and probably with relief.

On Armistice Day, November 11th, 1945, Gracie was in Italy singing for the troops at a concert in the Naples Opera House and immediately after that she and Monty Banks went back to Capri. During the next three years she starred in a series of radio programmes called "Gracie's Working Party" and made a number of records, all of which sold as rapidly as ever. But the British Press was still hostile to her and it was not until 1948, when she was fifty, that she returned to London for her first public appearance since the wartime tour of 1943. The venue she chose for this come-back was the London Palladium.

Lilian Aza said: "She was pretty nervous about it. She had to walk out on that stage at the Palladium, which held about 4,000 people, I think, and she wasn't to know how they were going to take to her or what was going to happen to her. And she came out and she sang 'Take Me to Your Heart Again' — you know, she was saying 'let everything be forgiven'. And when she'd finished I don't think there was anybody who wasn't crying. She had a standing ovation."

So now a belated peace was restored between Gracie and the Press. She did more concerts, made more records but by the end of the 1940s she decided to live permanently in Capri, where she and Monty Banks built a restaurant and a swimming pool. In 1950, however, with this enterprise still incomplete and while the couple were returning to Italy by train Banks collapsed and died of a heart attack.

Even if it had not been the most passionate of marriages, the bereavement left Gracie understandably depressed and lonely. As an antidote, she involved herself once more with concerts and recordings and between times kept her house in Capri well stocked with friends and family. It was there, in Capri, in 1951 that she first became acquainted with Boris Alperovici. He was a Bessarabian by birth, a resident of Capri since 1927 and now an Italian citizen. He was also a gifted but unambitious man who spoke five languages fluently, had studied architecture and physics and made his living by building and repairing electrical equipment. In fact he first met Gracie when he was summoned to her house to mend her radio set. Neva Hecker, who had been Gracie's secretary and companion in the Hollywood period, said: "I came over to Italy to stay in 1951 and I went to Capri and spent three weeks there and I knew then that she was interested in Boris. He came to lunch most days but she used to try and put him next to me, saying he was a good man and then one day I asked the maid where Gracie was and she said she was walking, downstairs. And I looked downstairs and there were the two of them swinging along hand in hand."

For the most part the relationship between Gracie and Boris was kept secret, largely at his instigation. "Gracie was travelling," he said in his slightly eccentric English. "She was a big star, she was very famous. I was just a normal, grey person living quietly in Capri. I was a bachelor, I had never been married before. I was an orphan. I lost my mother when I was three years old. I lost my father when I was seven. I was living alone quite quietly. I thought I was not made to be married."

In the end Gracie decided the only way to cope with this bashful orphan of forty-nine was to propose to him, which she did. He accepted and so in 1952 at the Catholic church in Capri Gracie, now aged fifty-four, became Mrs. Boris Alperovici. The announcement of the impending marriage came as a considerable surprise to her friends, particularly Lilian Aza.

"She rang up on Christmas Eve and said, 'Now listen to this song' and started singing 'I'm in love with a Wonderful Guy'. I said, 'Have you gone crackers or something?' and she said, No, and then she told me all about Boris. And I was very surprised. As a matter of fact she did a concert in Hamburg shortly afterwards and I flew over and saw her and tried to get her to promise she wouldn't marry him for twelve months. I said, 'You're not a child. It doesn't matter if you wait awhile. Just wait for twelve months and make sure you're doing the right thing.' And she promised she would but she went straight back and married him."

Lilian Aza's natural agent's caution was not, however, echoed by Gracie's family, including her mother, who took to Boris very well. "He's a very nice man," said Tommy Fields. "He's a very strong man, strong-willed, but he's also a very good businessman and he really looked after Gracie's interests during her life with him."

Curiously enough, although he was aware that she was a very big star when he married her, Boris had very little idea of the peculiar appeal she had. In Capri he had heard her sing snatches of opera and one or two of her comic songs, which he didn't like, but it was not until they were married and he accompanied her to England that he ever saw her perform in a theatre. It had a profound effect upon him. After the concert, Lilian Aza said, "He came back to me and he was really astounded. He said, 'I am very upset. Gracie sang "Christopher Robin is Saying his Prayers" and you could have heard a pin drop in the theatre. It was absolutely fantastic. And then as she went to finish the song the pianist moved his chair and made a noise and Gracie said to the audience, "Oh, excuse me, it's my tummy rumbling.'' I thought this was dreadful, this was dreadful.' But I said, 'You know, Boris, that's what people love. That *is* Gracie. That's what makes her so wonderful to the public.' But, you see, to him, it was just absolutely ghastly.''

From the time of her third marriage onwards Gracie was more or less in semi-retirement. She travelled a good deal and went frequently to England for concerts and recording sessions and for a while had her own series on television. But much of her time was spent with Boris on Capri where her stature was such that she was visited by royalty, including King Farouk of Egypt who, at lunch one day, asked whether he could stay with her if, as was becoming pretty well inevitable, he was ejected from his throne.

"Grace," said Tommy Fields, "was taken aback by this and took it all with a pinch of salt. She said, 'Well, yes. Yes, if you've got nowhere else to go we'll find room for you.' And she never thought any more about it. Well, of course, a year later he did abdicate and suddenly one morning she looks through the window and there's this yacht coming towards her with ex-King Farouk and his wife and all his henchmen.

"So, of course, she fixed them all up and later she talked to me and she said, 'He's very nice, he's a nice fat lad and his wife's a very sweet woman and everything, but,' she said, 'he'll have to go. You see, the trouble is he wants the swimming pool to himself. Nobody else is allowed to go there because he's still scared of being shot or something so he has all his henchmen round the pool and he's the only fellow having a swim. Well, I've got my clientèle to think about. I can't have this; he'll have to go.' And so she told him and he went."

Despite her stature on Capri, despite the fact that her restaurant and swimming pool were always well patronised, especially by British holidaymakers who often chose to go to the island simply in order to see Gracie, Lilian Aza believes she would have preferred to live in England towards the end of her life. "But I don't think Boris would have liked to live in England."

Gracie was much influenced by what Boris wanted. "She was fond of him and I don't think she would have liked to live apart from him. I don't think she liked to be without a husband. She liked to have a man around for company. She wasn't man-mad but she liked to have a companion."

Gracie Fields entered the last year of her life on a note, or rather several notes, of triumph. She was asked to open a theatre which had been named after her in Rochdale; she was given an ovation when she appeared, as a surprise item, at the Royal Variety Show; and she was created a Dame of the British Empire, Dame Gracie Fields. But in the late summer she was taken seriously ill with pneumonia. She left hospital earlier than was advisable, insisting in a letter to a friend that "the old girl's back on her feet again". But not, unfortunately, for long. Just after breakfast on September 27th, 1979, the old girl decided to take a nap and died in her sleep. She was eighty-one. She was buried on a hillside in the non-Catholic cemetery at Capri and, the common touch prevailing till the end, her pall-bearers were waiters from her restaurant.

When some months later I talked to the people who had known her well, they all spoke of her with genuine warmth and affection. She was a kind, generous, modest woman, they said, a marvellous person, great fun to be with. But was she a happy woman, I asked Lilian Aza, had hers been a happy life?

"Well," she said, "it wouldn't have been a happy life if it had been mine. You see, I don't think Gracie was capable of real love as I would be and I hope you would be. I think all her love went into her songs. If you hear her sing 'The House is Haunted' you feel absolutely the agony that a woman goes through when a man walks out on her. It really tears at you the way she puts it over and I think she put everything into her songs. I don't think there was much left for anything outside of that."

She also said: "Gracie was a wonderful person really and I think one of the most wonderful things about her was that she had absolutely no conceit. She never behaved in any way at all like a famous person. And yet in many ways I think she led a sad life really. She had everything — this marvellous applause, this marvellous acclaim — and yet she had nothing, no family of her own and not enough love. She was a very dominating personality with practically everybody except her menfolk and I consider that she allowed them to dictate to her."

Certainly her first two marriages were either unhappy or, at least, unsatisfactory affairs and she probably was dominated both by Pitt and Banks. But Boris maintained that her time with him had been happy and he spoke of her with obvious emotion and sense of loss. Indeed, her death — which in Rochdale, according to the *Daily Telegraph,* was likened to "having a bit of the old town knocked down" — brought a sense of loss generally.

"You see," said Mary Davey, "you can't really describe this fantastic thing she had with an audience. She was a genius, I think. You couldn't say, 'Well, either you love her or you hate her,' because everybody just loved her. When she was at the Palladium, for instance, a lot of her fans bought tickets for the whole week and they'd go on the first night and the second night and watch the programme all the way through, but after that they'd just come in at the end, just to see Gracie and when she came on there was, oh, a sort of electric feeling, everybody on the edge of their seats watching her and listening to her. You can't define what her influence was on people; it was something quite uncanny. You could laugh at her till you cried with laughing but also, no matter how tough you were, you wept at some of the serious numbers. I've done it night after night. I've been there at the side of the stage and I've heard her sing the same song, night after night, but come to a certain song and a certain phrasing and there you were again, bawling your eyes out. Grown men I've seen crying. She had, I don't know, some quality in her and in her voice that touched a nerve in a way that was amazing and unique."

Gracie Fields was, I think, quite simply a phenomenon, a marvellous singer, an able comedienne and by no means a negligible actress. But all those things together aren't enough to explain the extraordinary effect she had on her audience or the hold she had on the affections of the British public or the quality she had that made half a million people write to her when she was ill with cancer, or caused Parliament to rise early so its members could listen to her on the radio, or impelled a theatre audience on one occasion to carry her in triumph shoulder-high down the entire length of the Strand.

As long ago as 1933 J. B. Priestley wrote of her: "Listen to her for a quarter of an hour and you will learn more about Lancashire women and Lancashire than you would from a dozen books on the subject. All the qualities are there, shrewdness, homely simplicity, irony, fierce independence, an impish delight in mocking whatever is thought to be affected or pretentious."

When she died, the *Guardian* described her as "the Rochdale mill girl who was almost the exact double of Lady Churchill but at the other end of the social scale". What it might have added is that, even more than Lady Churchill, she transcended the social scale. Ardent admirers of Gracie Fields were to be found in the cobbled streets of Rochdale and also in Buckingham Palace. The quality of stardom, as I've quoted before in this book, is "that little something extra" but even that is not enough to account for Gracie Fields. This and future generations will probably never quite understand the adulation that was heaped on her because virtually all that is left of Gracie Fields the performer is on film and film never quite did her justice.

I've seen her on TV and on film and I've discussed her with my parents who were, give or take a decade, of her generation. I admired her; they adored her. But then they had seen her in the flesh, pre-war, when she was at the height of her powers. And in trying to explain her I'm left with the thought that she must have had that little something extra and then a little something extra on top of that — something intangible but amazingly potent because, whatever it was, it made Gracie Fields incomparably the most popular entertainer Britain ever had.

Leslie Howard

The image of the perfect English gentleman and a truly accomplished philanderer.

above: Leslie Howard and his wife Ruth, who rescued him from his
extra-marital adventures and even cured his boils.

opposite: With his son, Ronald, at Palm Springs enjoying the only
thing he really liked about California — the sunshine.

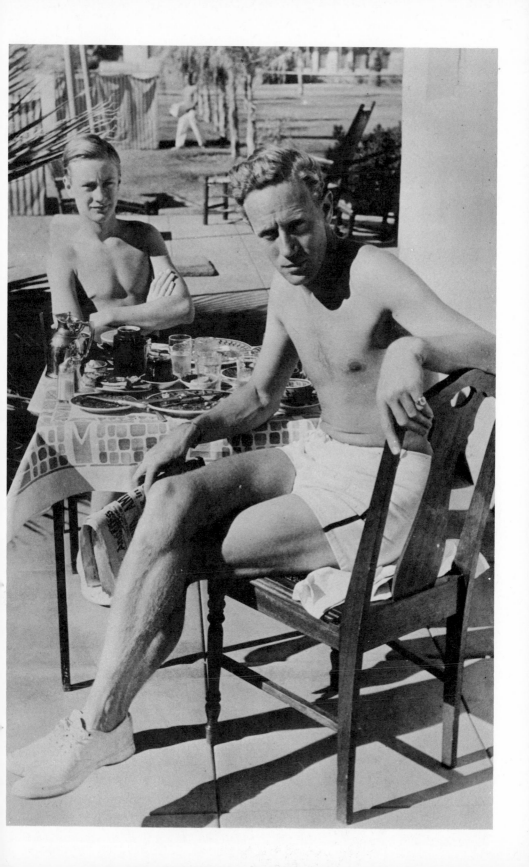

above : Howard at home in Surrey, living the life of a well-heeled country gentleman.

opposite above : Violette Cunnington in Pimpernel Smith.
Howard's relationship with her was "the most serious love affair of his life".

opposite below : Howard directing Pimpernel Smith *and dressed for his role as the professor who rescued intellectuals from the Nazis.*

Around midday on June 1st, 1943, a squadron of German fighter-bombers attacked and shot down a civilian airliner carrying thirteen people from Lisbon to London. The plane plunged into the sea about 180 miles off Cap Finisterre. There were no survivors.

Now why the Nazis chose to destroy this obviously neutral aircraft is one of the unsolved mysteries of the war. Many theories, none of them wholly satisfactory, have been put forward to explain what was quite simply an outrage, a callous disregard of one of the basic tenets of warfare; but it is just possible that one of the targets, one perhaps among several, was a fifty-year-old British actor, Leslie Howard, who had been lecturing in Spain and Portugal on behalf of the Ministry of Information and the British Council.

It's a romantic notion: the might of the Luftwaffe pitted against one unarmed, middle-aged Thespian and, to be fair, it is not the most popular explanation for the attack. And yet it's by no means entirely implausible. For just about three decades on stage and in the international cinema Howard had represented a version of the Englishman that was, in fact, romanticised but so skilfully projected as to appear archetypal: he was slightly vague, slightly shy, slightly — but never too obviously — intellectual and above all decidedly glamorous. To say that most Englishmen aren't really like that is merely to state the obvious; but to an international cinema audience the men of other nationalities weren't like that at all and therefore Howard served admirably as an Identikit portrait of the perfect English gentleman.

Such an image was not, of course, likely to endear him to the Nazis but on the other hand it could hardly, by itself, have enraged them sufficiently to set a whole squadron of fighter-bombers upon him. But in the early years of the war Howard was also a kind of talisman, a symbol of resistance, and his propaganda work for Britain in the form of broadcasts to America in the days when the United States was still neutral and in films like *Pimpernel Smith* and *The First of the Few* had earned him an honourable place on the Nazi hate list. So it's not altogether inconceivable that the Germans wished him dead and, given an opportunity to kill him, promptly seized it.

Whatever the reason for his death, the manner of it brought an appropriately tragic and romantic end to the life of one of the most popular and successful of all British film stars. In the words of George Cukor, who directed him both on stage and screen, he was "mysterious in a very odd way and his death was mysterious too.

He sort of went off in a cloud and one never knew what happened to him. He died a kind of heroic death and that was right."

Leslie Howard wasn't really mysterious, though, except perhaps in the context of Hollywood where the stars tend to reverse the policy of the iceberg and reveal at least nine-tenths of themselves to the public gaze. In such a place Howard might easily appear mysterious because he always retained a peculiarly British obsession with privacy. His emotions and his relationships — above all his relationships with women, which were many and varied — were matters that he regarded as being of interest and importance only to himself.

In Hollywood where, generally speaking, even a movie star's most casual one-night stand is accorded a blow-by-blow account in the gossip columns, Howard would indeed have been an object of curiosity, because while he was alive he was regarded as an impeccable husband, practising unswerving fidelity, and it was only after his death that he was revealed as an accomplished philanderer whose track record, in the considered opinion of Humphrey Bogart, was such as to make "Errol Flynn look like a fag". (Mind you, there are those who now suggest that Errol Flynn *was* a fag to which one can only retort that if this were so he did quite an incredible job of establishing heterosexual cover for himself.)

The antecedents of Leslie Howard, the accomplished but studiedly vague philanderer, do admittedly add another small touch of mystery to the story of his life and death. The standard account of his background is that he was born Leslie Howard Stainer in Forest Hill, London, on April 3rd, 1893. His father was Frank Stainer, Hungarian by birth, British by adoption, who worked in a stockbroker's office in the City and his mother was Lilian Howard. The *Dictionary of National Biography,* however, had a slightly different version according to which his surname was actually Steiner and his mother's original maiden name was Blumberg. Furthermore, Leslie Howard is accorded an entry in the *Encyclopaedia Judaica,* leading to the assumption that he was, if only on his mother's side, Jewish. It's not improbable that both accounts of the family surname are correct, that on arrival in Britain Frank Steiner became Stainer and Lilian Blumberg became Lilian Howard.

What is, however, certain is that soon after the arrival of their first child, Leslie, Steiner-Stainer and his wife, the ex-Miss Blumberg-Howard, moved to Vienna with the result that their son, who was later to represent everything that was English, spent the first few years of his life speaking only German. When the family returned to London, Frank Stainer — as he now was, whatever he may have been before — again found work in the City and he and Lilian had four more children, among them a daughter, Irene, who was considerably younger than her brother Leslie.

She remembered him as "a dreamy kind of boy, thinking of everything except what he should have been thinking about, certainly in the way of schooling". This schooling took place at Dulwich College, which Leslie disliked intensely on account of his shyness and where he indulged in the most un-British habit of writing plays in Latin. "He was always thinking and dreaming of something else," Irene Howard said. "He never seemed to be quite with one. But on the other hand he was very alert, he didn't miss much really."

The dominant figure in the family was Lilian. Frank Stainer appears to have been a rather stern paterfamilias to whom his elder son was never very close but Lilian, a frustrated actress herself, encouraged the boy to take part in amateur dramatics in which, once he had left school, he sought relief from the drudgery of the bank where his father had found him a job. He and the bank were by no means suited to each other and there were no regrets on either side when, in 1914, Leslie volunteered for the Army and became a subaltern in the 20th Hussars.

During an early leave at home he became engaged to a young woman whose name is now forgotten but who was known for some reason as "Buzz". At that time Leslie was not, according to Irene, at all a wordly man as far as women were concerned but clearly he had an innate ability to handle the sex because, on his return to his unit at Colchester, he struck up a friendship with Ruth Martin, a secretary in the local recruiting office and the daughter of a Regular Army officer. Such was the trust that women misguidedly placed in him that for some time he remained engaged to Buzz despite the fact that his letters to her were adorned by postscripts from Ruth, assuring the innocent fiancee that she was taking care of him.

A situation like that clearly could not last very long, even for the young Leslie Stainer, and eventually he discarded the unfortunate Buzz and became engaged instead to Ruth, whom he decided to marry at once. Irene Howard said: "There was a tremendous commotion going on because his Commanding Officer sent a telegram to my father saying, 'Your son intends to marry tomorrow.' So my poor father rushed down in a frenzy to see what it was all about. The CO, thinking he was going to help, put Leslie on some kind of guard duty but it was too late: Leslie and Ruth had got married the day before.

"So by the time my father arrived it was all over. And when he said, 'What on earth did you do this for?' Leslie said, 'I haven't the faintest idea.' So that was his idea of marriage. I don't think he realised what he'd done or why. It seemed a good idea at that particular moment, I suppose. You see, he was very lonely; he missed my mother a lot when he went into the Army and he wasn't the sort of chap who liked drinking in the mess with the boys. Ruth was very beautiful when she was young and I suppose he found her a sympathetic girl who seemed to adore him and so he could pour out all his thoughts and ambitions to her."

Fortunately for Leslie, Ruth continued to adore him and to cosset him for the rest of his life, though there were many times when it cannot have been easy for her. In the early days, Irene said, "She was great fun. I liked her very much because we went around together and she didn't seem to be bored, even though I was only a child. My mother was marvellous with her because she got on well with everybody. Ruth and my elder sister more or less ignored each other. I don't know that they disliked each other but they certainly didn't take to each other. Perhaps there was a little jealousy there because my sister and Leslie were very much of an age and I suppose they had been fairly close."

In 1916 Howard's regiment was sent to the front line in France and a year later, having lasted much longer than most subalterns, he was invalided out of the Army suffering from severe shell-shock.

Frank Stainer wanted him to return to the dull security of the bank but Lilian suggested that he might try to become an actor, a far more attractive prospect, and so later in 1917 Leslie Stainer, aged twenty-four, dropped his surname and became Leslie Howard, putative actor. In 1918, he also became Leslie Howard, father, when his son Ronald was born and soon after he was an established supporting player in the West End of London in Arnold Bennett's play *The Title*. Within another year he was appearing in short comedy films written by A. A. Milne and had enhanced his stage reputation in Milne's *Mr. Pym Passes By*.

Success had come fairly swiftly and painlessly to him and, not insignificantly, considering the future pattern of his activities, had already brought him to the attention of the postwar breed of newly-liberated young women. Suddenly Ruth found herself relegated to the unwelcome position of wife to a glamorous young actor while girls only a few years younger but a whole generation bolder than she began to pay court to her husband.

It was not, however, until 1920 when Howard first went to America that she can have fully realised the seriousness of her predicament. He went, initially, alone to appear in a play called *Just Suppose,* which turned out to be a highly prophetic tale about the Prince of Wales falling in love with an American girl. Both it and Howard were warmly welcomed in New York and within a few months he could afford to bring his wife and son over to join him. But by then the essential damage had been done and Howard had been discovered by American women — not a particularly difficult trick because he never exactly hid from them.

On the other hand, it doesn't appear to be true to say that Howard actually chased women; he just never seemed to have the energy, or indeed the inclination, to run from them. John Houseman, who co-directed Howard's *Hamlet* on Broadway in the mid-1930s, reckoned that like most great seducers he was a predator who disguised himself as prey. "His Don Juan operation consisted of never wanting to say 'no' and he was a man relentlessly pursued by ladies. The poor fellow was never left alone. They chased him and he would sort of demur mildly but then there came the day when he just didn't want to say 'No' any more."

The secret of this enviable appeal to women is as indefinable as the secret of star quality in an actor. Anybody who could isolate the formula for either and bottle it could become a multi-millionaire overnight. In his sister's view even Howard himself didn't really know what it was that he'd got. "He never looked upon himself as a great glamour boy at all. And he certainly didn't consider himself sexy. In fact he liked to think of himself as rather intellectual. Perhaps it was his very difference that appealed to the American women. He didn't dive at them straight away and so they thought it was up to them to do the diving."

In any event they were diving at him like kamikaze pilots by the time Ruth arrived in New York to begin tracing out what was to become the pattern of their lives. Over the next twenty years she and her husband, either together or separately, continually trekked back and forth across the Atlantic, dividing their time almost equally between Britain and America, while Howard climbed nimbly and without apparent effort to the top of his profession both in the theatre and the cinema.

And all the time Ruth had to cope with the fact that while he was unquestionably devoted to her and their children, her husband was quite incapable of resisting the temptations offered to him by other women. Like a man cheating on his own diet he was constantly nibbling chocolates between his balanced meals at home.

After the success of *Just Suppose,* Howard returned for a year or so to London but the news of his New York fame had made little impression there and in 1922 he went back again to Broadway, where he was in such demand and appeared in so many plays that one theatre critic was prompted to write: "Leslie Howard seems to have been in every first night I have attended."

In 1926 he returned again to London where again the success he had enjoyed in New York capriciously eluded him and so once more he returned to America, where his performance in *Her Cardboard Lover* had the first-night audience chanting his name in an ecstasy of enthusiasm and brought unanimous agreement that he was now among the foremost actors on the English-speaking stage. He repeated the role in London to rather less acclaim, largely because his co-star there was Tallulah Bankhead, who had become the object of a cult and whose hysterical devotees screamed so loudly that most of the dialogue was inaudible. The West End production was, however, notable for the fact that Howard failed to have an affair with Miss Bankhead, though not, apparently, for want of trying on her part.

"Poor Tallulah," said Irene Howard. "She couldn't make him out at all. She tried very hard, bless her heart, but he didn't want anything to do with her. She wasn't his type."

In 1930, after further stage triumphs in *Outward Bound* and *Berkeley Square,* Howard went to Hollywood for the first time. He had made no films since those early silent comedies but now Warner Brothers offered him the lead in the screen version of *Outward Bound.* It was the first of several of his stage productions — *The Animal Kingdom, Berkeley Square* and *The Petrified Forest* among them — to transfer successfully to the cinema. Howard's performance in the film *Outward Bound* looks, half a century later, to be distinctly over-theatrical and indeed over the top but the picture was well received and brought him into great demand among Hollywood tycoons.

In 1931 he appeared in four American films — *Never the Twain Shall Meet, A Free Soul, Five and Ten* and *Devotion* — usually in some kind of heart-throb role, as the cinema capitalised on his stage reputation.

But Howard never really took to Hollywood and the social life of

Beverly Hills. He enjoyed the climate and he enjoyed playing polo. At one time he had a string of six polo ponies and they and the sunshine were his main consolation for having to spend so much time there. Irene Howard said: "He wouldn't stay in Hollywood five minutes longer than he had to. He felt it was all a bit phoney and he had nothing in common with most of the people there. He was a funny man. He didn't really like actors very much. He was far more interested in writers or technical people."

Given his choice — and as far as the thing was possible he made quite sure that he was given his choice — he much preferred the life of a well-heeled country gentleman with Ruth, Ronald and Leslie (his daughter who was born in 1924) at Stowe Maries, his home in Surrey. Far more than any other British star, he skilfully maintained a thriving career for himself on both sides of the Atlantic and because he planned this rather than achieved it by accident he followed his initial flurry of Hollywood films by returning home to make his first British picture, *Service for Ladies* (or *Reserved for Ladies,* as it was called in the USA), for Alexander Korda.

But at this stage he was better known and more popular in America than he was in England and when the Korda film made only a slight impression at the box office in Britain he betook himself to New York again for another great success on the stage in *The Animal Kingdom.* This in turn rekindled Hollywood's interest in him and back he went for three more films. But he always retained a remarkable degree of independence. In an era when Hollywood's object was to sign its stars to exclusive contracts that left them with only a doubtful right to the freehold of their own souls, the longest contract Howard ever signed was a three-year deal for three pictures a year with Warner Brothers. This was negotiated in 1933 and he regretted it at once, on the grounds that though it guaranteed financial security it also guaranteed boredom and bad films. This was not an entirely charitable assessment because one of the pictures he made for Warners was *The Petrified Forest* which, thanks to the teaming of himself and Humphrey Bogart, is one of only a handful of his pre-war films that is familiar to modern audiences.

It was Howard, indeed, who was responsible for Bogart being given the role of the gangster, Duke Mantee. Warners didn't want him: they wanted Edward G. Robinson instead. But Bogart had played the role on Broadway and when Howard agreed to star in the film version he did so only on condition that Bogart should be in it, too. Furthermore, he stubbornly continued to insist upon this even when Warner Brothers put pressure on him to change his mind and Bogart, who was thus given his first significant chance in films, was so grateful that he later named his daughter Lesley in Howard's honour.

It was this kind of unshakeable resolution on Howard's part that also, I suppose, helps to explain George Cukor's description of him as "mysterious". On the face of it there was nothing tough about him at all. To those who knew him only slightly he gave the impression of softness. When she first started working with him Mary Morris, his co-star in *Pimpernel Smith,* thought there was "an old-womanish quality" about him but she soon came to change her mind and in the end she said: "I don't think there was anything soft or effeminate about Leslie. I think he was a man of steel really."

That view was echoed by Michael Powell, who directed him in *49th Parallel,* and said: "He always knew what he wanted. He was a very good businessman and a very strong man. My impression of Leslie is not of the slender, rather boyish-looking man that he appeared to be. I get the impression of a man made of steel, in mind as well as in body."

It was this slenderness, the lightness of his build, that perhaps gave the illusion of weakness but his son, Ronald, remembered him as "a physical man, although he was slight. He was proud of being a fairly physical personality, a sort of butch personality in a way, although he didn't look it."

But, on the other hand, Howard was clever enough, and perhaps steely enough, to appear to be weak and ineffectual whenever it suited his purpose. For example, in order to gain attention on those occasions when the people round him appeared, quite unreasonably, to have other things on their minds than his well-being, he would affect ill-health and indeed he was, in a small way, a practising hypochondriac.

Irene Howard said: "My mother had had a bad heart and he imagined he had a bad heart too. I remember there was one occasion when he and Ruth were having dinner in a Paris restaurant and Leslie suddenly thought he'd had a heart attack. He said he had to get out, get out of the room, get out into the air. So he fell over people's tables and stumbled outside and Ruth was in a great panic, of course, and said, 'Oh my God, Leslie's ill, Leslie's ill!' There was a friend with them, a man friend, and Ruth said, 'Oh, do go and see if Leslie's all right'. So the man rushed out through the swingdoors and Leslie was sitting on the steps in the street and the poor man fell over him and broke his ankle. And Leslie sat up and giggled at him."

But he also had in his armoury an even more potent weapon than hypochondria with which to attract attention and also to extricate himself from awkward situations and that was a carefully-cultivated air of vagueness. It was very much a pose, a mannerism that he adopted when, for instance, he was bored. "He was very vague on things he wanted to be vague about," said Douglas Fairbanks, Junior, who was both his friend and, on two occasions, his co-star in films. "But at the same time he could appear to be vague when in fact he was very alert. You could never be really sure that he had his mind concentrated on what he was doing." It was a characteristic noted and remarked on by all those who were in any way close to him but Mary Morris was not taken in by it. "I never believed in the vagueness," she said. "He'd say, 'Mmm? Oh, yes, yes', as if he wasn't paying attention but he would always go his own way in the end. Leslie's great thing was this gentle, quiet kind of personality and maybe he found that being vague was the best method of getting his own way."

John Houseman, the writer/producer/director, who in his later years turned character actor to such good effect that he won an Academy Award for his supporting role in *The Paper Chase,* was another who was not deceived by the pose: "He didn't strike me as a vague person at all. He was shrewd, he was very much alive and he was a very intelligent man."

In the autumn of 1936 Houseman and Howard co-directed *Hamlet* on Broadway, with Howard of course in the title role. He had never been greatly interested in the classics, although at this time he had just finished playing Romeo (after Robert Donat had declined the role) to Norma Shearer's Juliet in the lavish MGM production. Both of them — Howard, forty-three, and Shearer, thirty-six — were really too old for the parts, a thought which crossed the mind of the director, George Cukor. In the event, though, Cukor thought Howard gave an interesting performance: "He wasn't the fiery Romeo, he wasn't daring and dashing but he spoke it beautifully." At the same time Cukor was quite certain that Howard would not have made a classical actor: "He didn't have the voice, or the posture. He was a different kind of actor."

Nevertheless he was determined to play Hamlet, had spent months talking about it, had enrolled Houseman to share the directing and had even raised the money for the production himself. So, in the summer of 1936, he left Hollywood and went back to England to get ready.

"He went off," said John Houseman, "to prepare himself for this great task of performing Hamlet but when he came back to New York in the fall, ready to go into rehearsal, he really hadn't done a thing. He had done a little thinking but he hadn't learned his words even and this interested me very much because here was this man, quite arbitrarily taking on this gigantic task — it was his own money, his own operation, he didn't have to do it — and yet his indolence was such that he didn't learn the lines."

Houseman found this "terribly surprising" but, "The more I knew him the more I learned that he was this very strange mixture of great energy and great strength and of indolence. And above all he struck me as the most fatalistic man I had ever known. I had the curious feeling that he figured the whole business of his career as a miracle: he'd been born in England, lived in Vienna, became an actor and suddenly overnight had become this extraordinary matinee idol. I think he really thought, as many of us do in the theatre, you know, that he was a victim of one of those accidents that take place and that he was a man who had been favoured by destiny and that whatever happened was bound to happen anyway."

Even without the initial handicap of a Hamlet who didn't know his lines, the Howard–Houseman production was rather an ill-starred venture altogether. There were many delays while Howard got himself ready and there were a number of belated changes in the supporting cast and all these led to an ill-starred arrival on Broadway.

Houseman said: "His timing was such that his arrival in New York coincided with the arrival of John Gielgud in that great production of *Hamlet*, which simply could not fail. John had done it a dozen times before but this particularly had all the auspices: he had Lilian Gish playing Ophelia and he had Judith Anderson, I mean it was an absolute gilt-edged production. But Leslie blithely arrived in New York in competition with Gielgud. I urged him, I begged him not to do it. He could have gone on the road with *Hamlet* and made a fortune and eventually, when Gielgud was out of the way, come into New York with the reputation of his road tour behind him. But, oh no, he came into New York and into one of the biggest theatres in town; it was too big for any *Hamlet* and far too big for his. His whole performance of Hamlet was very interesting because it was beautiful but rather small, rather sinuous, very intelligent. After the try-out in Boston, where we played the Opera House, which is also a huge place, his friends came backstage and said, 'You were wonderful but you are going to make it bigger, aren't you?' So he started making it a little bigger and by the time he opened in New York he wasn't giving that original performance — he was like the frog who wants to blow himself up into an ox and so in New York he was by no means at his best.''

The critical reaction was bad. Quite apart from comparing his performance unfavourably with Gielgud's, the critics thought Howard was like ''a petulant schoolmaster'' or ''a peevish choirboy''. Houseman said: ''I mean, everyone was appalled at the audacity or foolishness of coming in to show himself, in competition with John who was the great Hamlet of his time.''

To be fair, Howard's performance was probably not as bad as the Butchers of Broadway said it was. After a disastrous run in New York, he took the production away, dusted it off, polished it up and then went on the road tour that Houseman had advised him to undertake earlier. ''By the time he reached Los Angeles five months later,'' Houseman said, ''he was back giving a very, very interesting and quite remarkable performance.''

On the face of it, Howard's determination to set himself up in competition with one of the great classical actors of this century was a gesture of pure arrogance, but if so it would have been very much out of character. Howard was a man who not only knew his limitations but also, as a rule, made a very shrewd calculation of the odds. A few years earlier he had been invited to co-star in a film with Greta Garbo, without doubt the biggest female star of her time, and to everyone's astonishment had turned her down with this explanation: ''She has a peculiarly dominating personality on the screen and that is why I declined the part. I should not hesitate to play opposite the most glamorous of stage actresses because a play can be depended upon to materialise as rehearsed. A picture is different. Added to the terrific competition of her personality, which no man has equalled, the film would naturally be cut to her advantage and then where should I be?''

In view of that very balanced assessment of the probabilities, it seems likely that he knew his Hamlet would be a gamble but took the chance anyway, either out of fatalism, as Houseman suggested, or, more probably, because he planned this one, big classical performance as his farewell to the theatre, for Hamlet was indeed his last appearance on the stage and he may well have intended it to be so from the start. Unlike most actors, Howard didn't really like acting. To both Douglas Fairbanks and his sister Irene he confessed that it embarrassed him, that he felt it was no way for a grown man to be earning a living.

Undoubtedly he enjoyed the material rewards that came with it and certainly nobody ever forced him to be an actor or to continue acting as long as he did. But the role of actor, and especially the role of matinee idol and star, made him uneasy. "I think he felt it was all right to start with," said Irene Howard, "when he was young and just getting going. But it didn't satisfy him later."

Stage acting in particular began to lose its attraction for him by the middle of the 1930s. His son, Ronald, believed that by then the constant repetition, night after night, of the same role bored him and drained him of physical energy. "The really physical actor enjoys it. He enjoys putting on the make-up, he enjoys the adrenalin charge he gets when the curtain goes up. But I think Leslie never quite recharged his batteries and after he'd been about six weeks in a production he'd explored all he could do with it, whereas in films there wasn't this repetition and boredom; every day brought a different set-up."

As time went by, even acting in films became less and less satisfying and his interest began to turn towards directing and producing. In 1939 he took his first step along that path by co-directing (with Anthony Asquith) Gabriel Pascal's film version of *Pygmalion,* in which he played Professor Higgins.

The picture was an enormous success (and is still absorbing to watch even today) despite the fact that Howard and the author, George Bernard Shaw, had serious disagreements about it. Irene Howard said: "Leslie tried to say that Higgins was obviously in love with Eliza but Shaw wouldn't have it. 'Oh, no, no,' he said, 'nonsense. He's just interested in her as an academic proposition,' and Leslie said, 'You don't realise what you've written. The man's in love with her. Couldn't we suggest this in one line at the end somewhere?' But Shaw still wouldn't agree. So Leslie had to suggest what he felt in the way he played the part and managed to get it over."

Shaw, much disgruntled by the way things had turned out, wrote when the film appeared: "It is amazing how hopelessly wrong Leslie is. However, the public will like him and probably want him to marry Eliza, which is just what I don't want." He was right about one thing at least: the public did like Howard. They also liked the film, though without Howard they might not have done. Wendy Hiller, who played Eliza, said: "It wouldn't have had a world market if Leslie hadn't played it. He was the only possible person at that time to do it. If you were criticising you could wonder whether, in the purely Shavian sense, he was entirely successful. But he *was* entirely successful for the film."

Pygmalion, however, did far more for Howard than merely confirm his status as a top-ranking romantic actor and open the way for a new career as a director. Indeed it had the most dramatic effect upon his life because during the course of it he fell in love. Up to this point — and with only one exception — Howard's extra-marital adventures had, broadly speaking and in the words of his son, Ronald, taken the form of "a sort of high-wire act with various attractive ladies. He had a kind of ethereal quality, there was always something held back, something intangible and I think women found this particularly fascinating. And he was very sensitive to admiration from women but I don't think he was too carried away. He always kept the thing in perspective and he was very discreet."

The only time he had come close to falling off the high-wire was in his affair with Merle Oberon. This probably started around 1934 when they made *The Scarlet Pimpernel* together, smouldered on for some while and then burst into leaping flames the following year when Howard was appearing on Broadway in *The Petrified Forest*.

He was then so taken with the lady that he left the family home in New York and moved into an hotel to be with her. This, in itself, was unusual. In the past when he was involved in one of his dalliances Howard might not have come home until dawn but at least he had come home. Now, however, he had broken away from wife and children and for the first and only time Ruth seriously considered divorce. She left New York for Los Angeles to give herself time for thought before she made any irrevocable decision and in the meantime the Oberon affair fizzled out.

It ended in most unromantic circumstances when Howard was afflicted with an attack of boils with which he coped far less philosophically than Job had done, though admittedly in rather different circumstances. Miss Oberon apparently was perfectly prepared to provide comfort and solace but Howard decided that in these dire straits there was only one woman who could really help him and that woman was Ruth. So he took himself and his boils back to her.

But it had, for a while, been quite a famous affair and, unusually, news of it had reached the Press. A reporter, approaching Howard on the subject, asked if there was any truth in the rumours of a possible divorce and Howard, bristling with self-righteousness, replied: "Certainly not. No man would throw away the sort of family life I enjoy. My wife and children are essential to my existence."

And indeed this was true. Howard was passionately fond of his children and, in his own way, of Ruth. But if they were essential to him so were his extra-curricular adventures. The accepted explanation for his conduct is that when a woman made him an offer he couldn't refuse he was too weak even to contemplate refusing it. But unless he suffered from satyriasis, which is possible but unlikely, there must have been some deeper psychological reason for his multitudinous affairs. Perhaps this endless parade of casual women scratched some philanderer's itch that otherwise he couldn't reach.

In any event he needed his family and he needed his women but, with the exception of the Oberon escapade, he kept his emotions, if not his appetites, under control until he made *Pygmalion* and fell in love with a young French woman named Violette Cunnington. She was the secretary and assistant to the producer of the film, Gabriel Pascal, and she was about twenty years younger than Howard, who was then forty-five, a dangerous age for a man to fall in love — or at least as dangerous as any other age.

By the end of the film Violette had become Howard's personal secretary and travelled with him to Hollywood where he was to make *Gone with the Wind*. Later, to avoid scandal and to kill off the rumours that were beginning to surround them, Howard brought Ruth and Leslie out to Hollywood and established them in a house in Beverly Hills, the only house he ever owned in California. But at the same time he set up Violette in another house only a few streets away and spent at least half his time living there with her.

About that relationship with Violette Cunnington, Ronald Howard said: "It was the most serious love affair in his life, without any question. She was the most charming girl, most attractive. In fact I fell for her myself. At that time [during the making of *Pygmalion*] I didn't realise how serious the affair was. I just thought that he was rather lucky at his advanced age to have such an attractive young secretary. I thought no more about it than that."

In those early days, first in London then in Hollywood, the affair was still comparatively discreet and probably accepted by Ruth as just another passing fancy on her husband's part. Howard, in any case, was much involved with playing Ashley Wilkes in *Gone with the Wind*. This is perhaps his most famous role but it is also the one that in a certain respect has done his reputation the greatest harm. He disliked the part intensely and resisted offers to play it for some time, arguing that "I haven't the slightest intention of playing a weak, watery character such as Ashley." In the end the producer, David O. Selznick, overcame his resistance by offering him, as a quid pro quo, the leading role (opposite the young Ingrid Bergman) in *Intermezzo* and — this was the clincher — agreeing to let him co-produce that picture.

That Selznick knew what he was about is proved by the success of *Gone with the Wind* and the excellence of Howard's performance in it. But that Howard, too, knew the dangers is equally proved by the fact that he is now largely remembered as Ashley, a fact that does a gross dis-service to his memory. Those who have only seen him in *Gone with the Wind* — and they must be counted in millions — will for ever think of him as "a weak, watery character" and will probably never realise that it's an immense tribute to his ability that, though he was not in the least weak and watery, he could project such an image so memorably.

While *Gone with the Wind* and *Intermezzo* were being made, Howard continued to lead his double life in Beverly Hills but by now it was the summer of 1939 and war in Europe was clearly inescapable. So together with his family — and Violette — he returned to England for good. He was planning to go there anyway to make a film (which never in the end got off the ground) called *The Man Who Lost Himself*. But his agent, not exactly an unbiased witness after all, capitalised on his client's move by extolling his "typically English, blind, unswerving loyalty to King and country" and indeed this was not entirely hyperbole. Howard by then was forty-six years old and he could easily have sat out the war in America. Many other British actors did so, after all.

But both Ronald Howard and Michael Powell believe firmly that in this time of national peril England was where Howard wanted to be. And so, inspired by patriotism as much as anything else, he returned to Britain and again set up two separate homes for himself: one in Surrey, where he deposited Ruth and his children, and the other in Denham, Bucks, where Violette was installed.

Ronald Howard said he knew then, for the first time, that the affair was serious. "He began to divide himself into two parts, as it were. He lived most of the week in Denham and came home to us at weekends."

Now at this point it may be wondered how Ruth reacted to this state of affairs and indeed how she had reacted over the years to all the other states of affairs in which Howard had involved himself. At times she seems to have been, quite understandably, extremely jealous of her husband's casual lovers.

But she always had, and must have known she had, an exceptionally strong hold on him. Marc Connelly, a member of the famous literary Algonquin set in New York, to which Howard had been an occasional visitor, once said: "Leslie is always afraid Ruth will go out in the morning before he's awake and forget to put the manacles on."

This is not, however, to suggest that Howard was at all henpecked; no husband who lived the way he did could possibly be so described. Rather did he use Ruth as a shield and a means of escape from difficult situations. The fact that until he met Violette he had never been inextricably involved with any other woman is probably due to his having allowed, or even encouraged, his wife to rescue him from entanglements that he didn't really want in the first place. Thus he was quite content to give the impression, to men as well as to women, that he was manacled to her.

"I think," Irene Howard said, "that she just sort of looked after him, mothered him, saw that he had everything that he wanted and of course he worshipped his children. He never would have broken up his home, of that I'm absolutely sure. And she would never really have gone off and divorced Leslie under any circumstances. Besides which, he was very discreet always. He didn't embarrass her." But he did use her; she was his excuse for his failure to do things he had never wanted or intended to do; she was the "heavy". If Howard let anybody down Ruth was always given the blame.

Douglas Fairbanks remembered her as the controller of the family finances. "I don't believe Leslie could sign a cheque by himself. He and I had a bet on something relatively trivial and he lost and he had an awful time paying me back. I didn't mind whether he paid me at all but his sense of honour required that he should. Nevertheless it took him about six or eight months to get around Ruth and explain what he wanted the money for. I think he was just allowed pocket money. Ruth took care of everything for him and paid the bills on his behalf. I think he was very dependent on her. I don't mean in a maternal sense, though he did seem to inspire the maternal instinct in women all over the world. They wanted to protect him and he didn't need any protection at all. But I think Ruth made herself over in such a way that he really would be dependent on her. I don't think she allowed him to be independent and I don't think he wanted to be either. He might have been frightened of her sometimes but on the other hand they did get along well and the marriage lasted a long time, so it was a good arrangement."

To John Houseman, Ruth was the stabilising influence in the marriage. She didn't, he thought, like her husband's philandering at all but she adjusted to it and as far as possible dealt with it. When the cast of *Hamlet* included "the most extraordinary collection of beautiful women", Ruth "simply didn't encourage the young ladies to moon around Leslie's dressing-room".

George Cukor, too, had the impression that occasionally Ruth fought off the women on Howard's behalf. "She was a very understanding lady but she didn't sit still all the time. There were some eruptions now and then, there must have been. To be married to a fascinating actor who has a roving eye is very difficult."

But if things had been difficult before they must have seemed well-nigh impossible when Howard fell genuinely in love with Violette Cunnington. That the matter was resolved without divorce, scandal or even bloodshed seems to be due entirely to the extreme tolerance and reasonableness of the two women. Of his mother Ronald Howard said: "She was a marvellous person. It's not all jam, you know, being the wife of a film star; you have to compensate for this butterfly you're married to and she compensated by being a very positive personality in her own right. She was very tolerant and understanding and I don't think Leslie would ever consciously have hurt her in any way. When we were young it was a very good marriage. It had its ups and downs with Leslie's flirtations and liaisons with various actresses but I don't think you can take that sort of theatrical relationship very seriously. Besides, he was successful in using his family as a sort of retreat, as an escape apparatus. Whatever happened he was always trying to get home and back to Ruth. That was his sanity really."

In the Violette Cunnington affair, however, matters were for once taken out of Ruth's hands and the compromise that was agreed upon was of Violette's devising. Ronald Howard said: "It was, let's say, a sort of French solution. Violette said, 'I will not break up your marriage, Leslie. We will do this in the French manner.' In France a man can have a mistress but he has to be married first and this was the case here." Violette accepted that Howard was firmly married and would not leave Ruth and so reconciled herself to the role of "other woman".

Ronald Howard said: "The protocol, the relationship between Ruth and herself was very good. They never clashed." Howard would return to his family at weekends and Violette encouraged him to do so. During the week he would live with his mistress. "On the surface everything went on perfectly equably. But of course underneath I presume Ruth was again very deeply hurt."

In the early war years, then, Howard divided himself neatly between two homes and otherwise devoted himself to helping his country in whichever way he could. He joined the "ideas committee" at the Ministry of Information and produced a document called "Notes on American Propaganda" in which he outlined his proposals for documentary films: "The first of these films should concern itself with placing the war guilt irrefutably upon the Nazis . . ."

He then put this theory into practice by co-writing, directing and starring in *Pimpernel Smith,* in which he played an English intellectual, a university professor, rescuing other intellectuals from Germany. The Germans hated this film, particularly Francis L. Sullivan's parody of Goering, and Howard was immediately placed on the Nazi blacklist.

While *Pimpernel Smith* was being made Howard had already started his series of "Britain Speaks", regular broadcasts to the United States whose object was to put the Allied case to the neutral Americans and enlist their sympathy and support.

That he was successful in this enterprise is evidenced by the fact that he earned the hatred of the German propaganda minister, Joseph Goebbels, and was denounced by the British traitor William Joyce, Lord Haw-Haw, who declared in his own broadcasts that once Britain was conquered Howard would be among the first people to be shot.

Undeterred by such threats Howard continued making films whose aim was at once to entertain, to raise morale and to plead Britain's cause to the non-aligned nations. *Pimpernel Smith* was followed by *49th Parallel,* directed by Michael Powell, and then by *The First of the Few,* which Howard directed and in which he played R. J. Mitchell, the inventor of the Spitfire. A critic later described it as "Leslie Howard's masterpiece and his monument".

When the film was completed he made what was to be his final public appearance, in the role of Lord Nelson, in a pageant entitled *In Praise of Britain* which was held on the steps of St. Paul's Cathedral and soon afterwards began work on producing and directing (though not acting in) *The Gentle Sex,* a tribute to the women's army, the ATS. But while that was in production Violette Cunnington became seriously ill.

It was the autumn of 1942 and she and Howard were now living in a cottage at Stoke Poges. The illness began with a small and apparently insignificant swelling on her nose. The swelling gradually became worse and more painful and finally she was taken to hospital where, after two days, she died of cerebral meningitis.

"Leslie was heartbroken, really heartbroken," Irene Howard said. "It was such a shock, you see, to everybody — we were all very fond of her and her death was the last thing anybody expected. She was quite young and seemed very healthy and Leslie was completely shattered."

At this dreadful time once again Howard's dependence upon Ruth and her own remarkable qualities of sympathy and understanding came into evidence. As soon as she heard that Violette was seriously ill in hospital, Ruth went to London to comfort her husband. And when Violette died and he was so distraught that he had to be tranquillised, Ruth took him back to Surrey and nursed him for two weeks. At the end of that time when the sharpest agony of his grief had been somewhat blunted Howard announced his intention of returning to the cottage he had shared with Violette.

By then *The Gentle Sex* had been completed by Maurice Elvey and Howard, anxious to get back to the studios and give himself something else to think about, began work on the production of *The Lamp Still Burns,* a hospital drama starring Stewart Granger. Howard approached Wendy Hiller to appear in it and, she said: "I noticed an enormous change in him; physically he'd aged and looked very frail. Later somebody who was closer to him mentioned that after Violette's death the poor man had taken to spiritualism and was earnestly and hopefully trying to get in touch with her. It sounded so tragic, as though he couldn't face up to her loss. So she must have had a great impact on his life."

Violette Cunnington was originally buried in the Mortlake cemetery, near the hospital where she died. But later Howard had her body moved to the churchyard at Stoke Poges — the churchyard of Gray's *Elegy* — because that was close to the cottage where they had lived together, the cottage which, he told Ronald, was "absolutely haunted. He kept hearing her voice and felt she was walking behind him through the rooms."

He had still not recovered from the loss of Violette when, in April 1943, he was invited to undertake a lecture tour — a propaganda tour, in effect — of Spain and Portugal on behalf of the British Council. He was reluctant to go on the grounds that lecturing was not his forte and agreed to do so only after the direct intervention of Anthony Eden who, after Winston Churchill, was the most senior member of the Government.

He was accompanied on the trip — an extremely successful one — by his accountant, Alfred Chenhalls, a burly man who somewhat resembled Churchill himself. Both in Spain and Portugal Howard was accorded a film star's reception wherever he appeared to lecture on *Hamlet* and to show *The First of the Few*.

The two men's travel arrangements were vague and right up to the eve of their eventual departure for home they had made no plans to return. It was only on that night that Chenhalls declared he could stay away no longer and made the reservations on Flight 777 from Lisbon to London.

There were, in fact, no vacancies available but Howard had flight priority — indeed he was the only person on the plane with that privilege and thus the only person who, once he had made his reservation, could be quite sure of a place aboard. And he and Chenhalls were given their seats only after two other passengers were taken off to wait for a later flight.

The following day, on June 1st, Flight 777 took off for London and three hours later was attacked and destroyed by the German squadron. Among the many theories that have been suggested to explain this action the most widely held is that the Nazis believed Alfred Chenhalls was indeed Winston Churchill. Churchill himself subscribed to it but there is no evidence to support it. And it does seem wildly improbable: what would Churchill have been doing in a totally unprotected aeroplane in the middle of the war?

The Germans put forward a number of contradictory reasons for the attack. First they said that Flight 777 was an armed plane, then that it was a fighter, then that it was escorted by bombers and finally that the whole thing was an error by unbriefed pilots. But none of them is plausible. With so many aircraft involved and in broad daylight there was no possibility of a mistake: the attack had been deliberate.

Ronald Howard, who did extensive research into the matter after the war, said: "I don't think they were only after Leslie. That was perhaps a plus for them, I don't know. But they were certainly after three other men who, I feel, were probably more important than Leslie.''

One of these men was the head of the petroleum company, Shell, and was also rumoured to be the head of the British Secret Service in Lisbon; another was the head of the London branch of the Jewish Agency for Palestine and had been involved in helping many Jews to escape from Europe; and the third was an important executive of the British steel industry.

Certainly the death of any of these three would have been more important to the Nazis than the death of a mere actor and it probably is too far-fetched to suggest that the plane was attacked on Howard's account alone. It's much more likely that he was merely one of a whole job lot of people whom the Germans preferred dead but, nevertheless, he was by no means an insignificant target. In 1945 the *British Film Year Book* described his wartime presence in England as "one of the most valuable facets of British propaganda" and propaganda, as the Nazis would have been the first to appreciate, was a vitally important weapon.

In Britain Howard's popularity was immense and his death was mourned more widely and more deeply than perhaps that of any other British star. In a dark and perilous time for the nation he had been a glitteringly romantic figurehead but he was also far more than that. Even without his wartime activities he would still have occupied a prominent place in any history of the British cinema, for he was a brilliant and versatile actor — not a heavyweight perhaps, but at the very least an outstanding middleweight.

He had great comic timing, a superb lightness of touch and innate humour, all of which made him ideal for sophisticated comedy. But he also had, or could assume, an air of gravity which made him equally at home in drama or tragedy. And there was, too, as his son said, that ethereal quality, an apparent detachment that meant that when he was on screen he was the one you watched, no matter who else was with him. To think of him only as Ashley Wilkes is to ignore the greater part of his ability.

In the international sense he was not perhaps a great star, rather he was, as Douglas Fairbanks put it, "a very fine co-star. When he made *Secrets* with my stepmother, Mary Pickford, it was considered a great coup for her to get him because of the prestige of his name, not because of his drawing power. He was not himself a great star but those who were great stars looked upon him with the highest respect and awe.''

That he was not a great star in the cinema — though he had certainly been one in the theatre — was entirely a matter of his own choice. The kind of superstardom that, in the 1930s, could be conferred only by the backing of a big studio which, in exchange for the exclusive use of his services, would have built him up and sustained him in the public eye by constant and careful exposure, was his for the taking. But it was not something he wanted. He refused to settle permanently in America, he refused to sign a long-term contract with any Hollywood company and in fact he only appeared in twenty-five films.

Always he preferred independence, the freedom to pick the roles he wanted and the wider enjoyment to be derived from pursuing his career on both sides of the Atlantic and in the theatre, until he grew bored with it, as well as the cinema.

Nevertheless, despite the comparative rarity of his screen appearances — it's interesting to note, for example, that while Howard was making his twenty-five films Clark Gable was appearing in forty-five — he occupies a special niche of his own. Just as Gable was thought in his time to epitomise America, so Howard with his grace and style, his wit and charm was firmly believed to epitomise England and though he may not have been the greatest movie star Britain has ever produced he was, in his own way, without equal.

Charlie
Chaplin

Chaplin in 1918 and already
earning 10,000 dollars a
week.

above : Chaplin's first wife, Mildred Harris. She was sixteen when they married in 1918. They were divorced by the time she was twenty.

below : Wife No. 2, Lita Grey. Another child bride and mother of his sons, Sydney and Charles Junior.

above : Paulette Goddard (wife No. 3) was a little mature by Chaplin's standards — comfortably into her twenties when they married somewhere in the Far East.

below : With his last wife, Oona, arriving in London in 1953. By then Chaplin had been driven out of America.

above : The Chaplin family at Cap St. Ferrat in 1957.

*opposite above : Charlie, the Tramp, the Little Fellow, has long
gone. What we have here is Sir Charles Chaplin, knight of the
realm.*

opposite below : The classic shot from the final reel of Modern
Times. *Chaplin and Paulette Goddard walk off, hand-in-hand, into
the sunset.*

I must begin with a confession: I have hardly ever laughed at Charlie Chaplin. I admire him enormously. I admire his grace, his ingenuity, his daring and his timing. I can sit awed and amazed at what he does on the screen. But he hardly ever makes me laugh.

Chaplin is generally regarded as a genius. Now this is a much-abused word too often applied to those whose abilities raise them fractionally above the mediocre, but in Chaplin's case it seems wholly appropriate. He *was* a genius, one of perhaps three undoubted geniuses the cinema has produced (the others being D. W. Griffith and Eisenstein). He was a genuine innovator who stretched the boundaries of what was possible in films. Almost every comic routine you ever see in pictures owes its origins to Chaplin and technically nobody has ever performed those routines better than he, although I believe others have performed them to greater comic effect.

I think it's the deliberate, carefully calculated pathos that destroys Chaplin's humour for me. He insists that you laugh at and cry for him virtually at the same time and it's too much to ask. Not that I object to pathos: there's a good deal of it in the work of Laurel and Hardy and I have been known to laugh at them so hard and for so long that people have refused to sit near me in cinemas. There is pathos in Stan's trusting simplicity and in Ollie's vast, pretentious dignity. But this is an understated pathos stemming from the fact that, come what may, this totally lovable, totally fallible odd couple are among the world's losers.

Chaplin's pathos is a colder, harder commodity. "Look at me," he says. "I'm the downtrodden Little Fellow, just like you. Weep for me, weep for yourself." But, in fact, he's not so downtrodden; he's not just like you and me at all. Chaplin's Little Fellow has a core of steel and in the end he always wins. He may not always get the girl but getting the girl isn't necessarily the ultimate objective in life. Failure to get her and being obliged to shuffle off alone down a straight, dusty road towards a new adventure may be cause for disappointment but it's not tragedy; it's not even truly pathos, though Chaplin would have us believe it is.

Besides, before we reach the long, lonely fade-out, Chaplin has won all the really important battles. All the villains, the big, fat, nasty men who have humiliated him and knocked him about, have had their come-uppance at his hands. Like a shabby James Bond, he invariably, inevitably metes out retribution to those who deserve it. Chaplin, in fact, is a winner disguised as a loser. Therefore I see no cause to weep for him and his demand that I should do so alienates me enough to make it difficult for me to laugh at him either.

And yet the man was a genius and, as is often the way, one who sprang from a most improbable source. He was born in Walworth, South London, on April 16th, 1889. Walworth at that time was a warm, teeming, poor community, rich in humanity perhaps but by no means in worldly goods and Chaplin's parents were as hard up as anyone else.

They differed from most of their neighbours, however, in that they were both in show business, Charles Chaplin, Senior, being a ballad singer and his wife, Hannah, a singer and dancer. At one time Charles, Senior, who came from an anglicised French Protestant family, was reasonably well established. He had appeared often in Europe and once in New York but if he was good at singing he was even better at drinking and most of the family income was dedicated to this hobby. Hannah, who had once appeared in a Gilbert and Sullivan production, was of part-Irish, part-gipsy descent and at the time Charlie was born already had a four-year-old son, Sydney, by a former marriage to one Sidney Hawkes, though probably for reasons of general tidiness and family solidarity young Sydney went under the name of Sydney Chaplin.

When Charlie was a year old his father walked out on wife and children and thereafter played no significant role in their lives. Indeed, by the time he was thirty-seven he was dead of dropsy. Meanwhile, Hannah was left in fairly dire straits. Recurrent attacks of laryngitis ruined her attempts to revive her music-hall career and she was reduced to earning what she could as a part-time dressmaker and part-time nurse. At the age of four, Charlie occasionally contributed to the family income by dancing for pennies outside the local pubs.

It was Hannah who had taught him to dance and it was from Hannah that he inherited the gift of mimicry. It was also Hannah who, aspiring even in adversity to something better in life, insisted that however poor they might be, her sons' speech and manners should be those of gentlefolk. Adversity was a constant companion at that time, for Hannah's sight began to fail her too, and in 1896 she was so destitute that she and her boys ended up in the Lambeth workhouse.

Now from such appalling beginnings, which sound remarkably like the opening chapters of some Victorian melodrama, it might be assumed that young Chaplin's life could only get better. But in fact it got worse. Having left the workhouse some months before, Hannah had a mental breakdown and was committed to a lunatic asylum and Charlie was returned to the workhouse.

Undoubtedly such early hardship had a most profound effect upon him and he described it brilliantly in the first, and far more fascinating, half of his autobiography. But his son Sydney was not entirely convinced that life was quite as bad as his father had remembered it.

He talked about his childhood, said Sydney Chaplin, "all the time" and what he talked about mostly was "the poverty. That impressed him. I mean, in his work and everything that impressed him. But, of course, I found out that he was poor such a short time that it wasn't so very horrible. Most kids don't know they're poor unless they're starving; you play with a stick or a rag in the street and you have your friends — Christmas . . . he used to tell us about Christmas because he said that was a nightmare. He said, 'If I got one orange for Christmas that was a marvellous present', and every year all of us kids we'd have to listen to that and we'd say, 'Well, next year we'll get you a box of oranges, Pa. You'll love it.'"

Whether or not Chaplin exaggerated the tribulations of his early days, they left him with a lifelong fear of poverty and insanity. And even allowing for exaggeration and the fact that poverty, like everything else, is relative and assuming that Sydney Chaplin was right and that the really hard years were comparatively few, Chaplin's childhood was by no means an easy or a conventional one.

By the age of eight he was already a professional entertainer, a member of a clog-dancing troupe called Jackson's Eight Lancashire Lads; at eleven he was peddling flowers in pubs and working as an errand boy. At about the same time his mother was committed once again to the lunatic asylum and at twelve he got his first engagement as a straight actor in the play *Sherlock Holmes*, wherein he played the page boy. He toured with this production for four years and thereafter appeared briefly in a music-hall act called Casey's Circus.

The desire to make his living on the stage was also inherited from Hannah and in her lucid moments nurtured by her. After all, it made sense: for a boy with his background and limited education the only occupations in those days that offered much chance to emerge from the ruck were prize fighting and show business and young Charlie had been on the books of a theatrical agency since his clog-dancing days.

So, too, had his half-brother Sydney and it was Sydney who made the first appreciable breakthrough. He joined Fred Karno's famous vaudeville troupe and, having established himself, introduced Charlie.

This was in 1906 when the younger Chaplin was still only seventeen and Karno was not greatly impressed by him, remembering him later as "a pale, puny, sullen-looking youngster". Nevertheless, Karno swiftly recognised the boy's talent as a mime and took him on to appear in a football sketch as assistant and stooge to the troupe's star turn, Harry Wheldon. Professionally the two worked well together, although privately they didn't get along at all. According to Karno Chaplin was dour and unsociable, not very likeable and with a horror of drink that must have made him very much the outsider in a music-hall company. Furthermore he quarrelled fiercely with Wheldon who, on one notable occasion, was heard to inform him: "I have more talent in my arse than your have in your entire body."

"Yes, that's where your talent lies," said Chaplin. Future events, of course, were to prove that Wheldon's original claim was as inaccurate as Chaplin's riposte was tactless but such an exchange can hardly have made for a happy relationship. It also tends to reinforce Karno's view that Chaplin was not an easy fellow to get along with, but even so he soon became one of the company's leading comics. And when the Karno troupe went to America to appear in New York in 1910 and again in 1912 it was he who attracted most attention.

Indeed, on that second visit he was approached by Mack Sennett, who offered him a contract at 150 dollars a week to make one- and two-reel comedy films. Chaplin accepted and so he arrived in Hollywood to take up this new career in December 1913, when he was twenty-four years old.

He began with a one-reeler called *Making a Living*, which won him a cautiously approving notice in the magazine *Motion Picture World*, and then rapidly started to make a name for himself after his second film, *Kid Auto Races at Venice*, in which he improvised the tramp outfit that was to become his trademark. He assembled it in a hurry and in response to a casual instruction from Mack Sennett to "put on a comedy make-up". The final costume was a ragbag of garments borrowed from other comedians: Fatty Arbuckle's trousers, for example, Ford Sterling's boots, a cut-down version of Mack Swain's moustache. To these he added a jacket and a bowler hat that were both too small for him and a walking stick, the emblem of the man about town. The *tout ensemble* at once gave the impression of down-at-heel gentility, the image of a man reduced by circumstances to the level of a hobo but still attempting to maintain standards.

Considering that it was, or he would have claimed it was, a perfectly haphazard collection of clothes, it became a remarkably successful outfit. But King Vidor, the director, who was one of Chaplin's earliest friends in Hollywood, is not so sure that it was haphazard. Vidor had another friend, a prominent psychiatrist who wanted to meet Chaplin. Chaplin refused to see him on the grounds, Vidor believed, that "he was afraid any analysis of his character would destroy his talent, his energy and his goals and motivation".

Chaplin insisted that he didn't believe in psychiatry, psychiatrists or psycho-analysis and also maintained, "I don't have any neuroses of any sort."

Vidor reported this conversation to the psychiatrist who replied: "My God, I've never seen anybody with more neuroses. The big shoes, the big pants, the baggy crotch to the pants, the Derby hat, the moustache, the cane — they're all symbols, neurotic symbols of the poor little fellow starving to death but wanting to be a socially prominent gentleman."

How much support you give to this view depends, I suppose, on what you think of psychiatrists but Vidor believed that in this case the psychiatrist was right and that what he had said summed up "the whole basis of Chaplin's life and character".

However, armed with the Little Fellow outfit and a huge repertoire of gags and slapstick routines from his London music-hall days Chaplin quickly began to prosper. In two years he made thirty-five pictures for Keystone before leaving to join the Essanay Film Manufacturing Company, who offered him 1,250 dollars a week and the opportunity to direct. Hal Roach, another of Chaplin's early Hollywood friends, said that "his contract with Essanay laid down that if he was making a picture on location, the company — not Charlie — had to pay for the meals for the crew and the actors. So every day about eleven thirty a.m. Charlie would think of a scene to shoot outdoors because then the company would have to pay for the luncheon."

This careful attitude towards money was again, no doubt, a residue of his poverty-stricken childhood but it was also one of his abiding characteristics.

He acquired and never lost a reputation for meanness but, like many apparently tight-fisted people, he could also be quite remarkably lavish. Douglas Fairbanks, Junior, said: "Charlie was famously frugal. He was said to have the first penny he ever earned. He parted with every penny as if it were his life's blood and he was a very good student of the dollar and the pound and the franc and the mark and so on and he was a very wise investor and a very shrewd businessman."

King Vidor believed that, because of his background, Chaplin was never able to convince himself that he was a rich man and thus he was never able to enjoy the delights of extravagance. "I think the house in which he lived in those early days in Hollywood was built by a studio technician and there were some things in it that were made for a film, so after a while all the plaster fell off but he never got it fixed. I remember he had a shower bath that didn't have a shower head on it, just a pipe coming out of the wall. One time, after a game of tennis, he said, 'You don't have to go home for a shower. Come and use mine.' So I got in this shower and I said, 'How do you work this thing?' and he said, 'Oh, I forgot to tell you. You take this pan and fill it from the pipe and then throw the water over yourself.' He never had it fixed, just never had it fixed."

On the same subject of money there is also the testimony of Hal Roach: "Charlie was one of the tightest guys I ever knew. I remember once we were eating in a cafeteria at lunchtime and we were going out to dinner together that night. Well, when the check came Charlie grabbed it — the first time I'd ever known him grab a check. It came to about thirty cents and he said, 'I'll pay this. You can take care of dinner.' And dinner would be about two dollars each."

Again Chaplin's son, Sydney, recalling an occasion much later in his father's life: "One night in Paris when he didn't have his glasses on he took out a 500-franc note, which was then about a hundred dollars, and gave it to the taxi driver and told him to keep the change. So the taxi driver, with a big laugh, took it and drove off. Well, my father thought he'd given him 50 francs and when he found out the truth he didn't sleep the whole night. I'll tell you, he was ill. He said, 'How could you, Christ, how could you let me do that? Couldn't you look and see what I was giving the man?'"

Around that time, too, when Chaplin was living with his fourth wife, Oona, in Switzerland, Sydney Chaplin said: "He lived like a rich man. He had a big house and a lot of servants and he denied himself nothing but he suddenly said to Oona one day, 'What are the meat prices here?' And she told him and he said, 'Well, that's it.

We're not going to eat meat any more. That's ridiculous — the servants and all of us eating meat at that price. We're spending a fortune.'

"And for three days they didn't eat meat. He was always relating back to the time when he was poor. But then, after a few days of not eating meat, he said, 'Let's have a steak,' and that was that."

Generally speaking, though, his attacks of meanness occurred when he was actually required to produce cash to pay for something. Sydney Chaplin said that if his father could sign a bill and didn't have to watch his own money grasped by other hands, he would quite happily take twenty people to dinner and be a most generous host. What is more, he would invest his own capital in his films and very few actors are prepared to take such a risk as that.

Hal Roach said: "That was an amazing thing. When he built his own studio and made his own pictures with his own money — that is, when he was with United Artists — Charlie, tight as he was in some things, would arrive at the studio at nine o'clock in the morning and decide that he didn't feel like acting or directing that day. And he would dismiss the entire crew and the very large bunch of actors he had for the film and that would cost him several thousand dollars."

One implication of all this is that Chaplin regarded money chiefly as sustenance for his work, which was always of paramount importance to him. "Comedy," he once said, "is the most serious study in the world." And partly perhaps because he learned this simple, though vital, lesson more quickly and more thoroughly than his contemporaries he soon began to outstrip them in popularity.

By 1915, when he was with Essanay, spin-off industries had sprung up around him, manufacturing Charlie Chaplin statuettes and Charlie Chaplin squirt rings. At the age of twenty-six he was already becoming very rich.

At Essanay his frequent leading lady was Edna Purviance, who was to appear in thirty-five of his films from *A Night Out* in 1915 to *A Woman of Paris* in 1926. The relationship between them was far more than merely professional and it was also long-lasting. Chaplin kept her on his payroll until her death in 1958 and it was surprising to many of their mutual friends that they never married. Hal Roach believed this was because "she didn't want to marry Charlie. Away from the studio I imagine Charlie was pretty boring because he probably wouldn't say a word for a couple of hours if he didn't want to and then he'd talk his head off about something that was way above her, like some gag he was trying to work out for a movie.''

Stan Laurel, on the other hand, was convinced that it was Chaplin who didn't wish to marry Edna Purviance because she was simply too mature and too grown-up for him. Certainly this is a point worth considering because Chaplin's taste was always for very young and very innocent girls. And this was a predilection that was to land him in trouble on several occasions throughout most of his life.

At the time he first met Edna Purviance, however, such problems still lay in the future. In 1915 he made the film that is generally regarded as the Chaplin classic, *The Tramp*, which is mostly significant for the fact that it was in this picture that he introduced the element of pathos that was to become as much his trademark as the Little Fellow costume was. By now he was in such demand that he could virtually dictate his own terms. He moved from Essanay to Mutual and from Mutual to First National and with every switch of allegiance his income soared.

There was a brief hiccup in this upward progress when America entered the First World War and letters began to pour into the studio demanding that Chaplin should enlist in the Army. In fact, he had already been turned down because he didn't meet the physical requirements, being only 5 feet 4 inches tall and weighing no more than 130 lbs. It was an unpleasant interlude for him (the receipt of white feathers through the post can hardly be an agreeable experience) but it made no appreciable difference to his box-office appeal because when he signed for First National in 1918 the contract gave him one million dollars — to say nothing of a 15,000 dollar signing-on bonus — to make eight films. One million dollars is quite a good fee now but in 1918 it was astonishing enough to merit worldwide publicity.

But to Chaplin what was even more important than the money was the fact that he also had complete control over the production of his pictures and could afford to build his own studios. So he acquired a five-acre lot just off Sunset Boulevard, put up an open-air stage, which he later roofed over, and then erected a row of mock-Tudor cottages to serve as the administration block. And there at last he set about making films the way he wanted to make them.

"Sometimes," said Douglas Fairbanks, Junior, "he would film a whole day's work as a rehearsal in order to be able to look at it the next day. Then he'd film it again a second time and sometimes it would take him three or four days to do one scene. Most people couldn't afford that but he was his own boss, he had very few overheads, he paid very small wages and he had a studio which was very inexpensive. People loved working for him. They could have got better jobs elsewhere but they would rather work for him for less than for somebody else for more.''

All this prosperity and success was not, however, mirrored in Chaplin's private life. In October 1918, he had acquired the first of a succession of child brides, a blonde, blue-eyed actress named Mildred Harris. He was twenty-nine and she was sixteen. More significantly, perhaps, she was also pregnant on their wedding day and a few months later gave birth to a son who died within three days. Soon after that Chaplin moved out of the conjugal home and by August 1920 the couple were divorced in an atmosphere of scandal and acrimony.

Mildred accused her husband of mental cruelty and neglect and claimed that he practised economy to such an extent that he even scrimped on funeral expenses for their child. Instead of hiring a hearse, she said, he had borrowed a car belonging to the Gish sisters. Chaplin refused to reply to what he described as ''these foolish charges''. This was undoubtedly the most dignified attitude to adopt but perhaps, with hindsight, it was not the most sensible, for the Mildred Harris episode was the first of several minor scandals which eventually were to help turn the American public against him.

While the divorce action was going on and Mildred Harris's lawyers were making ever more extravagant demands on behalf of their client, Chaplin was trying to finish his first full-length feature film, *The Kid*, in which he introduced the young Jackie Coogan to the screen. This became a difficult enterprise because, in order to stop the hostile lawyers from seizing such film as he had already shot, Chaplin had to keep moving from one location to another. But it was worth all the effort for, when it finally appeared, it was such a critical and popular success as to wipe away the bad taste left by the divorce action.

By then, too, Chaplin was even more securely established for in 1919 and in company with Mary Pickford, Douglas Fairbanks, Senior, and D. W. Griffith he had established United Artists in order that the four of them should have greater control over the distribution of and the profits from their films, though because of his contract with First National Chaplin was unable to enjoy the complete independence offered by United Artists until 1923, when he directed Edna Purviance and Adolphe Menjou in *A Woman of Paris*, released in 1926.

One of his intentions in choosing this particular subject was that it should at last make Edna Purviance a star. But in fact it did very little for her and such stardom as it conferred went to Menjou.

Meanwhile, in 1921, Chaplin had made his first visit to England for eight years. He had been mobbed and fêted, introduced to James Barrie and H. G. Wells (and thus acquired an abiding taste for the company and friendship of distinguished writers) and been to Europe, where he met and had an affair with Pola Negri. An odd affair it must have been, too, because her English at the time was apparently limited to the somewhat enigmatic phrase, "Jazz boy, Charlie". But, despite the fact that this must have made their conversation rather stilted, they obviously got along very well because when she turned up in Hollywood a year later their engagement was announced. This, however, seems to have been much more her idea than his and the romance, if such it was, rapidly cooled down.

By this time Chaplin and his brother Sydney, who was by now his business manager, had brought their mother to America and established her in a home with a staff of her own. Mrs. Chaplin's state of mental illness had become permanent and, though Charlie continued to look after her until her death in 1930, he found it emotionally painful to spend much time with her, hence the separate homes.

He himself had moved into a house in Beverly Hills. Pola Negri had confidently expected to become the mistress of this establishment but in the event the first woman to move in on any seemingly permanent basis was Charlie's second child bride, Lita Grey, whom he married in 1924. He was thirty-five but Miss Grey, like Miss Harris before her, was only sixteen. He had first met her when she appeared as a twelve-year-old in *The Kid*. Later he put her under contract and wanted to star her in *The Gold Rush* but on location a more intimate relationship developed and they were married because, once again, Chaplin the lover had been more passionate than careful.

"This was a situation which had occurred before in Charlie's life," said Miss Grey. "Again he was in trouble with an under-age girl . . . pregnancy before marriage, and so forth. Most of the girls in Charlie's life were under age."

It was Miss Grey's family who insisted they should be married and, although he greatly resented the idea, Chaplin was obliged to agree because Lita Grey was legally below the age of consent. The wedding took place in Mexico and "he didn't want much said about it. He was pretty bitter in the beginning. On the way back in the train he was quite nasty. He made a remark that I, well, being so young and not feeling too well at the time anyway, I couldn't know whether he was serious or whether he was joking. I really couldn't tell. But he said, 'You know, it would be easy if you'd just jump.' We were standing out on the platform between two cars while the train was travelling and he said, 'We could end this whole situation if you'd just jump.' "

From this inauspicious and far from jolly start and pursued by scandal-seeking reporters the couple returned to Hollywood to await the birth of their son, Charles Chaplin, Junior. It was a strange situation with the newly-wed husband laying down a hard set of ground rules from the very beginning. "He said, 'I don't intend to be a husband to you. You have your mother live with us because you can't live alone all the time in your condition and I don't intend to be a husband to you.' And he wasn't because he'd stay out till all hours and when he came home we wouldn't have any meals together." Thus the young bride was left very much in the company of her mother and her grandmother, who had also moved in, and her hired tutors whom Chaplin had to provide since his wife was still of school-going age.

Even the professional contact between husband and wife quickly ceased for, as the signs of her pregnancy became increasingly evident, the new Mrs. Chaplin was withdrawn from *The Gold Rush* and Georgia Hale was signed to replace her.

Charles Chaplin, Junior, was born on June 28th, 1925, according to the official records but according to both Charles, Junior and his mother he was actually born on May 5th. Chaplin, apparently, had the records changed (by means of a 25,000 dollar bribe) to make it appear that the child had been conceived after and not, as was the case, before marriage. But whatever the true date of the birth, the relationship between husband and wife obviously improved a little because very soon Lita Grey was pregnant again and in March 1926, another son, Sydney, was born.

"When I was pregnant with Sydney," said Miss Grey, "Charlie became quite decent. He was beginning to be very nice then." But, alas, this state of affairs didn't last very long. A little while after the birth of Sydney, Chaplin began filming *The Circus* with, as the leading lady, Merna Kennedy. Miss Kennedy and Lita Grey had been schoolfriends and it was Miss Grey who persuaded her husband to give the girl a screen test. This was rather a grave mistake on Miss Grey's part because Chaplin not only gave her the test and the role but he also gave her a diamond bracelet, a present whose significance was not lost on his wife. She, too, had been given a diamond bracelet as a prelude to seduction.

"I knew then what was going on because it was a repetition of the same kind of treatment that I got. So I think that was the thing that really ended the marriage. I just walked into his room and told him I didn't care what the result was, I was just not going to live with him any more."

As the divorce action got under way Chaplin was faced by a forty-two-page document of complaint in which he was accused of threatening his wife's life, of infidelity, of mental cruelty and of all manner of other inhuman acts. The whole affair was conducted in an atmosphere of the most remarkable bitterness which, on Chaplin's part, burned so deeply and so permanently that in his autobiography he never once mentioned Lita Grey by name.

Half a century later, however, Miss Grey herself was able to look back on this brief and turbulent marriage with a far more dispassionate eye. He was not a cruel man, she said, nor particularly selfish, though he could be ruthless in defence of his career and his work. The main problem, the one that made him impossible to live with, was "enormous insecurity. Looking back, I realise how terribly insecure he was. He had trouble ordering food in a restaurant even; the waiters intimidated him. I think he never had real confidence; he never felt that anybody loved him. He said to me once, 'How can anybody love me? I'm not tall and dark and handsome and well-proportioned . . . why would anybody love me?' He never believed it was possible."

But along with the insecurity went a kind of arrogance. "One time he said to me, 'I'm the best. I'm better known than Jesus Christ' and at that age, of course, I thought, 'Oh, the vanity of this man! It's just unreal,' but as I've grown older I've come to realise that it was a pretty truthful statement. There were places in the world that knew Chaplin, where they'd probably never even heard of Jesus Christ."

The divorce finally cost Chaplin 850,000 dollars and a mild nervous collapse and caused him to delay opening *The Circus* until early 1928. Immediately after that he started work on another idea: a film about a blind girl to be called eventually *City Lights*. At this stage, however, talkies had been introduced to the cinema. How would Chaplin react to this new-fangled idea? Well, he reacted by ignoring it. In an article in the *New York Times* he maintained that silent films represented a universal art which could not and must not be ousted by the current "hysteria" for talkies. Action, he said, was more generally understood than words: pantomime was a universal language while speech as a form of communication was perforce restricted to those who could understand what was being said. In explaining this attitude to his son, Sydney, he said: "Words are cheap. The biggest thing you can say is 'elephant'."

Yet there was more to his hostility towards sound pictures than that, certainly in those days. Many of his best effects were gained by undercranking the camera and this was impossible with a sound camera which was run by a motor at a set speed of twenty-four frames a second. Just as much to the point, he also argued that English dialogue would limit, if not destroy, his enormous foreign market and when you consider that he could recover the production costs of his films from Japan alone this was clearly no small matter.

So he went ahead with *City Lights* as a silent movie and was completely vindicated when, on its appearance in 1931, it proved to be one of the most popular films of the year.

Now, until this time, his most frequent companion since his last divorce had been Georgia Hale but after *City Lights* opened in New York he went on an eight-month world tour, leaving her behind and that was more or less the end of that because soon after his return he met his next leading lady — and his third wife — Paulette Goddard. At least it is generally supposed that she became his wife (probably during 1936 when they made a lengthy trip together to the Far East) although both she and Chaplin were reluctant to say whether they were married or not. Miss Goddard, indeed, would not even clear up the matter in 1938 when the suspicion that she was merely "living in sin" with Chaplin aroused the enmity of the American Women's Clubs and thus, since Hollywood dared not defy these baleful ladies, lost her any outside chance she might have had of landing the role of Scarlett O'Hara in *Gone With the Wind*, a role she wanted quite as desperately as every other actress in Hollywood.

When she and Chaplin met in 1932 Paulette Goddard was, by his standards, a rather elderly divorcee of twenty-one but, generously overlooking her comparative length of tooth, he took her into his home and co-starred her in his next film, *Modern Times*. That was made in 1936 when Chaplin was forty-seven years old and it was, of course, a silent picture (if you overlook the fact

that Chaplin sang a song in gibberish). By that stage nobody else in
his right mind would have contemplated making a silent picture
but once again the public appeared to support Chaplin's belief that
actions spoke louder than words because on its release *Modern
Times* swiftly climbed to Number Four in the box-office top
ten.

Chaplin followed this success with another satire on the
contemporary scene, *The Great Dictator*, and by the time that was
finished in 1940, the war in Europe was on and his relationship
with Paulette Goddard was over. Unusually, considering his
previous track record, it ended without acrimony and indeed with
regret on both sides. They had been together for the best part of
eight years and she had been a kind and attentive stepmother to
Chaplin's two sons. But she was twenty-two years younger than he
was and their interests were not altogether compatible.

Tim Durant, who looked after Chaplin's investment at United
Artists, said: "Charlie liked his home and he liked to be looked
after and she wanted to go out much more than he did."

And King Vidor said: "She used to go out on dates with other
men and he'd be sitting at home, this great comedian, waiting. I
thought it was quite a tragic sight."

Thus, as the 1940s opened, Chaplin, now aged fifty-one, was
again alone and embarking upon the most troubled decade of his
life. In a sense *The Great Dictator*, though made with the most
patriotic intent, was the start of his problems. Partly because of the
slight physical resemblance between him and Hitler, his films had
been banned anyway in Nazi Germany but this latest picture, this
obviously satirical view of the Führer, aroused the Nazis to a state
of fury bordering on apoplexy. The caption under Chaplin's
picture in a German propaganda book read: "This little Jewish
tumbler, as disgusting as he is boring . . ." Chaplin, in fact, was
not a Jew, though he never bothered to say so on the grounds that
if he did he would simply be playing into the hands of the anti-
Semites.

But in America in 1940 there were a good many anti-Semites
and a good many Nazi sympathisers, too, and when the film
opened Chaplin began to receive threatening letters from such
people. Furthermore, he was attacked in the Right-wing Press for
insulting the German leader. The suspicion began to grow that
Chaplin was a bit of a Left-winger, a species of person always
viewed with much distrust in the United States.

And when America finally entered the war this suspicion

became a certainty in the minds of his adversaries for Chaplin lent his voice to the demand for a second front to be launched in Europe to take some of the pressure off the Russian armies.

In San Francisco he addressed a rally of 10,000 people, delivering a forty-minute speech that opened with the emotive word, "Comrades!" Of course, he explained, he meant nothing specific by this — "I am not a Communist, I am a human being" — but the use of the word "Comrades" along with an impassioned appeal for a second front — "Stalin wants it, Roosevelt has called for it, so let's all call for it, let's open a second front now" — led the Right-wingers to colour him, at the very least, pink. Then he followed the San Francisco rally by talking on the telephone to a mass meeting of trades unionists in Madison Square Garden, beginning with the words: "On the battlefield of Russia democracy will live or die." That may ring a little hollow now but it probably sounded quite plausible at the time, though again not to the Right-wing faction. Enmity towards Chaplin was building swiftly and his friends began to advise him to ease up on his pro-Russian speeches. Nor were they entirely wrong to do so, for he was already being ostracised in New York society.

While all this was going on the one thing that Chaplin did not need was to become involved in another sexual scandal but, alas, in 1943 this is precisely what happened; a paternity suit was brought against him by an actress named Joan Barry.

The background circumstances were wearily familiar: she was a good-looking girl of twenty-two and he was fifty-four; they had first met two years earlier when Miss Barry screentested for the leading role in *Shadow and Substance*, a film Chaplin was contemplating about an Irish girl who was a kind of modern Joan of Arc.

The picture was never made but, inevitably no doubt, Chaplin and Joan Barry became lovers. Unfortunately, Miss Barry also became highly neurotic and a drinker and a nuisance. Alarmed by the lady's unpredictable behaviour, Chaplin ended the relationship, gave her money and paid her fare back to her home in New York. A few months later, however, she returned to Hollywood, broke into Chaplin's home, was charged with vagrancy, sentenced to thirty days' detention and announced that she was three months pregnant. As an afterthought she declared that Chaplin was the father, which would have been an extremely neat trick on his part because the couple had not been together for some eight months.

What complicated matters even further was that since divesting himself of Miss Barry Chaplin had met and fallen in love with Oona O'Neill, the daughter of Eugene O'Neill, the playwright. The affection he felt for her was genuine and, as it turned out, lasting, but unfortunately Miss O'Neill was only seventeen and under American law still a child. So when news of this relationship leaked out in the Press Chaplin was involved in a double sexual scandal; a paternity suit being brought against him by one young woman while he was consorting with an under-age girl. There was only one solution — fortunately a solution that appealed to both of them anyway —and that was to marry Oona.

This Chaplin did at the town of Carpenteria in California in June 1943 after (a) an elopement and (b) a wild car chase in which the couple were pursued by a strong contingent of the American Press. After the wedding and a brief honeymoon in Santa Barbara the couple returned to Beverly Hills, where the new bride's first task was to help her husband prepare his answer to Joan Barry's paternity case.

In fact, he had a perfect answer. The result of a blood test showed quite conclusively that Chaplin could not possibly have been the father of Miss Barry's child. This convinced everybody except the law court which refused to accept the blood test as evidence. But, in any case, the paternity suit was not now the most urgent of Chaplin's problems because he was facing criminal charges as well, having been indicted on four counts under the Mann Act, which prohibited the transportation of women (in Chaplin's case Joan Barry) from one state to another for immoral purposes. The fact that any transportation of Miss Barry had been done with her happy consent and that the most immoral purpose she had served was to sleep with Chaplin was, apparently, neither here nor there.

The legal proceedings dragged on into April 1944 at which time Chaplin was acquitted on all counts, though not before he had been comprehensively vilified in the Press. Two years later the paternity case was reopened and Chaplin was found, against all the evidence, to be the father of the child and ordered to support it. The whole case, said Sydney Chaplin, was "an absolute frame-up. They proved it wasn't his child — I mean, medically proved — but they threw the proof out because the blood test wasn't accepted in California."

By the middle of the decade, then, Chaplin the great comedian had been transformed in the eyes of the American public into

Chaplin the Leftie, Chaplin the satyr, Chaplin the heartless seducer and impregnator of innocent young women and finally Chaplin the apparent tax dodger, since in the past few years he had been involved in constant disputes with the Inland Revenue, though not because he was trying to cheat but because, in Chaplin's view and that of his lawyers, he was being assessed unfairly.

While the war was still on and America and Russia were allies his apparent Left-wing sympathies probably did him no great harm but his taste for young women was never likely to make him popular. For all manner of complex reasons — jealousy perhaps on the part of other older men; insecurity on the part of older women — an elderly man who consorts with young girls is by definition a dirty old man. But what exactly is a dirty old man? And was Chaplin one? If seducing young girls and making them pregnant is evidence of dirty old manhood then doubtless Chaplin qualifies for the title. But, on the other hand, in the two cases when he certainly did seduce and make pregnant a young girl he also did the honourable thing and married her. That neither marriage lasted is beside the point; far more pertinent perhaps is the fact that those who knew Chaplin well do not believe he was a dirty old man or that he was attracted to his various youthful brides and girlfriends simply on grounds of lust.

Sydney Chaplin acknowledged that his father was physically attracted to youth ("I mean, the oldest woman he married was Paulette Goddard, who was an old bag of twenty-one or something") but insisted that what really appealed to him more was "the freshness, the non-sophistication of the young".

And Tim Durant said: "I don't think it was primarily sexual, I really don't. He wasn't one of those lascivious old men who are always pursuing women. He married all of them, remember that; and he fell in love with all of them, too. We get down to the sexual angle with everybody I suppose, but what I think he felt was that he could influence and mould these young girls. And I think he was less sure of himself with older women because they had more experience."

Hal Roach agreed with Durant that Chaplin was not essentially a womaniser: "All the time I knew him I never saw him chasing dames. And if he was doing it, why would he hide it from me? I was doing a little chasing myself."

Lita Grey who, as one of the girls Chaplin seduced and married, spoke with first-hand experience, believed that he was a romantic, a dreamer. "Throughout his whole life," she said, "he was attracted to the virginal girl. I think it was part of his creativity. He wanted to see the girl awaken; he wanted to create a person. He was intrigued, I think, by innocence. When he married Oona this was the pattern again but Charlie was a very lucky man because while the pattern may have been the same, Oona was different. She became his stability.

"Probably because of his age he'd slowed down a great deal and he needed her very badly. She was an insecure girl and I think they needed each other. She turned out to be a fabulous wife and mother and I think she brought Charlie the only real peace he'd ever known. I don't think he'd ever been a very happy man and she brought him a measure of contentment that he'd never had before."

Chaplin himself assessed the situation in very much the same way. To Tim Durant, who had introduced him to Oona O'Neill, he said: "I've been looking for somebody like her all my life. If I'd found her before I wouldn't have had all the problems I've had in the past."

However, in 1947 Chaplin, now married once more (and, as it was to prove, permanently), supporting a child that was not his own but at least cleared of criminal charges under the Mann Act, made his first film in seven years, *Monsieur Verdoux*, a black comedy based on the career of Landru, the wife murderer. The American public disliked it but by this time they disliked Chaplin anyway, regarding his political views as dangerously liberal. At a Press conference after the opening of the film he was questioned about his patriotism and his politics. And even though he insisted that he was not a Communist, had never voted in his life and indeed had no political persuasions at all, he was still accused by Right-wing publications of being "a card-carrying member of the Communist party" and a speaker in Congress demanded that he should be deported and his "loathsome pictures" be banned for fear that they might corrupt American youth.

Hollywood society now began to ostracise him in much the same way as New York society had done earlier. Living virtually in isolation, he spent the next few years planning and making his final American film, *Limelight*. By the time that was in production the very mention of his name was enough to arouse anger. Claire Bloom, the young actress who co-starred with him, said: "I used to get a taxi to the studio every morning and at first I'd say, 'I'd like to go to the Chaplin studio, please', and the taxi driver would say, 'Is that goddamn Commie still working in this country?' So finally I just gave them the name of the street and the number to avoid any wrangles. America was a fearful place at that time."

When the film was finished Chaplin and Oona decided to take a six-month holiday in Europe. Before they left he had to apply for a re-entry permit into the USA because in the forty years that he had been living there he had never become an American citizen. This was the opportunity that the anti-Communist, anti-Chaplin faction had been looking for. The authorities stalled, refusing to grant him the permit until he had been interrogated by the immigration officials and then issuing it only reluctantly. Nor was that the end of the matter, for when the Chaplins were already on board the *Queen Elizabeth* en route for Southampton the permit was rescinded and he was informed that he would not be allowed to return to the USA unless he faced an Immigration Board of Inquiry "to answer charges of a political nature and of moral turpitude". No less an authority than the US Attorney General described him as "a person of unsavoury character".

Well, now, what was all this about? In the first place, of course, there was the suspicion of Communism, which was clearly unfounded. In a rather grandiose way Chaplin would describe himself as "a citizen of the world". It was a romantic and perhaps naive idea but then politically he was rather naive, tending towards the liberal (with a small 'l') though by no means a committed liberal. He was, by instinct, always far more a capitalist than a Communist.

"He pictured himself as a radical," said King Vidor, "and yet he was far from that." Vidor recalled one occasion when Chaplin ran into union difficulties while making a film and insisted that he would never have any truck with union contracts again and that rather than do so he would stop making films altogether. "He wasn't really for the common man at all," said Vidor.

Douglas Fairbanks, Junior, said: "He never stopped talking politics but you couldn't take him very seriously. His opinions would change from morning to night, sometimes from hour to hour. He would say things just to be provocative and stir up discussion." As for being a member of the Communist party, Fairbanks said: "He never belonged to any party. I can vouch for that. He was far too stingy to pay the dues to join anything."

In the political climate of the time, however, the American authorities were not to be persuaded by such arguments. They were convinced that Chaplin was a fellow-traveller if not an actual

Communist and besides they were irritated by the fact that after all those years he still carried a British passport. Chaplin had never taken out American citizenship because he didn't feel it important. He was, remember, a citizen of the world and as he said to Douglas Fairbanks: "Why should I become an American? There are a lot of Americans who live in France or England or Germany and they're not asked to become Frenchmen or Englishmen or Germans. Why are Americans the only ones who say you have to become an American citizen? It's the only country in the world where they make a thing about it." That sort of attitude was hardly designed to endear him to the Attorney General's office either.

So, inspired by a crusading zeal to stamp out this dangerous radical clown in whatever way they could, the American authorities constructed a political case against him and — on a belt and braces principle — introduced allegations of moral turpitude as well. The Joan Barry paternity suit gave them a certain amount of fuel for this but in their enthusiasm they even went back to Lita Grey in an attempt to revive the sensational aspects of the divorce action a quarter of a century earlier. To her credit Miss Grey refused to dish the dirt.

Meanwhile, Chaplin, angry and bitter at the campaign against him, refused to defend himself and left America, as far as he was concerned, for good. When he arrived in Southampton he declared privately that he had "no further use for America. I wouldn't go back there if Jesus Christ was President." Oona though did go back — to sell the family home and transfer Chaplin's fortune to Switzerland where he had decided to live.

Looking back on that time Tim Durant said: "When I first met Charlie he was the genius of Hollywood, the greatest man that ever was in motion pictures. Everybody respected him and revered him. When he left, everybody was against him. Everybody was afraid to be associated with him. They all rejected him. Well, this was the McCarthy era and there was a general fear of guilt by association."

Chaplin himself behaved with considerable dignity during the whole tawdry episode, his only public comment on the affair — and that an oblique one — being implicit in his film *A King in New York* which he made in England in 1956. It's the story of a deposed European monarch who arrives a penniless refugee in America, which he believes to be a land inspired by ideals of freedom and democracy. He is, however, rapidly disillusioned. By the time the picture was made Chaplin had broken his final ties with the USA by selling his shares in United Artists for something more than one million dollars.

In Switzerland Chaplin and Oona had four more children to add to the four who had been born in America and by the time the youngest arrived Chaplin was seventy-three years old. A few years later his eldest son, Charles, Junior, died of a heart attack at the age of forty-three. He had long suffered from a drink problem and indeed his whole life had been burdened by the impossibility of living up to the name that had been imposed upon him. Without inheriting any of his father's talent, he had tried to be an actor and, not surprisingly, he had failed. Nobody could possibly blame him for that but to be called Charlie Chaplin and not to be a genius was more than he could bear and he had sought refuge, as so many sons of the famous have done, in alcohol.

It would, of course, be easy to blame the father for the fate of the son and perhaps if they had been closer things might have turned out otherwise. But Chaplin's contact with his two elder sons was necessarily limited, although he was, apparently, an affectionate enough parent. Although Lita Grey said he was not the kind to "bounce his children on his knee," Sydney remembered him as "awkward when embracing and touching and rather reserved. But he had a very good heart with his kids and he was very decent." And from her observations of the Chaplins *en famille*, Claire Bloom said: "He just adored his children and that's all there is to it."

In 1966 Chaplin, then aged seventy-seven, made his last film, *A Countess from Hong Kong*. He wrote it, directed it, composed the music and played a small part as a ship's steward. The stars were Sophia Loren and Marlon Brando. With Brando he had very little rapport and it showed in the picture, which was old-fashioned and somehow listless. Critical and public reception of it was generally unfavourable and Chaplin returned to Switzerland and family life. Although he busied himself with composing music for some of his silent pictures and negotiated a very handsome fee for the re-release of nine of his feature films he had no need to work for he was an extremely rich man. In 1972 his personal fortune was estimated at more than £7,000,000.

Also in 1972, twenty years after he had been driven out of America as an unsavoury character and a dangerous Communist, he returned to the United States by special invitation and in triumph. At the Lincoln Center in New York 3,000 people gave him a standing ovation when he appeared at a gala showing of two of his films and in Los Angeles a few days later (on April 10th) he received a special Oscar in recognition of the "incalculable effect" he had had in making motion pictures "the art form of the century". It was only the second Oscar he had received, the first having been for *The Circus* as long ago as 1928.

This second, belated award was presumably America's way of saying sorry for the treatment he had received twenty years earlier and, though it can hardly have wiped away all the bitterness he must have felt, it was at least a handsome apology and Chaplin accepted it graciously, although at the same time he was undoubtedly using the occasion to serve his own ends. Sydney Chaplin said his father was not at all impressed by Oscars and that once indeed he had rejected one, informing the Academy that it was not qualified to judge his work and didn't know a good picture from a bad one. The special Oscar attracted him though because "he had just re-released all his pictures and he said, 'This is good for business.'"

Whatever he may have felt about Academy Awards, however, he certainly took considerable pride in another, and rather different investiture at Buckingham Palace three years later when Charlie, the tramp, the little fellow, became Sir Charles Chaplin. But that, too, according to Sydney was an honour he had declined before.

"They offered him a knighthood years and years ago and he said then, 'It's ridiculous; I can't do it — the little fellow who is for the underdog and the average man and he's suddenly knighted. No, I can't do that. It's against my principles.' But at the end of his life I think he just felt, 'Well, it's an honour' and he accepted."

Charlie Chaplin, Sir Charles Chaplin, who said when he received his special Oscar, "I went into this business for money and the art grew out of it," lived to enjoy that honour for nearly three years. But on Christmas Day, 1977, he died at home in his sleep. He was eighty-eight years old.

As a macabre postscript to his life and death his body was later stolen from the tiny cemetery at Corsier in Switzerland where he was buried and was not rediscovered for several months. I somehow doubt whether the old and distinguished Sir Charles Chaplin would have found that very amusing. With age and honours he had acquired a certain pomposity, as the second half of his autobiography clearly shows. But I like to think that the young Chaplin, the one who told Harry Wheldon that his talent lay in his arse, would have derived a considerable degree of mirth from such a bizarre happening.

He was a rare and complex man, of great arrogance and great insecurity; a man who appears to have had immense charm and a fair number of the other, less engaging qualities which often walk hand-in-hand with charm. He could be calculating, he could be ruthless in defence of himself and his work, he could be pompous and he could be cold. But then the kind of talent that he possessed is never found in men of simple good nature.

In any event whether he was lovable or not is largely immaterial. What is important is that he may well have been, in the words of the equally immortal Buster Keaton, "the greatest comedian that ever lived". What Chaplin grasped more keenly than any other comedian was the fact that farce and tragedy are very often exactly the same thing, viewed from different angles. So in his films the humour and the pathos (whatever you may have felt about the pathos) grew from the same root.

In the years since his death the inevitable process of cutting him down to size has flourished strongly. There are those who dismiss him merely as a superb mime — assuming that a superb mime is simply to be dismissed. He was not, they say, a great actor at all, nor was he a great director: he didn't even understand camera angles. Well, perhaps he didn't. But what he did understand far more than any of his critics ever did was the value of simplicity. "I remain one thing and one thing only," he said, "and that is a clown. It places me on a far higher plane than any politician." And he also said, just as pertinently: "All I need to make a comedy is a park, a policeman and a pretty girl."

For anyone less than a genius that could have been a recipe for disaster; for Chaplin it was the recipe for greatness. And if I, and perhaps others like me, find him far more admirable than funny the loss is ours and not his. In his own field Chaplin, like Jeeves, stands alone.

The famous Hollywood sign, high in the hills overlooking the movie capital and now restored to its original condition after the third O had begun to droop — rather as Hollywood itself has done.

above: An aerial view of the MGM lot at Culver City. MGM was the studio that boasted "more stars than there are in heaven".

opposite page:

above left: Jack Warner who, according to George Raft, ran his studio "like Alcatraz".

above right: Darryl F. Zanuck of 20th Century Fox. "There was only one boss I believed in," he said. "And that was me."

below: Harry Cohn, head of Columbia Studios, of whom it was said "You had to stand in line to hate him."

above: MGM's emblem is a roaring lion. This is how the roar was recorded.

opposite page:

above: Sam Goldwyn, the glove salesman from Minsk, who invented the Goldwynism — as, for example, "Gentlemen, include me out."

below: Louis B. Mayer, boss of MGM, seen here looking young and sinister and (inset) old and sinister.

On the wall of the production office of MGM studios during the great and golden days of Hollywood there hung a most remarkable chart. It listed every actress on the company payroll from the biggest star to the youngest starlet and against each name were the details of the lady's menstrual cycle. This very intimate information which, generally speaking, might be thought to be of interest only to the actress herself, was not of course for public consumption. Indeed, to the public, MGM, like every other Hollywood studio, presented the ladies as creatures who were rather more than merely human; if the public believed that it could see daylight between an actress's feet and the ground as she moved around, MGM was not about to disabuse it. And certainly the studio had no intention of presenting its female stars as people who were subject, like anybody else, to the inconveniences of internal plumbing.

The existence of the chart, in fact, reflected an aspect of Hollywood that is often overlooked: the studios were actually run on a coolly businesslike basis. Dream factories they may have been but the people at the top put as much emphasis on the factory as the public did on the dream. Or, to put it another way, the denizens of this particular factory town may have been, as somebody once said, engaged in an occupation akin to putting the skin on baloney, but they were determined to put that skin on in as cost-effective a manner as possible.

Thus, the interest in an actress's menstrual period was not personal but professional, a matter of business efficiency. "If the producer of a film knew that his leading lady was going to get the curse on Friday," said George Sidney, one of the most efficient of MGM's directors, "then Friday was the day the hero would chase the villains over the bridge, while the lady stayed at home. That way you didn't lose a day's shooting."

MGM was not, of course, typical of Hollywood studios, nor could it be because it was the biggest, the most powerful, the most glamorous. But it established the pattern on which the other studios were modelled and its rise and fall more or less mirrors the rise and fall of Hollywood itself. Furthermore, the way in which the company was created was, at least, fairly typical of the way in which its main competitors, Warner Brothers, Columbia, Paramount and 20th Century Fox, were also created.

It was established in 1924 by Marcus Loew, the head of Loew's Incorporated, a film exhibitor and cinema-owner based in New York, and it was brought into existence to provide products for

Loew's theatres. MGM was, in fact, like most of the other studios, the result of a merger or a series of mergers. Loew acquired Metro Pictures, a Hollywood production outfit which had been formed in 1915, and then the Samuel Goldwyn Studios. Finally he took over Louis B. Mayer Productions and thus Metro-Goldwyn-Mayer was formed, with Mayer himself as studio chief.

To the public, the studios which built the stars, made the movies and attracted the publicity, were the controllers of the film industry, the cinemas where the pictures were ultimately shown being merely a necessary adjunct. But, in truth, the tail wagged the dog. Financial control always remained in New York with the parent companies which ran the cinemas and arranged the distribution. In the 1930s and 1940s, when Hollywood flourished as it had never done before and never would again and when Louis B. Mayer appeared to be the most influential man in the entire business, he was actually far less powerful than Nicholas Schenck, who had taken over as president of Loew's Incorporated. And so it was with the other major studios. At Warner Brothers, for example, Jack Warner in Hollywood was the figurehead but it was his brother Harry in New York who had the power.

Nevertheless it was not the businessmen, the Nicholas Schencks and the Harry Warners, who created the Hollywood of fact and myth and legend. This was the work of the studio chiefs, men like Mayer and Jack Warner and Harry Cohn of Columbia, and they ran their studios like medieval baronies or small dictatorships, not always benevolent. These were the men the stars had to placate and whose rules they had to follow if they wished to thrive or even survive. The fact that the moguls in turn were subject to the whims and dictates of the New York office and the stockholders didn't really matter. In Hollywood itself the moguls were the law.

"They developed the system of patronage," said Dore Schary, who in the early 1950s replaced Mayer as head of MGM studios. "They were the *patrons* and everything was fine so long as the help did as they were supposed to do. If they didn't, well, they weren't given the best seats at the dinner table any more; they might even be fired. It was considered bad form not to do what the *patron* wanted you to do."

Any hint of megalomania which shines through that is by no means illusory. Without the stars the studios were nothing, but the studios controlled the stars. They controlled them by means of contracts and options. The contracts were usually for seven years, which gave the impression of security but the options, which could

287

be exercised by the studios every six or twelve months, took the security away. And on top of that there was the suspension clause. A star who refused to do a film he had been offered by his studio was automatically suspended without pay for the duration of the time he stayed away from work.

Moreover, the length of time he was on suspension was added to his seven-year contract, always assuming the studio wished to keep him when the seven years were up. And that clause was skilfully manipulated by the studio chiefs, who used it as a form of coercion to force stars to make films which were unsuitable for them or even downright trashy.

The system worked rather like this: a young actor, carefully nurtured by his studio, had at last been accepted as a star. Right, said the studio, you must now live like a star: you must buy a bigger house, a bigger car; you must build a swimming pool and a tennis court; you must dress expensively and hire a butler and maids and gardeners. Very soon the actor would be living up to and beyond his income. And at this point the studio would offer him a film that he knew was entirely wrong for him. He would refuse to do it, the studio would suspend him; the bills would continue to flow in — but the salary would not. Within a very few weeks the new young star would be willing to make any film if only the studio would take him back.

"Sometimes," said Joan Fontaine, "they would use the suspension clause in other ways too. Very often they would offer you a picture that was absolutely wrong for you on purpose because they didn't have anything worthwhile for you and didn't want to pay your salary for a few weeks. So you'd say No to the film and they'd suspend you."

As to the personalities of the men who operated this ruthless system, opinions vary considerably. Now, when they are all dead and films are perhaps only the third most important entertainment medium in Hollywood after television and the record industry, there is a general nostalgia for them, a feeling that with their passing there passed the age of giants. But they were by no means so beloved when they were alive.

There is a story that when Louis Mayer died a vast crowd, far exceeding all expectations, attended his funeral and when a bystander enquired the reason for so many mourners he was told: "We just want to make sure the bastard's really dead." That may be apocryphal but it is certainly true that when Harry Cohn died an extremely large number of people turned up at his funeral. "My

God," somebody said to the writer and director Joseph L. Mankiewicz, "look at this crowd. What are they doing here?"

"Well," said Mankiewicz, "give the public what they want . . ." (This remark is often attributed to Red Skelton but Mankiewicz insisted to me that it was he who said it and I'm not here to call Joe Mankiewicz a liar.)

It was of Cohn that the Hollywood gossip columnist Hedda Hopper said: "You had to stand in line to hate him," and that George Jessel, the producer-actor-entertainer, said: "He was a great showman and a great son of a bitch." Cohn's own best-remembered comments about himself and his work were: "It's better than being a pimp," and: "I don't have ulcers — I give ulcers." In much the same way Darryl F. Zanuck, who ran 20th Century Fox, once remarked: "People don't threaten me — I threaten people." And of Louis Mayer, Joe Mankiewicz said: "He was in many ways one of the most evil, one of the most dreadful men I've ever known in my life. He was ruthless and he could be utterly unfeeling."

Mankiewicz again on 20th Century Fox studios: "It was run like a sort of Uganda with Darryl Zanuck as a kind of Idi Amin at the head of it." And George Raft on Warner Brothers: "That was like Alcatraz. That was a tough studio, believe me. I mean, Jack Warner was a nice guy in the living room but in the studio he was a tough man. We had to do what he said."

The emerging picture of the Hollywood moguls, the founding fathers of the modern film industry, as so many tyrants or prison governors is, however, only partly accurate. The fact that they were all hard and forbidding men was only one thing that they had in common. They also had in common the fact that they were all very short. It has been said that if you had gathered all the Hollywood moguls together in one room and swung a sword five foot six inches above the ground you wouldn't have touched a hair on the head of any one of them. But, apart from being small and tough, they shared one other, far more valuable, quality: they were all utterly devoted to the movie business.

Having dismissed Mayer as evil, dreadful, ruthless and unfeeling, Joe Mankiewicz added: "But he could have run General Motors or ICI as well as he did MGM. He was a brilliant, brilliant executive."

"There are many things," said the director Richard Brooks, "that can, I suppose, be said about the so-called Hollywood moguls. They were pirates, some of them, monsters some of them but I guess that one of the most important things was that they loved movies, they cared about movies.''

They were not themselves artists these men, nor were they necessarily creative. Most of them had been hustlers in other areas — junk dealers, glove salesmen, furriers — before they moved into the movie industry. But they had the ability to hire artists, to recognise creative talent. ''They hired,'' said Joe Mankiewicz, ''the best bloody intellects they could find. They didn't respect them but they hired them. There wasn't any piece of fictional material being written and published — and sometimes even unpublished — anywhere in the world that the studios didn't know about. They had story departments in London, Paris, Budapest, Copenhagen, anywhere you care to name and everything that was written was distilled into long synopses, shorter synopses, still shorter synopses and finally one-page synopses and these would find their way into every studio in Hollywood. And the studios would hire writers like William Faulkner and Robert Sherwood and Scott Fitzgerald and get them to convert these synopses of synopses into screenplays.''

Or, to sum them up, these Hollywood moguls, the way Richard Brooks did: ''They had tremendous egos, tremendous personalities. They were overwhelming in their tenacity, in their ebullience and in their style. You were impressed by the fact that they were attractive. They weren't good-looking men in the sense that an actor was good-looking. They were attractive in the sense you wanted to be around them. They told good stories; they told them well and they could be tough. Oh yes.

'' *You* couldn't break a contract but *they* could. They knew how. I suppose many of the stories are apocryphal about the things they did and didn't do and the people they broke and didn't break, but they *could* break people and they could do it in such a way that you almost liked them for doing it. They could be difficult with people, they could be difficult on contracts and they would never forget. They were vindictive to a degree and they knew how to fight in the clinches. They were street fighters, alley fighters but with it all the least they had was their love of movies. I never met one of them who didn't want to know what the movie — your movie, his movie — was about. They'd go down into the cutting room and hang on to the cans of film like they were personal pints of blood.''

With such formidable men in charge it is perhaps not to be wondered at that the stars regarded themselves — and were regarded by others — as the best-paid slaves in history. They were cosseted to a degree that nobody ever was before or ever has been since. At MGM, for instance, there was a special restaurant where the best food in Hollywood was served, free, every day to the top forty or so stars on the payroll. MGM, it was said, was the only place in the world where you could get 5,000 dollars a week and all found. Now this may be the kind of slavery that many people would welcome but the fact remains that, because of the contract system with its options and suspension clauses, the stars had hardly any control over their own destinies.

"There was very little," said Richard Brooks, "that a star ever did — except drink — that was not under the supervision of the studio. Very little, especially for the women. The studios brought them along, groomed them, even educated them. The studios decided with whom they would go out, organised their social life as well as their professional life; became involved in their medical life, their health problems, their babies, if they were having any, their abortions, if they were having any. There were some marvellous young actresses who were practically born into the business: Elizabeth Taylor, Jean Simmons, a number of others of that kind, who were naturals. Well, they never even learned how to go shopping or buy their own clothes by themselves."

On the other hand, Dore Schary (who was, it must be remembered, a studio head himself, after all) denied the allegation that the stars were simply chattels. "It's nonsense," he said. "They were chattels in that they were under contract and if the studios had a quarrel with them, like Warner Brothers often did with Cagney or Bogart or Bette Davis, they'd be put on suspension. But even when that happened the studio would be around after a while to make sure the stars weren't really in trouble, weren't injuring themselves. They'd be offered another deal, another contract. The studios really looked after them."

Even so, this sounds very like brainwashing; a paternalism that could by turns be stern and benevolent. The recalcitrant star would first be broken and then welcomed back with all his sins — real or most often imaginary — generously forgiven. An excellent case in point is James Cagney who, in the mid-1930s, quarrelled with Warner Brothers and set out to make his own, independent productions. Jack Warner was not pleased and let the word be known around other studios and — even more importantly — among the exhibitors and distributors that he was not pleased. Cagney's independent productions failed, financially, because he couldn't get mass distribution for them, and within a very short time he made his peace with Warner and was welcomed back into the contractual fold.

Ironically, though, if the stars had but known it and, more to the point, had known how to use their knowledge, the power within Hollywood really lay with them. The moguls would insist that it was they who made the stars but this was never really true; the moguls gave actors and actresses the opportunities, the vehicles, in which they might become stars. But the accolade of stardom itself was conferred, as it always has been, by the cinema-going public. Sam Goldwyn, for instance, spent years and a fortune trying to make Anna Sten, an import from Russia, into a star but it didn't work. The public looked at her and, as a star, simply found her wanting.

In the 1930s and the 1940s, however, the stars were conditioned to believe that anything good that happened to them, such as fame and popularity, was benevolently bestowed by the studio and the diminutive tyrant who ran it. If the tyrant said, "I made you: I can break you," the stars believed it and so, like birds hypnotised by the dance of the weasel, they gave their full attention and even their love to the moguls who controlled their destinies.

Richard Brooks said that the one thing the studios didn't control was the drinking habits of the stars but in some cases even that wasn't true. June Allyson, America's archetypal girl-next-door and for many years a contract star at MGM, said: "L. B. Mayer was the giant of the industry and he loved being called our father [not, presumably, to be confused with Our Father as in the Lord's Prayer? Oh, I don't know, though] and he really treated us all like children. We weren't allowed to drink, we weren't allowed to smoke and we had to go out with the gentlemen that he thought were proper for us."

This paternalistic attitude — "You are all my children" — was a particular gambit of Mayer's. Robert Taylor, having felt underpaid for some time, finally plucked up the courage to burst into Mayer's office and demand an increase in salary. When he came out again a friend asked: "Well, Bob, did you get the raise?"

"No," said Taylor, "but I gained a father."

Oddly enough, the stars hardly ever seemed to resent this obvious confidence trick. June Allyson certainly didn't. "Mayer was the only family I ever really had and it was nice to be told, 'Now this is good for you and this is not good for you.' I never found him an ogre. I loved him. I truly did."

Yes, I said, but surely there were those times when he wanted you to play a part in a film that you didn't like, that you felt was wrong. What happened then?

"Well," she said, "he would call you up to his office and he'd get you a sandwich and a glass of milk and tell you what a good little girl you were and how he wanted only the best for you and how he couldn't understand how you could go against his wishes. Then he'd start to cry and by the time you left the office you really felt you'd done something terrible and so you agreed to make the film."

The ability to summon up tears whenever they were likely to be handy was Mayer's greatest stock-in-trade. In many ways he was a far better actor than most of the stars on his payroll. Joe Mankiewicz recalled the time when Myrna Loy decided to rebel against a role that was being foisted on her against her will. A rebellion by a major star such as Miss Loy was regarded by Mayer as a threat to the very foundations of the studio and was therefore something he had to quell very smartly.

Mankiewicz was present when Mayer called Myrna Loy into his office to persuade her as to the error of her ways. "Mayer," he said, "suddenly collapsed physically. His face turned grey and he tottered and Myrna said, 'Oh my God, L. B., what's the matter?' He said, 'Nothing, nothing,' and Mayer's secretary was there and she said, 'I'm gonna call Dr. Jones.' And the doctor came over and there was this big business of getting Mayer onto his couch and Myrna knelt beside him and she was terribly upset because she and this man had been arguing so vehemently and she said, 'Oh God, I did something to him!' And there was Dr. Jones taking Mayer's blood pressure and saying, 'L. B., please don't talk,' and L. B. looked at Myrna and the doctor looked at Myrna and she said, 'L. B., look, I'll play the goddam part, really I will. I'll play it, L. B.' And he said, 'No, no. I don't want you to. No, no, you're not gonna play the part just because I got sick. You're doing it out of pity. You're not doing it because you want to play the part. No, no, Myrna, that way I don't want it, that way I don't want to run the studio, that way I don't want to control other people's lives.' So Myrna said, 'L. B., believe me, I want to play the part,' and he said, 'No, my God, this I can't believe,' and she said, 'L. B., on my mother's life, I swear I want to play the part.' 'Oh,' he said, 'oh, if I could only believe that!' She said, 'Please, L. B., please believe me — I do want to play the part.' He said, 'All right, all right,' and the secretary said, 'Myrna, I think you'd better leave now,' and Myrna left, in tears, and as soon as she'd gone L. B. jumped off that couch like a jack-in-the-box and said, 'Okay, who's next? Who's waiting out there?' I couldn't believe my eyes, I couldn't believe the performance he'd given."

In thumbnail sketches of the three main ogres of Hollywood, Jesse Lassky, Junior, a writer and son of one of the founders of Hollywood in the silent days, said: "Mayer was a great sentimentalist. He wept as easily as a crocodile. He was deeply moved by the sight of the American flag; he was a confirmed patriot; he was the self-appointed guardian of the nation's morals. But aside from this surface sentimentality, his apparent charm and warmth and love and his habit of going around patting the little girls on the back (and other places) he was as ruthless as he needed to be — a very strong man indeed under a cloak of mellowness and kindness.

"Harry Cohn was even tougher. He was almost a brute. He didn't care about anybody's feelings. But again he was an iron leader who exercised complete control. Sometimes he hid microphones on the film stages so he could sit in his office and hear every word that was said, on and off the set. And yet he had a curious kind of taste, a shrewd instinct for knowing what was good and what was bad.

"Jack Warner was a joker. He fooled a lot of people. He shared with Mayer this feeling of being the guardian of the safety of the United States but he was also a jester and his jokes could be very cruel. And again he was ruthless. Once he barred his own son from the studio because the boy had upset him. But at the same time he was good at seeing the value of people, at discovering which star could do a certain thing well and then developing him or her in that kind of picture. They were different kinds of people, those studio chiefs, but they were all showmen."

Another difference noted by the producer Pandro S. Berman, who worked for both Mayer and Cohn, was this: "Mayer respected the people he hired and generally he gave them a great deal of leeway. But the minute you went to work for Harry Cohn he despised you. He figured that if you were foolish enough to make a deal with him, you couldn't be any good."

It was Cohn who, when asked to describe in a few words what the movie business was all about, said: "It's about cunt and horses." Mayer would have been horrified. To Mayer it was about glamour and beauty and romance and, said Berman: "He was the most far-sighted man I've ever known in the picture business. I'll give you an example: one day he called me up and said he'd like me to leave RKO and go work for him. I was flattered and amused at the same time because I'd just signed a new three-year contract and I told him so. He said, 'Did I ask you when?' I said, 'No, you didn't.' He said, 'Well, I mean when you're available whether it's tomorrow or three years from now.' He had patience. He looked ahead."

George Sidney had a similar tale to relate. "When I was a test director at MGM, I made a test of a sixteen-year-old girl from the south called Ava Gardner. She'd just come up from the cotton fields and she was raw, believe me. I mean, shoes and she were not friendly at that time. But Ava was a girl who had innate talent. It was in an undeveloped state and it had to be brought out because, for one thing, she couldn't speak the language — she had this terrible Southern accent, which had to be worked on. But we made this test and Mayer said, 'Good, make another test when she's seventeen and another when she's eighteen. Just keep on going.' Because, you see, we were shooting for the potential she would have when she was twenty, twenty-one."

But, meanwhile, as the studios waited patiently for the potential to develop and carefully groomed their starlets, a rigid discipline was imposed.

June Allyson: "You never questioned Mr. Mayer."

Me: "Why? He didn't like that?"

J. A. : "No. You would get punished."

Me: "What was punishment?"

J. A.: "Punishment was getting suspended or being taken out of a film or not being allowed to do a film you wanted to do."

Me: "Were you ever suspended?"

J. A.: "No, but I almost was when I wanted to marry Richard."

(Miss Allyson was first married to Dick Powell, who had begun his career as a very popular singer, dancer and light comedian. Later he was to become even more popular playing tougher roles such as private detectives and the like. But at the time of his marriage to June Allyson he was between these careers and little regarded in Hollywood.)

J. A.: "Mr. Mayer said, 'You're a bright new star and we can't have you marrying an old has-been.' Well, this was the only time I defied him. I said I was going to marry Richard and I did marry him."

Me: "How long did it take Mayer to forgive you for having defied him?"

J. A.: "Oh, a good five years. When he saw that my marriage was going to last and that Richard was becoming successful again, that's when he forgave me. Mr. Mayer didn't have too much respect for people who weren't successful. But when he saw that things had worked out well for Richard and me he would hold me up as a very good example to all the new kids on the lot, saying, 'Now see, this is the way you should run your life — marry an intelligent man.' And all the time he was the one who had tried to talk me out of it."

Occasionally the bigger, older, most secure stars would rebel and sit out the resulting suspension because, having been around a long time, they could afford to do so. Humphrey Bogart, for example, suffered many a suspension because he had been careful from the start to build up what he called his "Fuck you" fund.

For the younger stars this was not so easy. Though they were well paid, they were encouraged by the studios to live well, so it was financially important to them that their options should be picked up regularly. It might be thought, of course, that at a time when the industry was thriving and Hollywood was turning out close to 800 feature films a year, being dropped by one studio was not such a crisis. There were, surely, other studios that would be eager to pick up a discarded but established star. This, however, was not necessarily so. The moguls might, and often did, betray and double-cross each other but in the face of a recalcitrant star they presented a solidarity that would be the envy of any militant trade union. If a star was dropped because he had displeased his own studio the word would go around that he was trouble, that he made waves, that nobody else should touch him.

Even a nest egg was not proof against this kind of treatment, although in a community that used wealth as a yardstick not only for success but also for merit, it did entitle an actor or an actress to a degree of respect.

Ann Rutherford, another MGM contract player, best known perhaps for playing Mickey Rooney's girlfriend in the Andy Hardy series, was one of the comparatively few actresses who swiftly realised the advantage of having independent means. She learned the lesson early in one of her first films as a teenager at Republic Studios. When she reported for work on that film, *Waterfront Lady*, starring Ben Lyon, she discovered that among the bit-part players was one Jack La Rue. Now in the days of silent films this La Rue had been quite a star, the idol of Ann Rutherford and her schoolmates. She was, therefore, shocked to see him fallen so low.

"He was playing, like a bartender or something, and I was quite horrified because he had only two or three days' work. So I asked the assistant director, 'Why is he playing such a tiny role?' and he said, 'Well, the man's got to eat. If he'd saved his money when he was at the top he wouldn't have to be doing this stuff. He could have just sat back and waited for the right part to come along.'

"And this taught me something very important. The other young contract stars were buying cars and furs and spending their money and going into cardiac arrest every time their options came up for renewal. But I went to the studios by bus. I didn't drive my money or wear it; I saved it. And later at MGM when Mr. Mayer would call the young players in and tell them how much he loved them and what big plans he had for them and then add, sadly, that unfortunately things weren't going too well at the studio and if he kept them on it would have to be at the same salary as before, they couldn't do anything but accept. But I'd pull out my little bank book and look into it and cough delicately and say, 'Mr. Mayer, I've saved my money. If you don't have plans for me, I'll just have to go someplace else.' It was like poker, a game of bluff and I always won. I always got my raise in salary."

But if she really had saved her money and acquired a measure of independence, surely it wasn't bluff at all?

"Well, yes, it was bluff, because I didn't want to leave MGM. I mean, where else would you go? If you were at MGM you were at the White House. It was the tops. It was the best of the Hollywood studios so you didn't want to mess around and spoil your chances there. You wanted to stay. You didn't want to go out into the cruel, cold world. MGM was the White House because it had the best talents and took the best care of them. They weeded, hoed, watered that talent. I remember when they first took on Ava Gardner. They gave her diction lessons, dancing lessons, singing lessons. Not that they wanted her to be a singer or a dancer; they wanted her to learn how to move gracefully, pitch her voice properly. The other studios didn't do that; they just let you sink or swim."

So, in terror of being dropped entirely or even of being loaned out to some inferior studio, Ann Rutherford, for all her independent means, played the game according to MGM's rules.

"We were expected to maintain a certain amount of decorum, a certain amount of dignity and always to dress immaculately. If you wore white gloves and there was a speck of dust on them, somebody would reprimand you because you were not upholding the standards of Metro-Goldwyn-Mayer. As a contract player you represented the studio and it did not bode well for your future if you let the studio down in any way. They set a certain standard and we were all required to live up to it."

And this standard was also applied to the actresses' private lives. Even the men they went out with were sternly examined to make sure they met with L. B. Mayer's approval. "The studio got wind of the fact that John Garfield was trying to get my telephone number. They didn't want me to go out with John Garfield. You know why? He was quite a bit older than I was and they thought it wouldn't look well for my image as Andy Hardy's girlfriend if I went out with a man that much older."

Miss Rutherford, therefore, did not go out with John Garfield. Did she not resent this appalling intrusion into her life? "No, I was very grateful for the studio's interference. I didn't want anything to jeopardise this marvellous life I was living. To me it was like a passport to the world. It opened doors for me that never would have been opened otherwise."

And indeed it was a marvellous life. Joan Fontaine said: "The so-called 'golden age' of Hollywood, between 1935 and just after the war, was unbelievably opulent and glorious. Everybody had yachts and race horses and all that. This was before taxes came in to the extent they have now and we were making so much money we didn't know how to spend it. You thought, 'What shall we do with it this week? Let's charter a yacht and go somewhere. And then what will we do with all this money next week?'"

But if the studios offered the carrot of wealth with one hand, they still brandished the stick of fear with the other. Suspension, for example, did not merely mean that the weekly paycheck stopped coming in; it also meant the suspended player was unable to earn any money anywhere else. Joan Fontaine said: "Your contract forbade you even to get a job as a waitress or sell ribbons in a department store. So you simply sat waiting for the phone to ring, waiting for them to forgive you for being a naughty girl. Also in Hollywood you never knew from one day to another whether you were going to be fired or not. Even when I was making *Rebecca* (her fourteenth film in five years) Alfred Hitchcock kept coming up to me and saying, 'You know I'm rooting for you but you're on trial.' I was constantly being told I was on trial and might be replaced."

Replaced, though, by whom? Surely a star, an established star, had some power, some ability at least to argue that although somebody else might be able to play his or her role, nobody else could bring quite the same qualities to the film? Yes, but ... "The studios had a very tacky system," said Ann Rutherford. "They always had a threat coming along to everyone else. There was always a new Joan Crawford or a new Judy Garland waiting in the wings. This was sort of nervous-making but it kept everyone on their best behaviour. For instance, when Mario Lanza was giving the studio a problem, he set foot on the lot one day only to find someone who looked startlingly like him and wearing the costume that he was to wear for his next picture going into the adjoining dressing-room where somebody said, 'Your test is being shot this afternoon at two.' Well, little experiences like that were liable to make an actor or an actress shape up pretty fast."

Always it was drummed into them that they were only as good — or as bad — as their last film, that their careers were fragile things that could fall apart under the onslaught of a bad review or the frown of a studio head. "The rewards," said Jesse Lassky, Junior, "were so enormous. You could earn so much when you were successful. But you could be cut off and go down faster than you'd come up."

Hollywood, somebody once said, was the only place in the world where you could be forgotten while you were out of the room going to the toilet and this is not too much of an exaggeration. To Jesse Lassky the place was a jungle. "Like a jungle it looked very beautiful but like a jungle it was full of danger. There were serpents lurking in every tree. One mis-step and down you went. An actor who took an extra drink could be branded as an alcoholic and not get the job he was after. A writer who said something careless could be dismissed as mentally unstable. And so it went all the way up the ladder. People didn't only live in glass houses; they wore glass suits."

The director Richard Brooks said: "Failure is the biggest fear in Hollywood. People die of failure here. The death certificate might say cancer or heart attack but they get the cancer or the heart attack only after they've failed."

The studio view of this system of iron control was, not surprisingly, different from that of the stars. The studio view was that they were exercising a sort of stern, but kindly, guardianship, protecting these strange, erratic creatures they employed; they were offering them security. And, indeed, there was a degree of security for those who understood the system and, through not bucking it too overtly, made it work for them.

Speaking from the point of view of the writer and director, Joe Mankiewicz said: "There was the kind of security that, as a creative person, you never expected to have. Let's take writing, for instance. Since the beginning of time writing has been something that somebody does by facing a blank block of paper with a pen, pencil or typewriter and just putting down whatever it is that he or she wants to write. But having written it, you've then got to sell it, to earn your living from it. In Hollywood for the first time you were paid by the week just to write. And if your writing was no good you didn't have to give the money back. Again the director was hired for fifty-two weeks of the year. It gave you a tremendous sense of security."

Along with the security went the protection, the kind of protection that no other industry ever has, would ever have dared or ever could provide for its employees. When Clark Gable, monumentally drunk, drove his car into a tree it was the studio, MGM, and not the police who were called to clear up the mess and get him to hospital for treatment. The police were never involved at all. When Spencer Tracy, equally drunk, smashed up a store window it was the studio who bailed him out and made sure no inkling of the affair ever reached the Press. They might have balked at covering up murder, armed robbery or acts of terrorism, but for anything less they ensured that a star whose pictures were making money was virtually immune from prosecution. The studios employed heads of publicity, heads of security and even heads of police whose job it was to rescue the stars from potential trouble with the law.

"If a star was picked up for rape," said Joe Mankiewicz, "the chances were that the studio had somebody with contacts at the downtown District Attorney's office and he made sure the case never got to court or the newspapers. When Jean Harlow's husband, Paul Bern, committed suicide Louis Mayer was so accustomed to controlling the police that he got to the house before they did and picked up Bern's suicide note and put it in his pocket. He'd have taken it away and destroyed it if Irving Thalberg hadn't pointed out that it was material evidence and that it might have looked bad for Jean if there was no suicide note. If you were a star you knew that in your private life you were guarded all the time. Anything went wrong in your home, you sent for somebody from the studio to fix it — the stove, the plumbing, the electricity, whatever."

Pandro S. Berman said: "My God, the studios did everything. They had such good contacts with the police, the mayor and the newspapers that often when something happened involving a star it was years before news of it came out."

But did the studios actually bribe the law and the Press to cover up the peccadillos of the stars? Dore Schary, himself a studio head, I would remind you again, though in the less palmy days of Hollywood, flinched a little at the use of the word "bribe". He said: "Let's say the studio had friends in the police department. If anything happened — somebody driving while drunk or being caught in a bedroom doing something he shouldn't be doing — you'd call your friends in the police and they'd cover it up. You didn't have to bribe them. Gifts might be exchanged but you wouldn't call it bribery."

Sometimes, however, incidents occurred which the studios were quite unable to cover up, a case in point being the night when Robert Mitchum was "busted" for smoking pot. As soon as he was arrested, long before he was brought to trial, the gossip columnists such as Louella Parsons and Hedda Hopper began a campaign against him, inspired by self-righteous hypocrisy. They wanted to have his films banned on the grounds that it was injurious to the mental and psychological health of young America to be subjected to movies that starred a man who smoked marijuana. Indeed, in odd places around America Mitchum's pictures were banned and his future as a star looked, to say the least, distinctly shaky. But here was one case where the studio system worked for the star and not against him. At the time he was tried and convicted of his crime, Mitchum was under contract to RKO and thus to Howard Hughes. Although it became fairly apparent that the marijuana was either planted on him by the police or a police informer or that, at best, the police were intent on arresting him as an example of the immorality of Hollywood, Mitchum was sent to prison and it was firmly believed that this would be the end of his career.

But, to most people's surprise, Howard Hughes stood by him. Robert Parrish, the director, said: "Hughes called Mitchum's agent and said, 'I'm sending a cheque for 50,000 dollars immediately to take care of his family while he's in jail. And when he comes out I'm giving him a new contract and he's going to be the biggest star on the lot.' And he was. So there's one actor whose career was saved by the studio."

The Mitchum episode happened in 1948 and by then, admittedly, the power of the studio was already in decline and the power of the star was in the ascendancy. The event that caused this shift in the balance and was a major contributory factor in the decline of Hollywood itself had occurred four years earlier when

Olivia de Havilland, a star who had been so frequently on suspension that her seven-year contract looked like extending into eternity, took Warner Brothers to the Supreme Court to challenge the studio's right to add suspension time automatically to the duration of the contract. The Supreme Court found in her favour. The law was changed and from then on a seven-year contract was precisely that and could not be extended, save by mutual agreement. The position of the studios was dramatically weakened. Television in America was already robbing the cinemas of a huge proportion of their audiences and the stars were the biggest weapon Hollywood had left. But now that a star could, if he so wished, sit out his entire contract on suspension knowing that his term of durance was legally limited, the studios were obliged to hide the stick and offer more carrot. Agents who, hitherto, had been little more than intermediaries between studios and stars began to exert more muscle on behalf of their clients, demanding ever more lucrative contracts and even percentages of the profits. The freelance star, asking for one film what previously he would have been happy to accept for a whole year, began to flourish. By the end of the 1940s the golden age of the studios — and consequently of Hollywood itself — was virtually over.

Perhaps it wouldn't have happened, would never have been allowed to happen, in the heyday of the moguls but by 1950, a year in which American cinema attendances were lower than they had been since 1933 and the depths of the Depression, the moguls were getting old. Mayer was sixty-five, Cohn fifty-nine, Warner fifty-six. They were by no means ancient and far from senile but there had been too many fat years behind them. They had grown accustomed to virtually unchallenged power; had become set in their ways. The opportunity was there for them to move in and control the amusing, new-fangled toy called television and if they had done so the power of the Hollywood studios would have been greater than ever. But, instead, they treated it with contempt in the belief that either it wouldn't last or, if it did last, it would never rival the movies. They treated it with such scorn that they helped to cut their own throats by selling the backlog of their old pictures to it.

Even so, despite TV and despite the shattering of the suspension clause, the studios might still have survived had it not been for the introduction of the anti-Trust laws which stipulated that the same company could not make, distribute and exhibit films. Thus, cut off from their parent companies in New York and, more essentially, from a guaranteed outlet for their products, the studios were isolated and doomed.

And yet, despite all, the swiftness of the decline might have been halted had there been a new generation of Mayers, Cohns, Warners and Zanucks to take over and bring fresh enthusiasm, a fresh hunger to the battle to keep the cinema pre-eminent as the medium for mass entertainment. But, alas, there was no such younger generation and, as George Sidney said, that was the weakness of the system.

The moguls had always been careful and avid to groom new stars to replace the older, fading ones but they never thought to groom anyone to take their own places. Perhaps this was deliberate policy. In such a competitive business, why take chances, why train somebody to have the ability and desire to grab your job, possibly before you wanted to relinquish it? Or perhaps they thought themselves irreplaceable and, if not immortal, so different from other men that their powers would never fade. Or perhaps, just as likely, they never even thought about it.

"They were so confident," said George Sidney, "You know — how could there be a day when Mr. Mayer wouldn't be sitting at the helm? How could there be a day when Harry Cohn wouldn't be in the office, or Jack Warner, or Sam Goldwyn? So they never took anybody else and trained him to run the store and in the end two things happened simultaneously. One, which they couldn't help, was something called age and the other was a mechanical device called television, which just moved in and took over and bingo, the movie industry was down the drain and the whole dynasty of moguls just vanished."

Ironically, the first of the moguls to fade away was also the greatest of them, L. B. Mayer himself. By the late 1940s the impact of television had brought about a sharp slump in the picture business and coincidentally the standard of MGM's films had fallen off, too. Mayer had to find somebody who could pull the studio's products back into shape. With the approval of Nicholas Schenck, the president of Loew's and thus Mayer's boss, the job was offered to and accepted by Dore Schary, a former writer at MGM who had become production chief of RKO-Radio. Unfortunately it was soon clear that Mayer and Schary could rarely agree about how things were to be done. There was frequent conflict; there were fierce arguments in which Schenck had to intercede as peacemaker.

A similar situation had often prevailed in the 1930s when Irving

Thalberg was the incumbent of the office now occupied by Schary, but Mayer had held Thalberg in much higher regard than he did his successor and the differences between them had never become so bitter. Mayer and Thalberg learned to co-exist; Mayer and Schary never did.

In 1951, with the atmosphere at the studio deteriorating day by day, Mayer played what he believed to be his trump card and told Schenck that he had to make a choice: either Schary went or he, Mayer, did. Schenck chose — and Mayer went.

It was impossible, unbelievable. MGM without Mayer simply couldn't be. And if it was possible and really had happened, then it could only denote that the end of the world was nigh. And in a sense, of course, this is precisely what it did denote — well, not the end of the world exactly but the end of Hollywood as everyone had hitherto known it and to the inhabitants of Hollywood the end of Hollywood and the end of the world amount to pretty much the same thing. Schenck's decision, though drastic, was not, however, illogical. Mayer was sixty-six; Schary was only forty-six. In an era when everything was changing so fast and so bewilderingly, it made sense to put a younger man, a man who belonged to that time, at the helm. Unfortunately, for all his abilities, Schary was no Mayer, nor was he another Thalberg, and by the end of 1956 he, too, had been fired.

Meanwhile, if the events at the rival studios were, generally speaking, less dramatic, the effects were much the same. As their influence and income waned, so did their assets. The star system went, as indeed did the whole policy of long-term contracts, and the land went, too. In 1940, for example 20th Century Fox owned about 280 acres; today most of that area is covered by the tower block settlement of Century City and the studio only leases the sixty-three acres on which the sound stages are built.

Hollywood — to use that name as the generic term for the American film industry — still survives, of course, but it survives in a different form, a truncated form. The inmates have taken over the asylum; the stars, the agents, the accountants and, in a few celebrated cases, the directors hold the power. They put together the packages; the studios provide the backing.

Once there was such a thing as an instantly identifiable MGM picture, or Warner Brothers picture, or Columbia picture. Each studio had its own style and the style derived from the man at the top. This is no longer so because the man who is at the top today is probably not the man who was at the top yesterday nor the man who will be at the top tomorrow. With most of the studios merely minor subsidiaries of multi-national conglomerates, with their headquarters in New York, the security of the man in control depends on the latest trading figures. He is required only to be a businessman; it is no longer thought necessary that he should really care about films in the way that Mayer, Cohn, Goldwyn and the others did. Today there are simply pictures and any picture could have come from any studio.

But what did they actually achieve, these little baronies or dictatorships, back in the days when each had its own separate identity and the stars couldn't think how to spend all the money they earned and movies were still the greatest medium for mass entertainment that the world had ever known or could ever envisage? What influence did they have on public opinion, on the politics and mores of America or any other country where their products were shown?

The answer, in truth, is very little really. Occasionally films would deal with important political and social issues — but only occasionally. As Sam Goldwyn said, messages are for Western Union.

"I don't think," said Dore Schary, "that Hollywood had anything much to do with politics." Nor did Richard Brooks believe that it had, in any way, "changed the character of the people. Movies don't set social trends. We like to think they do, but they don't. I believe that in those areas movies are ten or fifteen years behind the times."

Where Hollywood had its most profound effect on the lives of the people in the audience was on the superficial level, the cosmetic level. Hollywood provided the model and led the way in fashion, in make-up, in hair-styling and in interior décor. In all else, in all important matters such as political, social, cultural and philo-sophical developments it trailed behind, reflecting rather than setting trends.

Well, perhaps that is all one could have expected of it. It wasn't there to lead crusades; it was in the entertainment business. Its function was to make money by building dreams and fantasies for people who hadn't the imagination to build such things for themselves. The films provided an opiate, escapism, and though this may be a minor role in the history of a nation it is not an unimportant one. Jesse Lassky, Junior, believed that during the Depression the cinema "kept the American dream alive. Even though much of the country was on the breadline people could still go to the movies and feel it was possible some day to end up with a Cadillac. The films gave them the impression of safety, of substance, and the belief that the old, lush goodness that lay behind the American dream was still there somewhere."

To a large extent, then, Hollywood thrived because it reflected the capitalist society within which it was created and perhaps it faded simply because it only reflected, rather than led, that society. A capitalist society has, like any other society, perforce to change. Hollywood marked and recorded those changes only after they had happened and when the changes came along that affected itself it marked, recorded — and absorbed — them too late to save itself.

The great studios dealt in illusion; it was their stock-in-trade. And illusion is, by its very nature, an intangible and fleeting commodity: now you see it, now you don't. A whole town devoted to turning out illusion on a conveyor belt is very easy to mock and deride and yet in its own way it was providing a much-needed service. Anyone offering dreams for sale will always find customers, and Hollywood offered more dreams more cheaply than anyone else has ever done.

Ann Rutherford said: "For thirty-five cents you could go into a motion picture house and watch Joan Crawford go from a girl working in the five and dime store to someone living in a penthouse. It was true, escapist entertainment. It gave everybody hope. There's nothing wrong with escapist entertainment because for the majority of people life is real and life is earnest. It was a marvellous thing that for a few hours you could go into a movie house and be transported to a never-never land, a happy world, where all the men were handsome and all the women were beautiful and all the families were happy."

Nobody (or very few people) thought of what they were doing as art, though sometimes their work became that. But if it did, it happened by accident. Hollywood never took itself all that seriously and that was one of its charms. It had a product to turn out and it tried to make each picture as good as it could be. Sometimes the ingredients blended and the cake rose; sometimes they didn't and the cake fell. Well, never mind: there was always another cake to be baked next week and another the week after that.

Sometimes today, indeed quite often today, it's possible to see a film that has cost ten times more money than most people have ever dreamed of earning and to leave the cinema feeling ripped-off and cheated, not simply because it was a bad film (with the best intentions in the world anyone can end up making a bad film) but because it was an empty film, cynically made by cynical people to a basic, lifeless formula that followed the latest trend. In its great days Hollywood was never guilty of turning out films like that: it made bad movies, certainly, but it made them nevertheless with hope and enthusiasm. The moguls may have been monsters; the star system may have been a form of gilded slavery; but there was wealth and fame to be earned and there was magic to be made. And there was a great, huge, audience out there to be wooed and won and enchanted.

That such a place as Hollywood was could not last is not surprising. Looking back on the ruins of it now, the main surprise is that it ever existed at all. It came, it flourished and then it died.

No doubt this was inevitable; it had happened before, after all. Indeed, the whole history of entertainment is a continuing story of change and impending disaster for the established form. The coming of radio was going to kill off the theatre; sound movies were going to kill off radio; television was going to kill off the movies; now satellite TV or pay TV or cable TV is going to kill off the kind of television to which we have all become accustomed. Happily, however, the worst has never yet happened. Theatre, radio, films may not thrive as they did before their newest rivals came along but, nevertheless, they still exist and they still have a significant part to play. History teaches us that eventually every empire must crumble and the many little empires that once flourished in a certain suburb of Los Angeles were no exception. But films are still made there and, as far as one can foresee, will continue to be made there. And at least the name remains — Hollywood — a name that conjures up an image of a place that was unique. The world had never seen its like before and will certainly never see its like again.

Index

Page references in italics denote illustrations

Abdication, The, 83
Actors' Studio, 35, 36
After the Ball (Renoir), 163
Adler, Jane *see* Robinson, Jane
Adventures of Tartu, The, 190
Agate, James, 218
Alhambra Theatre, 209
All About Eve, 16, 30, 31
Allan, Rupert
  and Marilyn Monroe, 29, 39, 40
    and Arthur Miller, 37
    and Yves Montand, 43
    and suicide theory, 52, 53
Allen, Irwin, 107
Allied Film Makers, 129
Allyson, June
  and L.B. Mayer, 292–3, 295–6
Alperovici, Boris, *202*
  and Gracie Fields, 219–21, 222
American Academy of Dramatic Art, 145
Anderson, Judith, 239
Andy Hardy series, 296, 298
Angels One Five, 127
Animal Crackers, 99, 100, 101, 110
Animal Kingdom, The, 235, 236
Anti-Nazi League, 153
Anything for a Quiet Life, 127
Arbuckle, Fatty, 261
Applecart, The, 125, 129
Asherson, Renee, *174*
  and Robert Donat, 178, 179, 191
    marriage to, 194, 196
    his ill health, 195
Askey, Arthur, 218
Asphalt Jungle, The, 16, 30, 31, 43, 44
Asquith, Anthony, 214
Astoria Studios, 99
Attenborough, Richard, 129
At the Circus, 104, 105
Autumn Crocus, 122
Aza, Lilian
  and Gracie Fields, 206, 219, 220
    and Archie Pitt, 207, 208
    and John Flanagan, 211
    and Boris Alperovici, 221
    and children, 216
    and films, 212
    as artiste, 209
    character of, 222

Badel, Alan, 70
Bacall, Lauren, 136
Baer, Max, 35
Balcon, Michael, 128

Bankhead, Tallulah, 235
Banks, Monty, *202*
  and Gracie Fields, 213, 215, 222
    marriage to, 216, 217–18
    death of, 219
Banky, Vilma, 148
Bannen, Ian, 82
Bardot, Brigitte, 21
Barrett, Eletha *see* Finch, Eletha
Barrie, J.M., 267
Barry, Joan, 272–3, 277
Barthelmass, Richard, 148
Bassey, Shirley, 80
Beau Geste, 121
Bennett, Arnold, 233
Bennett, Constance, 218
Benson, Frank, 179, 180, 185
Bergman, Ingrid, 244
  The Inn of the Sixth Happiness, *175*, 196, 197
Berkeley Square, 235
Berman, Pandro S.,
  and studio chiefs, 294–5, 300
Bern, Paul, 300
Bernard, James, 178, 179
Bequest to the Nation, 83
Bianchi, Mario *see* Banks, Monty
Big Store, The, 105
Birds of Prey, 123
Black Clock (Cézanne), 163
Blackmer, Eunice Murray
  and Marilyn Monroe, 47, 48, 49–52
Black Rose, The, 127
Bloom, Claire, 70
  and Charlie Chaplin, 275, 278
Blumberg, Lilian *see* Howard, Lilian
Bogart, Humphrey, 291, 296
  and Leslie Howard, 231, 236–7
  and Edward G. Robinson, 157–8
Bogart, Lesley, 237
Bonnie Prince Charlie, 126
Boulting, John
  and Robert Donat, 176, 192, 193–4, 195
Bowery Boys, 107
Boys Town, 187
Brando, Marlon, 126, 128, 278
Brickhill, Paul, 66, 67, 85
Bridge on the River Kwai, The, 129
Bright Shawl, The, 148
"Britain Speaks" broadcasts, 247
British Film Yearbook, 250
Britton, Tony
  and Peter Finch, 67, 76–7, 79, 80, 85
Bromley, Sydney, 121, 130

Brooks, Richard
  and Hollywood, 299, 305
    studio chiefs, 289, 290
    treatment of stars, 291, 292
Brothers Karamazov, The, 33
Bus Stop, 36
Buzzell, Edward
  and Marx Brothers, 104, 105–6, 112

Café de Paris, 209
Cagney, James, 291
Cambridge Festival Theatre, 173, 180, 181
Campbell, Major Jock, 63, 64, 81
Candida, 125
Capone, Al, 148
Capra, Frank, 159, 164
Capri
  Gracie Fields and, 211, 212, 216, 219, 220, 221, 222
Captain Blood, 183
Captain Boycott, 192
Casey's Circus, 260
Cash, 182
Casson, Lewis, 121
Chandler, Charlotte
  and Groucho Marx
    childhood and mother, 94, 95
    Erin Fleming, 110
    Monkey Business, 102
    and money, 99
    and women, 97, 108, 109, 113
Chandler, Raymond, 8
Chaplin, Charles Snr. (father), 259
Chaplin, Charles Jnr. (son), 254, 268, 271, 278
Chaplin, Charlie, 6, *253–7*
  childhood, 259–60
  music hall career, 261
  first films, 261–2
  first marriage, 266
  second marriage, 267–9
  third marriage, 270–1
  Joan Barry paternity suit, 272–4
  marriage to Oona O'Neill, 275
  death of, 279
  and Edna Purviance, 264–5
  as father, 278
  attitude to money, 262–4
    politics, 272, 275–7
    women, 274–5
  his humour, 258–9
Chaplin, Hannah, 259, 260, 267
Chaplin, Oona, *255*, 263, 276, 277
  marriage to Charlie Chaplin, 273, 275, 278
Chaplin, Sydney (brother), 259, 261, 267
Chaplin, Sydney (son), 254, 270, 271, 278
  birth of, 268
  and Charlie Chaplin's childhood, 260
    as father, 278

  attitude to money, 263, 264
  attitude to women, 274
  Barry paternity suit, 273
Charburn's Young Stars, 206
Chayevsky, Paddy, 164
Chekov, Michael, 32
Chenhalls, Alfred, 249
Chevalier, Maurice, 218
Churchill, Lady, 223
Churchill, Winston, 217, 249
Cincinnati Kid, The, 167
Circus, The, 268, 269, 279
Citadel, The, 187
City Lights, 269, 270
Clair, René, 185
Clash by Night, 32
Cleopatra, 80
Clift, Montgomery, 43
Coconuts, The, 99
Cohn, Harry, 28, *283*
  and Columbia Studios, 287, 288, 289, 294, 302
Colbert, Claudette, 148
Coliseum theatre, 209
Columbia Studios, 9, 286, 287, 304
  and Marilyn Monroe, 28, 29, 30
  and Edward G. Robinson, 152–3
Connelly, Marc, 245
Consolidated Film Industries, 22
Conte, Richard, 129
Coogan, Jackie, 266
Countess from Hong Kong, A, 278
Count of Monte Cristo, The, 182, 184
Crawford, Joan, 33, 299, 306
Cronin, A.J., 187
Cronyn, Hume, 124
Cruel Sea, The, 127–8
Cukor, George, 33
  and Leslie Howard, 230, 237, 238, 246
Cunnington, Violette, *228*
  and Leslie Howard, 243–7
  death of, 248, 249
Cure for Love, The, 174, 190, 192, 194
Curtis, Tony
  and *Some Like It Hot*, 38, 39, 40–2

Dailey, Dan, 129
Daily Express, 215
Daily Telegraph, 222
Dangerous Years, 27
Daphne Laureola, 70, 71
Dark Hazard, 152
Darkness at Noon, 161
Davey, Mary
  and Gracie Fields, 205, 216, 217, 218
    as entertainer, 222–3
Davis, Bette, 219
Day at the Races, A, 104
Day, The, 80
Dean, Basil, 121
  and Gracie Fields, 212, 213

Dear Octopus, 123
de Haviland, Olivia, 126, 302
de Mille, Cecil B.
  and Communism, 163
  and foundations of Hollywood, 8–9
de Sica, Vittorio, 129
Devotion, 235
Dictionary of National Biography, 231
Dietrich, Marlene, 45, 126
  and Robert Donat, 186–7
diMaggio, Joe, *17*
  and Marilyn Monroe, 32, 33, 46, 50
    marriage to, 34–5, 36, 54
Dinner Table (Matisse), 163
Disney, Walt, 71
Donat, Brian, 188
Donat, Ella, *173*
  and Robert Donat, 177, 179, 186, 187,
    197–8
  marriage to, 180, 181, 188–9
  divorce from, 188, 192
  and Hollywood, 188, 192
Donat, Ernst Emil, 178, 189
Donat, Joanna, *173*, 184, 188
Donat, John, *173*
  and Robert Donat, 180, 185, 188, 189,
    191, 192
  health of, 195, 196
Donat, Robert, 5, 123, *171–5*, 238
  childhood and early career, 178–9, 181
  first marriage, 180, 188, 189
  second marriage, 194, 196
  first films, 182
  Hollywood, 183–4
  Red Knight, 185–6
  Goodbye Mr. Chips, 187–8
  The Magic Box, 192–4
  The Inn of the Sixth Happiness, 196–7
  his illness, 194, 195–6
  and death, 197
  as actor, 176–7, 190, 197–8
  character of, 191–2, 194
Donat, Rose Alice, 178, 189
Dostoevsky, F., 148
Double Indemnity, 157
Dougherty, James, 39, 53
  marriage to Marilyn Monroe, 23–6
Dr. Ehrlich's Magic Bullet, 155
Dr. Kildare TV series, 132
Duck Soup, 102, 103
du Maurier, Sir Gerald, 209
Duncan, Isadora, 64
Dundy, Elaine, 63
Durant, Tim
  and Charlie Chaplin, 271, 274, 275, 277

Ealing Studios, 70, 127, 128
East is West, 149
Eden, Anthony, 249
Edward VIII, 217

Edwards, Blake, 137
Eighth Army News, 217
Eisenstein, S.M., 258
Elephant Walk, 73, 74
Elusive Pimpernel, The, 126
Elvey, Maurice, 123, 212, 248
Encyclopaedia Judaica, 231
England Made Me, 82
ENSA, 190
Essanay Film Manufacturing Company
  and Charlie Chaplin, 262, 264, 265
Eureka Stockade, 69, 70
Evans, Edith, 70
Evening News, 123

Fairbanks, Douglas, Jnr.
  and Leslie Howard, 238, 241, 245, 250
  and Charlie Chaplin, 263, 265, 276, 277
Fairbanks, Douglas, Snr., 187, 266
Fallen Idol, The, 126
Far From the Madding Crowd, 81
Farouk, King, 221
Faulkner, Trader
  and Peter Finch, 63, 67, 76
    childhood, 64, 81
    attitude to women, 78
    and Vivien Leigh, 74, 75
Faulkner, William, 290
Festival of Britain, 192
Fields, Gracie, 5, *199–203*
  childhood, 204–5
  early career, 206–8, 209–10
  first marriage, 208–9
  and John Flanagan, 210–12
  in films, 212–13, 218
  Hollywood, 214–15
  second marriage, 216, 219
  and Second World War, 216, 217
  third marriage, 219, 220, 221
  death of, 222
  character of, 218, 222
  as entertainer, 204, 220–1, 223–4
Fields, Tommy, *200*
  and Gracie Fields, 221
    childhood of, 205, 206
    marriages of, 208, 217–18, 220
    popularity of, 210, 218
    generosity of, 214
    illness of, 215, 216
    and John Flanagan, 211
    and films, 212
    as entertainer, 209
Finch, Anita, *58*, 71, 73, 82
Finch, Bloody Finch (Elaine Dundy), 63
Finch, Charles, *58*, 80
Finch, Christopher, 81, 83
Finch, Diana, 81, 83
Finch, Eletha, *59*
  and Peter Finch, 62, 74
    marriage to, 81, 83–4

Finch, Peter, *57–61*
  childhood, 63–6
  early career and first marriage, 68–70
  reunited with parents, 71–3
  and Vivien Leigh, 73–5
  second marriage, 79–80
  third marriage, 83–4
  Far From the Madding Crowd, 81
  Sunday, Bloody Sunday, 82
  as actor, 62, 85–6
  character of, 67–8, 75–8
Finch, Samantha, *58*, 80
Finch, Tamara, *59*
  and Peter Finch, 77, 82
    marriage to, 68–9, 70, 71, 72, 79
    and Vivien Leigh, 73–4, 75
Finch, Yolande, *58*, 74, 81
  marriage to Peter Finch, 79–80
First National Studios, 265, 266
First of the Few, The, 230, 247, 249
Fisher, Art, 92
Fitzgerald, Scott, 290
Five and Ten, 235
Five Star Final, 152
Flanagan, John
  and Gracie Fields, 210–11, 212
Fleming, Erin, *91*
  and Groucho Marx, 109, 110, 112,
    113
Flight of the Phoenix, The, 82
Flynn, Errol, 184, 231
Fontaine, Joan, 5
  and suspension clauses, 288, 298
Forbes, Bryan
  and Jack Hawkins, 129, 135, 136, 137
Ford, John, 153
49th Parallel, 237, 247
Four Just Men, The, TV series, 129
Fred Karno's Troupe, 261
Free Soul, A, 235
Frend, Charles, 127

Gable, Clark, *19*, 177, 251, 300
  and Marilyn Monroe, 43, 44, 46
Garbo, Greta, 45, 240
Gardner, Ava, 295, 297
Garfield, John, 28, 156, 298
Garland, Judy, 299
Gentlemen Prefer Blondes, 16, 32
Gentle Sex, The, 248
Ghost Goes West, The, 185
Gielgud, Sir John, 83
  and *Hamlet*, 239, 240
  and Jack Hawkins, 123, 125, 135
Gifford, C. Stanley, 22
Girl with Green Eyes, The, 80
Gish, Dorothy, 148, 266
Gish, Lilian, 239, 266
Goddard, Erwin, 23
Goddard, Grace, 22–3

Goddard, Paulette, *255, 257*
  marriage to Charlie Chaplin, 270, 271,
    274
Goebbels, Joseph, 247
Goldenberg, Emanuel *see* Robinson,
  Edward G.
Goldenberg, Morris, 144, 145, 147
Goldenberg, Sarah, 144, 147
Gold Rush, The, 267, 268
Goldwyn, Sam, *284*, 292, 305
Gone with the Wind, 243, 244, 270
Goodbye Mr. Chips
  Robert Donat and, 176, 187–8, 189, 190
Gorcey, Kay *see* Marx, Kay
Gorcey, Leo, 107
Go West, 104
"Gracie's Working Party" radio series, 219
Granger Stewart, 192, 248
Grant, Cary, 177
Graumann's Chinese Theatre, 33
Gray, Charles, 134
Great Catherine, 134
Great Dictator, The, 271
Green, Rose Alice *see* Donat, Rose Alice
Greene, Milton, 35, 36, 38
Greenwood, Walter, 190
Grey, Lita, *254*
  and Charlie Chaplin, 277, 278
    marriage to, 267–8, 269
    and women, 274–5
Griffith, D.W., 258, 266
Guardian, The, 223
Guiles, Frederick, 48
Guthrie, Tyrone
  and Robert Donat, 179, 180, 184, 187

Hale, Georgia, 268, 270
Hamlet, 123, 125, 184, 249
  Robert Donat in, 172, 179
  Leslie Howard in, 234, 238–40, 246
Harding, Olive
  and Peter Finch, 62, 81
    marriages of, 78, 80
    and Vivien Leigh, 73
    and attitude to women, 79
    and his children, 82
Harlow, Jean, 300
Harris, Mildred, *254*
  marriage to Charlie Chaplin, 266, 267
Harrison, Rex, 80
Hatchet Man, 152
Hathaway, Henry, 126, 133
Haver, June, 27
Hawkes, Sidney, 259
Hawkins, Andrew, *118*, 129
Hawkins, Caroline, *118*, 128
Hawkins, Doreen, *118*
  and Jack Hawkins, 121
    marriage to, 125, 126
    throat cancer of, 130, 132, 133, 135–6,
    137

Hawkins, Jack, 5, *115–19*
  childhood, 120–1
  first marriage, 122, 123
  first films, 123
  second marriage, 125, 126
  Mandy and *The Cruel Sea*, 127–8
  Bridge on the River Kwai, 129
  fight against cancer, 130, 132–5
  final illness and death, 136–8
  as actor, 120, 127, 138
  character of, 130–2
Hawkins, Nicholas, *118*
  and Jack Hawkins, 129, 132, 135, 136
Hawkins, Susan, 123, 124, 126
Hayworth, Rita, 29
Hecker, Neva, 219
Hello, I Must Be Going (Charlotte
  Chandler), 94
Hepburn, Katharine, 45
Her Cardboard Lover, 235
Hertford, Eden *see* Marx, Eden
Hiller, Wendy, 242, 248
Hitchcock, Alfred, 123, 185, 186, 298
Hole in the Head, A, 164
Hole in the Wall, The, 148
Hollywood
  beginnings of film industry in, 8–9
  MGM Studios in, 286–7
  studio chiefs, 287, 289, 290, 294–5
  treatment of stars, 288, 291–4, 295, 301
  decline of, 302–5
  achievements of, 305–7
Hollywood Greats, The (Barry Norman), 5
Hollywood Reporter, The, 62
"Hollywood Ten, The", 160
Holy Matrimony, 218
Hope, Bob, 113
Hopper, Hedda, 9, 43, 301
  and Harry Cohn, 289
Horse Feathers, 102, 103
Horseman on Beach (Gauguin), 163
Houseman, John
  and Leslie Howard, 234
    and *Hamlet*, 238–40
    and Ruth Howard, 246
House Un-American Activities Committee
  (HUAC)
  Arthur Miller and, 36–7
  Edward G. Robinson and, 158–61
Howard, Irene
  and Leslie Howard, 237
    childhood of, 232
    Ruth Howard, 233, 245
    and attitude to women, 234, 235
    and Violette Cunnington, 248
    and acting, 241
    and Hollywood, 236
Howard, Leslie, *225–9*
  childhood, 231–2
  early career, 233

marriage, 232–3, 245–7
affairs, 234, 235, 242–3
  and Violette Cunnington, 243, 244–7,
    248–9
and Hollywood, 231, 236
Hamlet, 238–40
activities during war, 244, 247, 249
death of, 230, 249–50
as actor, 241, 250–2
character of, 237–8
Howard, Leslie (daughter), 236, 243
Howard, Lilian, 231, 232, 233
Howard, Ronald, *227*, 233, 236
  and Leslie Howard, 241, 242
    and Violette Cunnington, 243, 244,
      246, 247, 248
  death of, 249–50
Howard, Ruth, *266*
  marriage to Leslie Howard, 232–3,
    234–5, 236, 237–8, 243, 245–6
  and Merle Oberon, 242
  and Violette Cunnington, 244, 245,
    246–7, 248
How to Be Very, Very Popular, 35
How to Marry a Millionaire, 32
Hughes, Howard, 301
Humour Risk, 98
Huston, John, 28
  and *The Asphalt Jungle*, 30
  and *The Misfits*, 20, 43, 44–5
Hutton, Betty, 29
Hyde, Johnny, 29–30, 31, 32

I'll Say She Is (Broadway show), 98, 99
Intermezzo, 244
Importance of Being Ernest, The, 123
Ingle-Finch, Alicia Gladys, 63, 64, 71–3
Ingle-Finch, Charles, 65
Ingle-Finch, Dorothy, 65
Ingle-Finch, George, 63–4, 71, 72
Ingle-Finch, Laura, 64–5
Inn of the Sixth Happiness, The, *175*, 196–7
In Praise of Britain, 248
Italia Conti Drama School, 121
Italian Woman (Corot), 163
It's a Bargain (revue), 207

Jackson, Glenda, 83
Jackson's Eight Lancashire Lads, 260
Jaffe, Sam
  and Edward G. Robinson, 145, 154, 159,
    162
  and Edward G. Robinson, Jnr., 165
Jessel, George, 289
Johnson, Ruth *see* Marx, Ruth
Journey's End, 116, 122
Joyce, William (Lord Haw-Haw), 247
Just Suppose, 234, 235

Karno, Fred, 261
Keaton, Buster, 280

Keep Smiling, 215
Kelley, Tom, 29, 31–2
Kennedy, John F., 47
Kennedy, Joseph, 49
Kennedy, Merna, 268
Kennedy, Robert
  and Marilyn Monroe, 7, 48, 51, 52, 54
Kerr, Deborah, 190
Kerr, Bill, 67, 68, 76
Key Largo, 157, 158, 169
Keystone Studios, 262
Kid Auto Races at Venice, 261
Kid, The, 266, 267
King in New York, A, 277
King Lear, 123
Kipling, Rudyard, 76
Knight Without Armour, 186
Koestler, Arthur, 161
Korda, Sir Alexander
  and Robert Donat, 182, 186
  and Jack Hawkins, 125, 126, 128
  and Leslie Howard, 236
Krasna, Norman
  and Groucho Marx, 96, 100, 106, 111–12

Ladies of the Chorus, 28, 29
Lady to Love, A, 148, 149
Lamp Still Burns, The, 248
Landi, Elissa, 183
Lang, Fritz, 157
Lanza, Mario, 299
La Rue, Jack, 296–7
Lassky, Jesse, Jnr., 294, 299
  on Hollywood, 305–6
Laughton, Charles, 182
Laurel and Hardy, 258
Laurel, Stan, 265
Laurence Olivier Productions, 70
Lawford, Peter, 47, 48
Lawrence, Doreen *see* Hawkins, Doreen
Lawrence of Arabia, 130
Laye, Evelyn, 218
League of Gentlemen, The, 129, 130
Lean, David, 131
Lease of Life, 195
Le Blanc, Bert, 68
Le Crotoy (Seurat), 163
Lee, Jack
  and Peter Finch, 76, 78, 85
    his rootlessness, 67, 77
    life in Mill Hill, 79
    and Rank contract, 75
Lee, Rowland, 182, 183
Legend of Lylah Chase, The, 81
Leigh, Vivien, 69
  and Peter Finch, 73–7
Lejeune, C.A., 215
Le Malade Imaginaire (Molière) 69
Lemmon, Jack
  and *Some Like it Hot*, 38, 39, 40–2

Let's Make Love, 17, 43
Levin, Leo, 94
Limelight, 275
Lincoln Center, 278
Lipman, Annie, 208, 209
Little Caesar, 152
  Edward G. Robinson and, 149–50, 155, 169
Little Giant, The, 152
Liverpool Playhouse, 179
Lloyd, Gladys *see* Robinson, Gladys
Loder, John, 213
Lodger, The, 123
Loew, Marcus, 286, 287
Loew's Incorporated, 286, 287, 303
Logan, Joshua, 36, 55
London Film Productions, 182
London Palladium, 219, 223
Lord Jim, 131
Loren, Sophia, 21, 278
Lost Horizon, 83
Louis B. Mayer Productions, 287
Love Happy, 29
Love, Life and Laughter, 213
Lower, Ana, 23, 25
Loy, Myrna, 35
  and L.B. Mayer, 293–4
Lumet, Sydney, 85
Lusitania, 146
Lyon, Ben, 26, 27, 296
Lytess, Natasha
  and Marilyn Monroe, 28, 20, 32, 33, 36, 39

Macbeth, 184
MacGowran, Jack, 131, 132
Mackendrick, Alexander, 62, 127
MacLaine, Shirley, 130
MacMurray, Fred, 157
Madame Pimpernel (Paris Underground), 218
Magic Box, The, 176, 192, 195
Magwood, Mrs. Flavia
  and Peter Finch, 77, 82
    childhood and parentage of, 63, 67, 71–2
Mailer, Norman, 20, 48
Maitlands, The, 123
Making a Living, 261
Malvern Festival, 181
Man Behind the Statue, The, 191, 192
Mandy, 127, 128
Mankiewicz, Joseph L.
  and Marilyn Monroe, 30–1, 55
  and 20th Century Fox, 289
  and studio chiefs, 290
    Louis B. Mayer, 293–4, 300
  and artistes in Hollywood, 299–300
Man Who Lost Himself, The, 244
Marilyn Monroe Productions, 35, 38

Marilyn (Norman Mailer), 48
Martin, Dean, 47
Martin, Ruth *see* Howard, Ruth
Marx, Andy, 113
Marx, Arthur, *89*, 98, 113
  and Minnie Marx, 95
  Marx Brothers' names, 92
    Chico, 100
    Zeppo, 101
  Groucho Marx's childhood, 94
    marriage, 106, 107, 108
    attitude to money, 99, 111
    and Thalberg, 104
Marx, Chico (Leonard), *88*, 106
  childhood, 94
  as Marx Brother, 92, 102, 107
  love of gambling, 100, 101, 103, 104,
    105
  and women, 96, 99
  death of, 109
Marx, Eden, *90*, 108, 109, 112
Marx, Groucho (Julius), 29, *87–91*, 92
  childhood, 93–4
  in vaudeville, 94–7
  first marriage, 98, 106
  first films, 99–103
  with MGM, 104–7
  second marriage, 107
  third marriage, 108–9
  and Marx Brothers revival, 110
  his meanness, 111–12
  death of, 113
Marx, Gummo (Milton), 101, 109
  childhood, 94
  as Marx Brother, 92, 97
  and Harpo, 100
  death of, 113
Marx, Harpo (Arthur), *88*,
  childhood, 94
  and Minnie Marx, 95
  as Marx Brother, 92, 107
  his popularity, 100–1
  death of, 109
Marx, Kay, *90*, 107, 108
Marx, Manfred, 94
Marx, Marion, 107
Marx, Melinda, *90*, 107, 112
Marx, Minnie, 93, 94, 95, 109
  death of, 99–100, 101
Marx, Miriam, *89*, 99
Marx, Ruth, *89*
  marriage to Groucho Marx, 98, 106–7
Marx, Sam, 93, 109
Marx, Susan, 100, 106
Marx, Zeppo (Herbert), 95, 107, 110, 111
  childhood, 93, 94
  as Marx Brother, 92, 98, 101, 102
  and Chico, 100
  attitude to women, 96, 97, 98–9
Mason, James, 129

Mayer, Louis B., 104, *284*
  as MGM studio chief, 287, 288, 289, 302
    treatment of stars, 292–3, 294, 295,
      297, 298
    end of career, 303–4
McLaglen, Victor, 215
McQueen, Steve, 167
Melson, Inez
  and Marilyn Monroe, 32, 48–9, 52
Menjou, Adolphe, 267
Men of Tomorrow, 182
Mercury Theatre (Sydney), 69
Metro Goldwyn Mayer (MGM), 9, 148,
  238, *282*, *285*
  formation of, 286–7
  treatment of artistes, 291, 295, 296, 297
  decline of, 303, 304
  and Robert Donat, 187, 190
  and Gracie Fields, 214
  and Marx Brothers, 103, 104, 105
Metro Pictures, 287
Middle of the Night (Chayevsky), 164
Miller, Arthur, *17*, 20, 32, 35
  and HUAC, 37
  marriage to Marilyn Monroe, 36, 40, 42,
    43, 45, 46, 49, 54
Miller, Gilbert, 122
Mills, Sir John
  and Robert Donat, 185–6, 190, 192, 197
Milne, A.A., 233
Miniver Story, The, 70
Misfits, The, *19*, 20, 43–5
Mitchell, R.J., 247
Mitchum, Robert, 301
Modern Times, *257*, 270–1
Monkey Business, 101–2
Monroe, Gladys Pearl *see* Mortensen,
  Gladys Pearl
Monroe, Marilyn, *15–19*
  childhood, 22–3
  first marriage, 23–6
  first films, 27–9
  early successes, 32–3
  marriage to Joe diMaggio, 34–5
  marriage to Arthur Miller, 36–45
  Some Like It Hot, 40–2
  The Misfits, 43–5
  appearance of, 20
  as actress, 54–6
  as sex symbol, 21, 33, 34
  and drugs, 44–5, 45–7
  and Johnny Hyde, 30–1
  unpunctuality of, 38–9
  death of, 6–7, 48–54
Monsarrat, Nicholas, 127
Monsieur Verdoux, 275
Montand, Yves, *17*
  Let's Make Love, 43
Morris, Mary, 237, 238
Mortensen, Gladys Pearl, 22, 24–5, 26

Mortensen, Norma Jean *see* Monroe, Marilyn
Moscow Strikes Back, documentary, 158
Motion Picture World, 261
Mr. Pym Passes By, 233
Mr. Samuel, 149
Mr. Tower of London (revue), 207, 209, 210
Mr. Winkle Goes to War, 156
Muni, Paul, 156
Murder in the Cathedral, 195
Murray, Don, 36
Mutual Studios, 265

Neame, Ronald, 193
Negri, Pola, 267
Network, 61, 62, 84, 85
Never the Twain Shall Meet, 235
Newcombe, Pat, 49, 50
Newsweek, 158
New Yorker, The, 100
New York Herald Tribune, 156, 157
New York Times, 157, 158, 270
Next of Kin, 124, 127
Niagara, 32
Night at the Opera, A, 104
Night in Casablanca, A, 107
Night Out, A, 264
Night Ride, 148
Nijinsky, 64
Nobile, Umberto, 82
No Business Like Show Business, 35
No Highway, 126
No Love for Johnny, 78, 79
Norma Jean (Frederick Guiles), 48
Norman, Leslie, 78, 128, 134
Nun's Story, The, 82

Oberon, Merle, 242, 243
Oh What a Lovely War, 135
Old Vic, 123, 187, 195
Old Vic Company, 184
Olivier, Sir Laurence, 122, 168, 186, 187
   and Robert Donat, 177, 193, 194
   and Peter Finch, 69, 70, 73, 74–5
   and Marilyn Monroe, 36, 38, 42
O'Neill, Eugene, 273
O'Neill, Oona *see* Chaplin, Oona
Othello, 125, 187
   Peter Finch in, 70–1
O'Toole, Peter
   and Jack Hawkins
      Englishness of, 120, 138
      and illness of, 133, 134, 135
      Lawrence of Arabia, 130–1
      Lord Jim, 131–2
Outside the Law, 149
Outward Bound, 235

Paper Chase, The, 238

Paramount Studios, 9, 256
   and Marx Brothers, 99, 101, 103
   and Edward G. Robinson, 148
Parrish, Robert, 301
Parsons, Louella, 301
Pascal, Gabriel, 241, 243
Perelman, S.J., 97, 102
Perfect Strangers, 190
Peter Finch – A Biography (Trader Faulkner), 63
Petrified Forest, The, 235, 236, 242
Photoplay magazine, 32, 33
Pickford, Mary, 250, 266
Pimpernel Smith, *228*, 230, 237, 247
Pirandello, L., 148
Pirates of Penzance, The, 121
Pitt, Archie, *201*
   and Gracie Fields, 207, 212, 222
      marriage to, 208, 209, 210, 213
Powell, Dick, 295, 296
Powell, Michael, 237, 244, 247
Power, Tyrone, 126
Precious Bane (Mary Webb), 181
Price, Vincent, 151, 163
Priestley, J.B., 223
Prince and the Showgirl, The, 18, 20, 36, 37–8
Private Life of Henry VIII, The, 182
Public Prosecutor, The, 129
Pumpkin Eater, The, 80
Purviance, Edna, 264–5, 267
Pygmalion, 241–2, 243

Queen Elizabeth, 276
Queen of Hearts, 213

Rabin, Yitzak, 84
Racket, The, 148
Raft, George, 282, 289
Raid on Entebbe, 84
Rains, Claude, 161
Rank Organisation
   and Peter Finch, 75, 76, 79
   and Jack Hawkins, 128
Rats of Tobruk, 69
Rattigan, Terence, 36, 83
Rebecca, 298
Redford, Robert, 128
Red Knight, 185
Red Tent, The, 60, 81, 82
Reliance Studios, 183
Remick, Lee, 47
Republic Studios, 296
Richardson, Sir Ralph, 123
Rietty, Robert, 134
Rivals, The, *173*
RKO Studios, 104, 294, 301, 303
Roach, Hal
   and Charlie Chaplin, 264, 274
      his attitude to money, 262, 263

Robbery Under Arms, 67, 75, 78
Robert Donat: A Biography (J.C. Trewin),
176
Robin Hood, 71, 183, 184
Robinson, Edward G., 6, *139–43*, 236
 childhood, 144–5
 early career, 146
 first marriage, 147, 153, 154
 first films, 148–50
 Little Caesar, 149–50
 career during war, 155–7
 HUAC investigation, 144, 158–61
 divorce settlement, 162–3
 second marriage, 164
 death of, 168
 as art collector, 150–1, 162, 163
 as father, 152, 154–5, 164, 166–7
 his film roles, 169
Robinson, Edward G., Jnr., 152, 165
 alcoholism of, 163, 166
 relationship with Edward G. Robinson,
 154–5, 166–7
Robinson, Gladys, *140*, 149, 164, 165
 marriage to Edward G. Robinson, 147,
 153
 birth of son, 152
 illness of, 154, 161–2
 divorce settlement, 162, 163
Robinson, Francesca, 150, 162
 and Edward G. Robinson, Jnr., 166–7
Robinson, Jane, *142*
 and Edward G. Robinson, 168
 marriage to, 164, 169
 and HUAC, 159, 161
 and art collection, 163, 165
 and Gladys Robinson, 154, 162
 and Edward G. Robinson,
 Jnr., 166
Robson, Dame Flora
 and Robert Donat, 180, 192, 197
Rochdale
 Gracie Fields and, 204, 211, 215, 221,
 222, 223
Rochdale Hippodrome, 205
Rogers, Will, 214
Romeo and Juliet, 126
 Robert Donat in, 184
 Leslie Howard in, 238
Room Service, 104
Rooney, Mickey, 296
Roosevelt, F.D., 272
Rosmersholm, 180
Rosten, Norman, 38, 54
Royal Variety Show, 222
Russell, Jane, 33
Rutherford, Ann
 and L.B. Mayer, 296–7
 and MGM, 297–9
 and Hollywood, 306
Ryskind, Morris, 103

Sabotage, 186
Sally in Our Alley, 212
Sammy Going South, 168
Samuel Goldwyn Studios, 287
Scarlet Pimpernel, The, 242
Schary, Dore
 and Hollywood, 305
 and MGM, 303, 304
 and studio bribery, 301
 and studio chiefs, 287
 and treatment of stars, 291
Schenck, Nicholas
 and MGM, 287, 303, 304
Schenk, Joseph M., 27–8, 29
Schlesinger, John, 81, 82, 85
Scudda Hoo! Scudda Hay!, *16*, 27
Secrets, 250
Selznick, David O., 244
Sennett, Mack, 261
Service for Ladies (Reserved for Ladies), 236
Seven Year Itch, The, 34–5
Shadow and Substance, 272
Shalako, 134
Shaw, George Bernard, 121, 125, 148
 and Leslie Howard, 241–2
Shearer, Norma, 238
Sherlock Holmes, 260
Sherwood, Robert, 290
Shipyard Sally, 215
Shiralee, The, 78, 79
Show's the Thing, The (revue), 210
Sidney, George
 and MGM, 286, 295, 303
Signoret, Simone, 43
Silver Dollar, 152
Simmons, Jean, 291
Simpson, Mrs. Wallis, 217
Sinatra, Frank, 156, 164
Skelton, Red, 289
Small Back Room, The, 126
Smart Money, 152
Smith, Jean, 48–9
Snyder, Whitey
 and Marilyn Monroe, 39, 48
 and children, 38
 and drugs, 46–7, 52
Some Like It Hot, 38, 39–42
Something's Got to Give, 19, 46, 48
Something to Hide, 82
S.O.S., 209
Soylent Green, 167, 168
Spigelgass, Leonard
 and Edward G. Robinson, 147, 152
 and financial problems, 151, 162
 and Oscar, 168
 and Edward G. Robinson, Jnr., 166
 and Gladys Robinson, 154
Squaw Man, The, 9
Stainer, Frank, 231, 232, 233
Stalin, J., 252

Stanislavski, Constantin, 32
Stansfield, Betty, *200*, 210
Stansfield, Fred, 204, 215
Stansfield, Jenny, 204, 215
  and Gracie Fields, 205, 206
  and Archie Pitt, 207, 208
Stanwyck, Barbara, 157
State Secret, 126
Steiner, Frank *see* Stainer, Frank
Sten, Anna, 292
Sterling, Ford, 261
Stevens, George, 169
Stewart, James, 126
St. Joan, 116, 121, 122
Story of Mankind, The, 107
Strasberg, Lee, 35, 36
Strasberg, Paula
  and Marilyn Monroe, 28, 36, 38,
   39, 40
Stravinsky, Igor, 64
Streetcar Named Desire, A, 126
Sullivan, Ed, 35
Sullivan, Francis L., 247
Sunday, Bloody Sunday, 62, 82
Sunday Graphic, 128
Swain, Mack, 261
Sydney Sun, 66

Talmadge, Norma, 28
Tamarind Seed, The, 137
Tandy, Jessica, 126, 130
  marriage to Jack Hawkins, 122, 123,
   124–5
Taylor, Elizabeth, 74, 80, 291
Taylor, Robert, 292
Tchinarova, Tamara *see* Finch,
  Tamara
Temple, Shirley, 101
Ten Commandments, The, 163
Terry, Ellen, 6
Thalberg, Irving, 300, 303–4
  and Marx Brothers, 103–4
  and Edward G. Robinson, 148–9
That Night in London, 182
Theatre Guild of New York, 147, 148
Thirty-Nine Steps, The, 176, 185
Thorndike, Dame Sybil, 121
Thunder in the City, 153
Ticket to Tomahawk, A, 29
Tiger Shark, 152
Title, The, 233
Town Like Alice, A, 67, 75, 78
Tracy, Spencer, 85, 187, 188, 300
Train of Events, 70, 71
Tramp, The, 265
Trewin, J.C., 176, 198
Trials of Oscar Wilde, The, 78
Trumbo, Dalton, 160
Turnbull, Yolande *see* Finch, Yolande

20th Century Fox, 9, 21, 190, 286, 289, 304
  Gracie Fields and, 214–15, 218
  Marilyn Monroe and, 26–7, 28, 29, 31,
   35, 36
  Something's Got to Give, 46, 47–8
Two Loves, 130
Two Seconds, 152

Ullman, Liv, 83
United Artists, 9
  and Charlie Chaplin, 264, 266, 278
Universal Artists, 9, 28, 128, 148
Ustinov, Peter, 191, 192, 197

Vidor, King, 187
  and Charlie Chaplin, 271
   and attitude to money, 263
   and politics, 276
   and tramp costume, 262
Voysey, Ella Annesley *see* Donat, Ella

Wallace, Edgar, 129
Wallach, Eli, 36, 37
  The Misfits, 43–4
Wallis, Hal
  and Edward G. Robinson, 149, 150
Walter, Francis, 144, 160
Warner Brothers, 9, 286, 287, 291, 292,
  302, 304
  and Robert Donat, 184–5
  and Leslie Howard, 235, 236, 237
  and Edward G. Robinson, 149, 151, 152,
   153, 155, 157
Warner, Harry, 287
Warner, Jack, *283*
  as studio chief, 287, 289, 291, 294, 302
Waterfront Lady, 296
Watt, Harry, 70
Webb, Mary, 181
Welles, Orson, 70
Wells, H.G., 267
We're Going to be Rich, 215
West, Mae, 214
Wheldon, Harry, 261, 279
Where the Rainbow Ends, 121, 130
Whole Town's Talking, The, 152
Widow from Chicago, 149
Wilder, Billy
  and Marilyn Monroe, 34–5, 36, 54–5, 56
  Some Like It Hot, 38, 39–42
Wilding, Michael, 136
William Morris Agency, 29
Winslow Boy, The, 192
Woman in the Window, The, 157
Woman of Paris, A, 264, 267
Wooden Horse, The, 70
Wooley, Monty, 218
Woollcott, Alexander, 100

Yes I think So (revue), 206

You Bet Your Life (quiz show), 107–8
Young, Freddie, 196
Young Mr. Pitt, The, 190
Young Woodley, 121

Zanuck, Darryl F., *283*
  and 20th Century Fox, 289
    and Gracie Fields, 214, 218
    and Marilyn Monroe, 31, 32